GRGICH HILLS
ESTATE

Happy Holidays

and

Best Wishes for the New Year

from our family to yours!

GRGICH HILLS ESTATE

1829 St. Helena Hwy. • Rutherford, CA 94573 • Tel: (707) 963-2784 • www.grgich.com

WINE & CHEESE PAIRING GUIDE

Your Exciting Search for Wow! Combinations

by

Norm & Barbara Ray

Rayve Productions
Hoffman Press Division

Cover design: Heidi Would
Cover illustration: Filomena Booth

Rayve Productions Inc.
Hoffman Press Division
Box 726, Windsor, CA 95492

Quantity discounts and bulk purchases of this and other Hoffman Press books
are available through Rayve Productions Inc. For more information and to place
orders call toll-free 1-800-852-4890 or fax 707-838-2220.

Library of Congress Cataloging-in-Publication Data
Ray, Norm, 1940 -
   Wine & Cheese Pairing Guide: your exciting search for Wow! combinations / by
Norm and Barbara Ray,
     p. cm.
   ISBN-13: 978-1-877810-00-8 (alk.paper)
   ISBN-10: 1-877810-00-2 (alk.paper)
   1. Wine and wine making. 2. Cheese--Varieties I. Ray, Barbara, 1941-. II. Title
III. Title: Wine and cheese pairing guide
   TP548.R2894 2006
   641.2'2--dc22
                              2006048272

Thank you Filomena Booth, Jenny Helman, Betsy Fischer, Lori Ray, Rhonda Ray, Cynthia Thomas, and Heidi Would for your special contributions to the *Wine & Cheese Pairing Guide*.

And a big *merci beaucoup* to friends, relatives, winery tasting room personnel, cheese experts, and the many participants in our wine and cheese pairing events for giving us your excellent "hands on" opinions regarding specific wine and cheese pairings. We especially enjoyed witnessing your **Wow!** pairing discoveries.

*"With more than a thousand wines
and a thousand cheeses in the world today,
the number of potential pairings is mind-boggling."*

—Norm Ray

CONTENTS

PAIRING BASICS

PAIRING RECOMMENDATIONS

JOURNALS

Introduction

It's great fun to discover a taste sensation that makes you say *"Wow! This is fantastic!"* and that sensation is readily available to you when you successfully pair wines and cheeses.

With more than a thousand wines and a thousand cheeses in the world today, the number of combinations is mind-boggling ... literally, over a million potential combinations. But, what an excellent opportunity for you and your friends to enjoy the pleasure of searching for specific combinations of wines and cheeses that give you the "Wow!" experience.

Since everyone has a unique set of taste buds and olfactory nerve cells, the perfect pairings of wines and cheeses are ultimately a matter of personal preference. Hence, the goal of this book is to give you information to help in your quest for *your* excellent pairings. This quest, by the way, is a very pleasurable ongoing experimentation process – a pursuit that you can repeatedly enjoy individually, with a friend, or in a group.

We encourage you to have "Wow! tasting parties" where the participants compare a wine with a selection of cheeses, compare a cheese with a selection of wines, or compare a series of wines with a series of cheeses. Listen to the variety of expressions by participants as they describe their individual tasting sensations or express your own declarations that "this wine definitely enhances the flavor of this cheese" or "this cheese balances perfectly with this wine" or "this wine blends perfectly with this cheese resulting in an extraordinary new flavor" or just "Wow! This is fantastic!"

Although we recognize and emphasize that perfect pairings are a matter of your personal preferences, we make pairing recommendations in this book based on many sources, including our personal experiences, tasting events with other people, recommendations by wine experts, recommendations by cheese experts, and various analytical pairings.

In other words, we have not personally tasted all of the potential combinations of over 150 wines and 340 cheeses described in this book (over 50,000 potential pairings) ... but we're working on it. Yes, we know "it's a tough job," but it's a challenge we enthusiastically accept.

An effective way to keep track of your personal favorites is to use "My Favorite Pairings Journal" in this book. We are confident you will discover additional wonderful pairings that we have not included in this edition, so we would certainly appreciate your telling us about your Wow! discoveries (as recommendations for future editions). Please email your suggestions to us at *rayvepro@aol.com* or write to us through our website *rayvepro.com*.

Thank you ... and enjoy!

CHEESE BASICS

Cheese is a living, breathing substance. Some say cheese is the purest and most romantic link between humans and the earth. Others argue that wine is also a living, breathing substance ... and is *obviously* the most romantic link between humans and the earth. What a dilemma!

But, alas, what an opportunity to personally explore this conundrum, enhancing your research by enjoying both of these "most romantic links" simultaneously while pairing cheeses with wine.

Cheeses of the World

Since there are more than two thousand types of cheese in the world, produced in at least 48 countries, you have an exciting opportunity to savor an enormous variety of wonderful cheese flavors and textures.

More than 30% of the world's cheese is manufactured in the United States, whose cheese vendors also import hundreds of additional cheeses that are produced in other countries. You'll find cheese vendors at local cheese shops, local markets, supermarkets, artisan cheesemaking farms, and online.

"Age is not important unless you're a cheese."
–Helen Hayes

History

Cheesemaking was underway thousands of years ago. Mesopotamian sculptures from the third millennium BC show men tending and milking goats, and cylinder seals from that era depict women churning. In the second millennium BC, the Bible records Job asking, "Did you not pour me out like milk, and curdle me like cheese?" (Job 10:10). The Bible also records King David being served a variety of foods including honey, butter, and cheese (2 Samuel 17:29). Cheese was also mentioned in Homer's *The Odyssey* circa 700 BC.

It is speculated that cheesemaking was discovered about 4000 BC when nomadic shepherds traveled with their milk supply in storage pouches made from the stomachs of sheep, camels or goats. Cheese would coagulate in the heat of the day, having absorbed microbes from the air that turned the milk sugar into acid, leading to coagulation, which was also accelerated by the natural presence of the enzyme rennin (now commercially "rennet") in the animal-stomach travel pouch. The requisite churning leading to the separation of curds and whey was the natural outcome of the shepherd's bag swinging back and forth during travel on foot or riding on the back of an animal.

It is believed that nomadic cattle-breeders from Central Asia subsequently brought cheesemaking to Europe where cheese production and consumption were abundant in Ancient Greece. Then, during the era of the Roman Empire cheesemaking processes were expanded in that milks from different sources began to be blended and seasonings added to produce a variety of flavors. Italy became Europe's cheesemaking center and the Roman Legion spread the art of cheesemaking across Europe and England.

During the Middle Ages production and consumption of cheese diminished, but cheesemaking processes were preserved by innovative monks in European monasteries who refined curing and ripening techniques. Early successes were Brie and Camembert.

Cheese came to America with the Mayflower and its cargo of goats in 1620 and continued as America's first cows arrived in 1624. Individuals or local farms produced America's first cheeses until the first cheese factories were established. In 1841, Anne Pickett established Wisconsin's first cheese factory. In 1851, Jesse Williams formed New York's first cheese factory in Oneida County.

Emigrants from excellent cheese producing countries of the British Isles (Cheddar), Holland (Gouda), France (Chèvre), Germany (Limburger), and Scandinavia ("Swiss-type") began making the wonderful cheeses they had made in their homelands. Now there are hundreds of artisan cheesemakers in the United States producing exquisite mouth-watering cheeses.

Cheese Styles

Cheeses are described and categorized using a variety of terms, which sometimes seem to overlap but are extremely valuable in helping you anticipate what you will likely experience when you store, serve and eat specific cheeses. Considering the huge variety of cheeses and complexity of their creation processes, classification confusion seems inevitable; but it's fun and educational to delve into the various forms of classification terminology to experience what the describer is communicating. You may be thinking that this same statement can be made about terminology used to describe the enormous variety of wines ... and you are right. But more on that later.

A popular set of terms to describe cheese styles is *soft* (retain most of their moisture), *semi-soft, semi-firm, firm* (retain little moisture), and *extra-firm* (least residual moisture).

Cheese style descriptors that focus on the rind are *fresh* (no rind), *natural rind* (wrinkled rind with bluish grey mold), *soft white* (white fuzzy rind), *semi-soft* (brownish orange to thick greyish brown), *hard* or *firm* (thick, dense rind often waxed or oiled) and *blue* (gritty, rough, dry or sticky with various colors).

Cheeses are also differentiated by the type of milk from which they originate: *cow, goat, sheep, buffalo, horse, camel, yak* and *reindeer*. Cheesemakers also decide (sometimes guided by legal regulations) how they will use that milk: *raw, skimmed* or *pasteurized*. In the United States a cheese that is going to be aged less than 60 days must be made from pasteurized milk.

Here is another set of adjectives to describe cheese styles: *very mild, mild, strong* and *very strong*.

You can also describe cheeses by the nature of their physical behavior or status when you serve them: *loose curds, runs or oozes; readily spreadable; crumbles; clings to knife; springy; slices smoothly;* and *easily gratable*.

Here's yet another popular set of cheese classification terms: *fresh* (uncooked and unripened, with texture ranging from thick and creamy to heavy curd); *fresh ripened* (white and no rind); *soft-ripened* ("bloomy rind" cheeses inoculated at the curd stage, ripening from the outside in, usually creamy and spreadable, edible rind); *washed rind* (outside rind has been wiped with a liquid such as wine, beer, or brandy); *semi-soft* (cooked or uncooked, smooth, usually creamy, little or no rind, pressed into a form); *firm* or *semi-firm* (they have been cooked and pressed but not aged as long as *hard* cheeses); *hard* (cooked, pressed and aged until hard and dry, generally aged two to four years and pressed with weights during aging to extract whey).

"There are many ways to describe cheese styles."

Basic categories of cheeses can also be described as *fresh* (no cooking and usually no ripening); *soft-ripened* (bloom of white mold rind with a buttery interior); *washed rind* (bathed, dunked or rubbed with a brine or beer, wine or brandy); *cooked pressed* (milk, culture, and rennet mixture is heated, and the resulting curds are pressed); *uncooked pressed*; and *blue-veined*.

In addition, there are the double- and triple-cream cheeses where extra cream has been added to soft-ripened cheese. *Triple-crèmes* have a fat content of at least 75% and *double-crèmes* have at least 60% fat content.

Ripened cheeses are classified by texture. *Firm* (*hard*) cheeses are cooked, pressed and aged for long periods (usually at least two years) until they become hard and dry (examples: Parmesan and Pecorino). *Semi-firm* cheeses are firm but not crumbly (examples: Jarlsberg, Edam, Cheddar). *Semi-soft* cheeses are pressed but can be either uncooked or cooked. They are soft but sliceable (examples: Monterey Jack, Gouda, Tilsit). *Soft-ripened* (*surface-ripened*) are not cooked or pressed, but are sprayed with or dipped into bacteria that cause the cheese to ripen from the outside in. They grow a rind that is powdery white or golden orange (examples: Brie or Pont L'Eveque). *Soft-ripened* cheese ranges from *semi-soft* to *creamy* and *spreadable*.

Some cheeses are further categorized by the cheesemaking process. *Blue-veined* cheeses are inoculated or sprayed with spores of the molds *penicillium roqueforti* or *penicillium glacum* and sometimes punctured to encourage the mold to penetrate the cheese during the aging period. This results in cheeses with veins or pockets of flavorful blue or green mold. Flavor intensifies as the cheese ripens.

As you can see, there are many ways to describe cheese styles and it becomes even more complex because the categories may overlap. A cheese can have an entirely different character when it is young than it does when aged. You may be thinking that this same statement can be made about wines as they age ... and you are right. But more on that later.

In this book we have chosen the following set of adjectives to categorize cheeses that we include in our pairing recommendations:

Fresh. They are neither ripened nor aged; often uncooked; texture can range from thick and creamy to heavy curd. Usually mild flavor. In the United States, the base milk is pasteurized, since the cheese is not aged at least 60 days. Highly perishable.

Soft (or soft-ripened). They are neither cooked nor pressed: bacteria ripen the cheese from the outside in; develop an edible rind; usually creamy, spreadable, and sometimes runny inside. Produced from pasteurized milk.

Semi-soft. Soft, but sliceable; pressed into form; cooked or uncooked. Generally little or no rind. High in moisture content and flavor ranges from mild to very pungent. Can be made from either pasteurized or raw milk, depending on cheesemaker decisions regarding aging and style.

Firm. Sometimes termed *semi-firm* or *semi-hard*; cooked; pressed; not aged as long as *hard* cheeses. Flavor ranges from very mild to sharp and pungent.

Hard. Cooked; pressed; aged until hard and dry. Commonly used for grating.

Blue. Often soft and crumbly; inoculated with penicillium spores, resulting in moldy bluish-green veins; flavor intensifies as cheese ripens.

Cheesemaking

Although hundreds of specialized techniques produce hundreds of distinct cheese flavors and characteristics, three basic steps comprise cheesemaking: (1) Proteins in milk are transformed into semisolid lumps called curds. (2)

Curds are separated from the milky liquid (whey) and are shaped or pressed into molds. (3) Shaped curds are ripened using a variety of aging and curing techniques.

To elaborate, cheese production begins as milk is allowed to thicken (often supplemented with the coagulating enzyme rennet and a starter culture containing a special bacteria that produces lactic acid) until it separates into whey and curds. The whey is then drained away and curds can be either allowed to drain further or pressed into various shapes. Applying heat is another cheesemaking technique used to increase the rate at which the curd contracts and squeezes out the whey. At this stage cheese is called *fresh* or *unripened* (examples: Cottage Cheese, Cream Cheese, Ricotta).

To produce *ripened* or *aged* cheese, the drained curds are cured by a variety of processes, such as being subjected to bacteria, heat and soaking. Sometimes curds are flavored with salt, spices or herbs, or colored with a natural dye (example: Cheddar). During this time, bacteria continue to grow and change the cheese's chemical composition which affects flavor and texture. Adding salt also inhibits the growth of undesirable microbes.

Sometimes another microbe is added to the cheese. Blue veined cheeses are inoculated with a *penicillium* spore.

After curing, natural cheese begins a ripening process whereby it is stored, usually uncovered, at a controlled temperature and humidity until the texture and character desired by the cheesemaker are obtained. As cheese ages it typically develops a stronger or sharper flavor. An exception is soft-ripened cheeses, which become softer and creamier with more pronounced flavors as they age (example: Brie).

In another special process, the cheesemaker gives the curd a hot whey bath, then kneads and stretches it to a pliable consistency, producing *pasta filata* cheeses (examples: Mozzarella, Provolone and Caciocavallo).

Whey cheeses are another special category. Instead of starting with milk, the cheesemaker uses whey drained from the making of other cheeses. The whey is reheated, usually with rennet, until it coagulates (example: Gjetost).

Cheese rinds are formed during the ripening process, either naturally or artificially. For instance, they may be brushed, washed, oiled, or coated with paraffin wax. Cheddars traditionally have a cotton cloth wrap.

The rind's primary function is to protect the interior of the cheese while allowing it to ripen to perfection. Heavily salted cheeses form a thick, tough outer rind.

Artisan vs. Large Scale Cheesemakers

Artisan cheeses are made by hand in much smaller quantities than large scale commodity-production cheeses. Artisan specialty cheeses vary according to season and region (terroir), as do wines. Contented cows grazing on the feed source in one region may well produce milk with characteristics much different from sister cows grazing in another environment. The happy result is that cheesemakers can achieve subtle (and not so subtle) cheese variations that are interesting for us to discover and enjoy.

Farmstead cheese is produced only from the milk of an artisan cheesemaker's own herd.

In contrast, commodity cheesemakers operate large sophisticated, fully integrated cheese processing factories where, for example, one cheesemaker annually produces a billion pounds of milk to produce a hundred million pounds of Cheddar, Monterey Jack, Mozzarella, and other cheeses.

Buying Cheese

You have many options regarding where to buy cheese. There are specialty markets, cheese shops, gourmet food stores, local farmers' markets, cheesemaker websites, cheese vendor websites, cheesemaker farms, and, of course, your favorite supermarkets. Each source could have an advantage for you, such as convenience, freshness of cheese, samples available before you buy, cut-to-order service, discussion with a knowledgeable cheesemonger or even a cheesemaker.

You certainly want to find consistently reliable sources to assure that cheeses you buy from them will be in excellent condition.

If you are cheese shopping in a store, study the package labels carefully, especially for fresh cheeses, to determine that the cheese is well within its expiration date. Analyze the appearance of the cheese to see that the interior is free of cracks, discoloration, and mold (blue cheese excepted). See if natural rind cheeses appear rustic and otherwise healthy.

It's best to taste the cheese before you buy it; but if that is not practical, buy the smallest portion possible to give it a try.

Check labels for type of milk (cow, goat, sheep, etc.) and whether it is pasteurized or raw milk.

Don't purchase cheese too far in advance. Try to buy the amount of cheese you intend to eat between then and your next visit to the cheese store. Of course, that's easier said than done, so in the next section we give you suggestions for storing your cheese for longer periods.

When you shop for cheese, you may want to have a small ice chest or other cooling container in your car for storing your cheese until you get it into your home refrigerator.

If the cheese you buy is wrapped in plastic, when you first open it, you should rewrap it in waxed- or parchment paper and then in plastic. That will allow air and moisture to keep the cheese in good condition while protecting it from picking up other flavors in your refrigerator.

Storing Cheese

Cheese contains living organisms (enzymes and bacteria) that need air and moisture to survive and to continue the cheese's ripening until it is eaten.

So, wrap cheeses to maintain moisture while allowing the cheese to breathe. A good approach is to wrap cheeses in waxed- or parchment paper, then aluminum foil, zip-close plastic bags or plastic wrap. If you use zip-close plastic bags, leave the zipper partway open so the cheese can continue to breathe while retaining moisture. To maintain cheese quality, wrappings should be changed if a cheese is stored for more than a week.

Except for fresh and soft-ripened cheeses, it's a good idea to store cheese in a large lidded plastic container in the warmest part of your refrigerator (between 35° and 45° F). The vegetable drawer at the bottom of your refrigerator is likely designed to provide extra humidity, which is just what cheese needs to stay at its peak. Some refrigerators also have cheese drawers.

To keep cheeses from picking up one another's flavors, you may want to have three separate lidded plastic containers: (1) blue cheeses, (2) washed rind cheeses, and (3) milder cheeses. This will discourage mold spores from spreading to other cheeses. It is also prudent to double-wrap all strong, pungent cheeses to keep their aromas from permeating other foods.

Fresh and soft-ripened cheeses should be tightly wrapped and stored in the coldest part of the refrigerator. Fresh cheeses are fragile and highly perishable. You should also store them in airtight containers, and eat fresh cheeses within two weeks. Semi-soft, firm and hard cheeses can usually be satisfactorily refrigerated for four to eight weeks.

In general, the harder the cheese, the longer it will stay fresh. Cut pieces of soft cheeses may last less than two weeks.

Freezing cheeses is not a good idea. The texture of frozen cheese can become crumbly when thawed, and its flavor deteriorates. Soft-ripened and bloomy-rind cheeses collapse when thawed after freezing. The exception is hard-grating cheese which can be successfully frozen and thawed.

If gray and blue molds appear on firm, semi-firm or semi-soft cheese, simply cut away the offending portion (plus a little extra) and discard the trimmings. Mold on fresh or soft-ripened cheese, however, signals that the cheese is ruined and should be discarded. Black and red molds should always be trimmed off and if they permeate the cheese, throw it away.

Do not store cheese with other strong-smelling foods. As cheese breathes, it will absorb other aromas that may spoil the flavors of the cheese.

Serving Cheese

Your tasting platter should include a variety of cheeses with contrasting flavors and textures. Generally, serve up to five different cheeses, ideally representing different milks, flavors, and textures. It is also fun to have a variety of sizes, shapes, colors, and foreign country origins.

Cheese generally tastes better if it is brought to room temperature before serving. In addition, its flavor will flow more freely when the cheese is warm. Remove it from the refrigerator one to two hours before serving, leaving it wrapped while it warms. An exception is fresh cheeses, which should be served cold.

Plan to serve eight to twelve ounces of cheese per person, with at least a one-ounce serving of each different cheese per person.

Strong, pungent cheeses should not be placed next to delicate-flavored cheeses. When practical, provide an individual knife for each cheese.

Edibility of cheese rind is a matter of taste and common sense. Unless you like the flavor of mold, trim it away. Most natural rinds may be unclean and are probably gritty and bitter.

Various serving tools will add to the ease and pleasure of your cheese tasting experience. They include a **cheese knife** with two sharp points (to facilitate handling the sliced cheese) at the end of a slightly bent blade, **wire cheese slicer** to easily thinly slice firm, semi-firm, or soft cheeses, **cheese grater** to easily grate hard cheeses, **cheese planer** to skim wafer-thin servings of firm cheeses, and for extra drama, a **serving board** of natural-looking materials like wood, marble, granite or slate.

A basket or plate of bread or plain crackers should also be part of the setup.

Tasting Cheese

The younger the cheese, the less flavor. Most cheeses taste best when they've been aged somewhere between bland youth and sharp maturity. As we eat cheeses, our flavor dynamic senses come into play — sight, touch, smell and taste. These senses translate appearance, aroma, texture and flavor into our responses to what we eat.

Appearance: Look for the nuances in color ranging from pale white to ivory, to buttery, golden or blue-streaked. Notice the moisture in the cheeses, causing them to range from soft and spoonable to firm or crumbly. Various appearances are soft, runny, hard, crumbly, dry moist, smooth, rough, crusty, moldy, white, yellow, ivory, and orange.

Aroma: Cheese aroma is created by many factors including the animal's feed and the butterfat content of the milk; type of starter culture and enzymes that the cheese recipe contains; length of time the cheese has been ripened or aged, and the amount of salting which helps to intensify aroma. Variously, aromas are mild, delicate, milky, fresh, creamy, salty, sweet, strong, pungent, earthy, and moldy.

Texture: Cheese ranges from very soft to very hard. The higher the moisture and milk fat of a cheese, the smoother the mouthfeel. Textures can be soft, firm, hard, moist, runny, crumbly, granular, creamy, buttery, rubbery, waxy, oily, chalky, and spreadable.

Taste: The sense perception we receive through our taste buds can be sweet, sour, salty, bitter, and umami. (Umami is the fifth primary element of taste found in substances like monosodium glutamate, MSG. substances like monosodium glutamate, *MSG*. Identified by Kikunae Ikeda in 1907. *Umami* means "delicious flavor" in Japanese.) Flavor is the quality that we experience as a blend of our taste and smell sensations. Tastes can be sweet, mild, milky, buttery, delicate, salty, sharp, acidic, tart, tangy, lemony, bitter, nutty, piquant, smoky, and yeasty.

Tasting sequences
- Tasting cheeses sequentially from mild to sharp will

help keep your palate from being overwhelmed, enabling you to especially appreciate the nuances in milder cheeses.
- Taste softer cheeses before harder.
- Start with cow milk cheeses, then progress to goat milk cheeses, then sheep milk cheeses, saving blue cheeses for the grand finale.

Tasting techniques

- Take a thin shaving of each cheese and let it melt on your tongue. Then try a larger chunk that requires chewing. Before putting a piece of cheese into your mouth, sniff it as you would a glass of wine. Take the first bite, breathing a little air into your mouth so the aroma fills the whole nasal passage. Notice any scent that distinguishes the cheese. Aroma and taste will combine to give you the flavor of the cheese.

- Don't chew and swallow quickly, but move the cheese around in your mouth to expose it to your taste buds. Note that some cheeses coat your mouth and others leave a clean palate. Analyze which tastes appear first, which tastes develop next, and which tastes linger.

WINE BASICS

Wine, like cheese, is a living, breathing substance. Some say wine is the purest and most romantic link between humans and the earth ... the other side of the "cheese romantic link" declaration in the first chapter.

Wines of the World

With thousands of varieties of wine produced in at least 25 countries, each wine having its own flavor and style, you have a very exciting opportunity to experiment, experience and savor.

History

Winemaking was underway thousands of years ago. The world's oldest existing wine jar dates to 5400-5000 BC and the earliest written account of viniculture is in the Bible (Genesis 9:20) where Noah planted a vineyard on Mount Ararat after the flood ... and he made wine.

Texts from tombs in ancient Egypt depict wine usage around 2500 BC.

Wine arrived in Western Europe with the spread of the Greek civilization around 1600 BC. Homer's *Odyssey* and the *Iliad* both have detailed descriptions of wine. Greek doctors, including Hippocrates, were among the first to prescribe wine for health improvement.

By 1000 BC, the Romans were classifying grape varieties and colors, recording ripening characteristics, diseases, and soil-type preferences. They also became skilled at pruning, irrigation and fertilizing techniques, and developed bottling, wooden cooperage, and storage systems.

After the fall of the Roman Empire, winemaking was kept alive during the Dark Ages mainly through the efforts of Christian monasteries, which developed some of the finest vineyards in Europe.

By the first century AD, Italy was exporting wine to Spain, Germany, England and France, all of whom developed their own vineyards. Over the next few centuries, France became dominant in the wine market. Exploration, conquest and settlement brought wine to Mexico, Argentina, and South Africa in the 16th and 17th centuries.

In 1769, Franciscan missionary Father Junipero Serra planted the first California vineyard at Mission San Diego and subsequently established eight more missions and vineyards, earning him the "Father of California Wine" moniker.

In the 1850s and 1860s Agoston Harazsthy imported cuttings from 165 great European vineyards to California, introducing about 300 different grape varieties.

From 1865 to 1885, a vine-killing phylloxera decimated nearly all vineyards of Europe. Since American vines were resistant to that disease, basically every wine grapevine in Europe was subsequently grafted onto American rootstocks, heading off the extinction of the European wine industry.

The American wine industry was nearly destroyed by the National Prohibition Act and the 18th Amendment to the

U.S. Constitution in 1920, which outlawed the "manufacture, sale, or transportation of intoxicating liquors." By the time of National Repeal in 1933, the American wine industry was basically ruined, although some wineries had managed to survive by making wines used for medicinal, sacramental, and non-beverage additive purposes.

Slowly, the American wine industry recovered, and in the past three decades, research and development in agriculture and technology have led to remarkably high quality wines and outstanding worldwide acclaim for American vintages.

Wine Categories and Styles

From the grape comes the wine ... and the grape exists in thousands of varieties. For example, Italy claims over 2000 indigenous varieties of grapes, and Spain has about 600.

There are basically two types of wine: Sparkling Wines and Still Wines. Sparkling Wines have bubbles; Still Wines do not.

General categories of wines are (1) Appetizer or Aperitif Wines, (2) Still or Table Wines, (3) Sparkling Wines, and (4) Dessert or Fortified Wines.

Appetizer or Aperitif Wines are customarily served before a meal to help stimulate the appetite. They often have flavors added to them. The best examples of these are Vermouth and Lillet. Vermouth is wine infused with herbs, alcohol, sugar, caramel and water. It can be dry (white) or sweet (white or red), or half-sweet.

Table Wines are generally categorized as Varietals, Proprietaries, Appellations, or Generics.

A **varietal** wine is made from a specific grape variety. In the United States, each varietal wine must generally contain at least 75% of its specific variety to be able to be named for that grape; however, this is not the requirement for varietal designations in every country. In the United States, the remaining percentage may be made up of grape varieties that the winemaker chooses in order to achieve a targeted flavor and/or color, or to manage production cost.

A **proprietary** wine is labeled with the winemaker's brand name. Proprietaries may be blended by the winemaker from multiple varieties of grapes to produce a unique body, flavor and aroma that can be found only in that particular wine at a targeted price point.

An **appellation** designates wine made from grapes grown in a specific region, which may or may not be where the wine is actually made. "Champagne" takes its name from the Champagne region in France, and "Rhine" is derived from the Rhine River in Germany. The name of the wine reflects the region in which the grapes are grown.

In 1982, the United States government established "American Viticultural Areas," specifying unique grape growing regions and the names for wines of those regions. These regions can be large, such as the entire Ohio Valley grape growing region; smaller, such as the Willamette Valley in Oregon or California's Green Valley, which is a sub-appellation of the greater Russian River appellation.

Use of an appellation requires that 85% of the grapes in the wine must come from that region. Furthermore, a wine label can specify the vineyard's name as part of the appellation if there is a minimum of 95% of the winery's own grapes, grown in that region, in the wine produced. "Estate Bottled" indicates that the winery either owns or controls the vineyard and is responsible for the growing of the grapes used in the wine.

"Wine & cheese are ageless companions ...
like good people and noble ventures."
–M.F.K. Fisher

Generic wines are named for the European locations where they were originally produced (such as Burgundy, Rhine, and Chianti). Generic wines are made from different wine grape varieties blended together with the resulting wine containing less than 75% of one grape varietal. The winemaker may use a single grape variety or a blend of varieties that may come from different regions or even different countries. Semi-generic wine is named for and made in the style of a European geographic district (e.g., "California Chablis" or "American Burgundy"). There are some very good generic or semi-generic blends, but there can also be great differences in the quality of wines. Although not required, some wineries list on the back label the varieties they blended to create that wine. It's a good idea to always taste-test generic wines before serving them.

Vintage is the year the grapes were harvested. It is often used to identify the quality of the wines created that year. The vintage year is very important in identifying European wines due to potentially dramatic fluctuations in weather in grape-growing regions. In America, weather in most grape-growing regions is less variable; but you are also well advised to research or ask wine sellers about the quality of American vintages that you are considering buying.

Sparkling Wines regularly produced in the United States are either Champagne or Sparkling Wine. In general, Champagne is made by the traditional European Champenoise method of aging the wine in the bottle. Sparkling Wines are made by the Charmat method, whereby wine is aged in large tanks before bottling.

Unlike Europe, where governments strictly control the use of the word "Champagne," in the United States the lines are somewhat blurred in that some wines that are aged in the bottle (Champagne?) are labeled Sparkling Wine; and some wines aged in tanks (Sparkling Wine?) are called Champagne.

These Champagnes and Sparkling Wines are available in the traditional blanc (white) and rosé (pink). They have varying degrees of sweetness:

- Extra Brut is the driest champagne or sparkling wine, with no hint of sweetness.
- Brut is dry, with little or no sweetness (the most common designation).
- Extra-Dry has a modicum of sweetness.
- Sec is slightly sweet.
- Demi-Sec is fairly sweet.
- Doux is sweet.

Dessert or Fortified Wines are classified as wines that have more than 14% alcohol and are generally served with dessert. Port, Sherry and Sauternes are popular dessert wines.

Varietal Wines reflect the recognizable taste of their specific grapes. Know the grape and you will know the wine.

The following seven grape varieties have tastes and smells sufficiently distinct and memorable to comprise internationally recognized varietal wines. We elaborate a bit on the flavors and aromas you may experience as you taste these popular wines; but remember, the recurring theme in this book ... everyone has a unique set of sensoromics (to coin a term), so your individual taste sensations may be different from the flavors mentioned. Analyzing and describing the flavors and nuances you taste in a wine are part of the fun of this adventure. There are no necessarily "right" or "wrong" taste sensations. What you taste and experience is irrefutably what *you* taste and experience.

Cabernet Sauvignon (ka-behr-NAY soh-vihn-YOHN / soh-vee-NYAWN) is a classic, full-bodied red wine with a rich, intense flavor. You may experience fruity undertones of raspberry, cherry, black currant; and/or coffee, dark chocolate, mint, bell pepper, green bean, olives, black pepper, and cassis notes with a long finish. Cabernet Sauvignon is widely considered the most complex of red wine varietals and most age 10 to 20 years extremely well.

Chardonnay (shar-dn-AY; shar-doh-NAY) is a medium-bodied white wine with a wide range of fruity flavors, from pineapple, peach, citrus, fig and red apple. You may also sense a bouquet of vanilla (if oak is used, such as aging in an oak barrel) and butteriness (from malolactic fermentation). Chardonnay can be semi-dry to dry, rich and intensely complex with a smooth finish. The most versatile of all white wines, and the most popular worldwide, Chardonnay goes well with any cheese that calls for a white wine. Aging potential is five to six years but most Chardonnays are ready for consumption upon release.

Gewürztraminer (guh-VURTZ-trah-mee-ner, geh-VEHRTZ-trah-mee-ner) is an American favorite whose name derives from Tramin, the Italian village believed to be the origin of the white grape used in the wine, and the German word *gewürtz* (spicy). This intense and distinctive crisp light wine is appreciated for its softness and richness. This dry to sweet wine has flavor descriptions that include spicy, floral, fruity (citrus, grapefruit, peach), lychee, and honey to jasmine tea. Late Harvest Gewürztraminer is very sweet and is ideal with or as dessert. Gewürztraminers are best drunk when relatively young as they generally do not age well past three to five years.

Muscat (MUHS-cat); **Moscato Canelli; Muscat Canelli** is a white wine that ranges from very dry to sweet with an intense fruity/floral taste – just like the muscat grapes from which it is made. Aging potential is two to five years.

Pinot Noir (PEE-noh NWAHR) is a popular red wine that pairs very well with many different cheeses and other foods.

Pinot Noir grapevines mutate easily, often changing the flavor of the grapes in the process. This presents a challenge to winemakers who have risen to the challenge by producing many excellent medium-bodied and silky wines with intense fruity (red cherry, strawberry, raspberry, black currant), spicy (black pepper, cloves) and smoky tones. When young, fine-quality Pinot Noir wines can exhibit simple, fruity characteristics of cherries, plums, raspberries, and strawberries. As these wines mature, they become more complex, with chocolate, figs, spices, and other intriguing flavors. Pinot Noirs from the cool California coast regions have incredible layers of aromas, flavors, and complexity. Aging potential is five to ten years.

Riesling (REEZ-ling, REES-ling) is a white wine known for its wonderful variety of flavors described as floral (honeysuckle), fruity (citrus, peach, apricot, pineapple and pear), and honey flavors that follow with a dry finish. This delicate, yet complex, light- to medium-bodied, very dry to very sweet wine is a perfect match with many cheeses. Riesling can age well for three to five years.

Sauvignon Blanc (soh-vihn-YOHN / soh-vee-NYAWN BLAHNGK) is also marketed under the name Fumé Blanc. It is light-bodied, quite dry, with crisp acidity and flavors of fruits (citrus, peach, pineapple, pear, apple, and apricot), and bell pepper, asparagus, green olive, and melon. Sauvignon Blanc is a good match with most cheeses calling for white wine. Fumé Blanc (FOO-may BLAHNGK) from the French *fumé* (smoky) and *blanc* (white), was originally coined by the Robert Mondavi Winery as a marketing designation for Mondavi's dry, oak-aged Sauvignon Blanc.

Additional Varietals – Red Wines

Barbera (bar-BEH-rah) is a dark red wine with a rich, fruity flavor.

Cabernet Franc (KA-behr-nay FRAHNGK), originally brought to the United States from France's Bordeaux region for blending, has now established its own recognition. Although quite similar to Cabernet Sauvignon, Cabernet Franc is not as full-bodied but is generally more aromatic.

Carignane; Carignan (kah-ree-NYAHN) is a heavy-bodied, rich table wine with fruity, spicy flavors. The grapes, which have a deep purple color and are high in tannins and alcohol, are often blended with softer grapes to enhance the wine's flavor.

Dolcetto (dohl-CHET-toh) is a soft, fruity, dry red wine, ideal for consumption while young.

Gamay (gam-MAY) refers to any of several related grapes used in making red wines, most notably, Beaujolais (Boe-zho-LAY), which is a light- to medium-weight, fragrant red wine. Delicately fruity, this wine often suggests the flavors of bananas, berries, and peaches. Gamay wines are best consumed young (within one to two years after bottling) as they do not age well.

Grenache (greh-NAHSH) is a grape used in both red wine and white wine, but "Grenache" used alone without a "white" or "rosé" adjective refers to the red variety. Grenache wines are sweet with strong fruity overtones.

Malbec (Mahl-beck) is a dark, dense, tannic, medium-bodied wine capable of excellent quality.

Merlot (mare-LOH, mer-LOH) wine is similar to Cabernet Sauvignon but has a mellow, softer taste. Merlot wines mature early and can be enjoyed sooner than many other red wines. Well-blended young Merlots are rich, velvety and delicious, medium to dark red in color, and often have complex nuances and smooth finishes of black cherry, plum, raspberry and chocolate.

Mourvèdre (Moor-VEH-druh) is an excellent dark, aromatic, tannic grape yielding medium-bodied, fruity wines.

Nebbiolo (nehb-YOH-lo, neh-bee-OH-loh) is an intense, complex, fruity, perfumed wine. Because it is quite tannic, it may age well for years.

Petit Sirah / Petite Sirah / Petite Syrah (peh-TEET sih-RAH) is a big, deep-colored, full-bodied wine with peppery overtones. It is also used to blend with other red wines to add body and character. It ages beautifully.

Sangiovese (San-gee-oh-VAY-zee) is a medium-bodied, tart wine with fresh berry and plum flavors and a hint of floral.

Syrah (sih-RAH), also called **Shiraz** in Australia (Sih-RAH, Shih-RAHZ), is a tannic, purple, peppery wine which matures superbly. It is often intense and earthy, with suggestions of black cherry, currant, and plum with spicy complexity.

Tempranillo (Tem-prah-NEE-yo) is aromatic. It is elegant in cool climates and beefy in warm areas.

Zinfandel (ZIHN-fuhn-dehl) is called America's signature wine since it has been cultivated more in the United States than anywhere else. Great Zinfandels have medium- to heavy-body with flavors of blackberry, raspberry, black pepper and smoky tones and a solid spicy finish. White Zinfandel wines, which are usually sweet, range in color from light to dark pink. Late Harvest Zinfandel, with its high sugar levels, is a popular dessert wine.

Additional Varietals – White Wines

Chenin Blanc (SHEN-ihn BLAHNGK) grapes are used to create a variety of delicious wines – dry, sweet, or very sweet, with significant acidity. Some Chenin Blanc wines age well; others do not.

Colombard (KAHL-uhm-bahrd) is slightly fruity, nicely sharp.

Kerner (Ker-ner) is a full-bodied wine resembling Riesling with a light, flowery bouquet and refreshing acidity.

Malvasia (Mal-VAY-zhuh, Mahl-va-SEE-a) is a sweet, fruity, soft wine that can be processed as white, red, or blush.

Marsanne (Marr-SAHN) is a soft, full-bodied wine that is rich in flavor and ages very well.

Müller-Thurgau (MUHL-er THUHR-gow) is an enticingly soft, light, aromatic, slightly sweet wine with low acidity.

Pinot Blanc (PEE-noh BLAHNGK), is a dry, crisp, fruity wine with slightly less flavor and intensity than its cousin, Chardonnay. Pinot Blanc is not aromatic.

Pinot Gris, also called **Pinot Grigio** in Italy (PEE-noh GREE, PEE-noh GREE-jzhee-o) wine may range from crisp, light and dry to heavy, full-bodied and sweet.

Roussanne (Ru-SAHN), with its floral aromas, can display great finesse and age well.

Sémillon (SAY-mee-yawn) is a light- to medium wine ranging from dry to semi-sweet. Often, it is blended with other varietals, particularly Sauvignon Blanc, resulting in balance, new flavors, and complexity. Whether sweet or dry, a top-quality Sémillon ages well for many years, the wine's flavor improving over time.

Seyval Blanc (SAY-vahl BLAHNGK) is a deliciously fruity, crisp, semi-dry wine.

Silvaner, Sylvaner (SEEL-vah-nay) is a light-bodied, gently fruity wine with light acidity and a delicate bouquet. It ages well.

Viognier (VEE-ohn-yay) is an aromatic, medium-bodied, complex wine with spice, fruit and floral components.

Selected dessert wines

Port (Pohrt) is a sweet, fortified wine customarily served after a meal. The best Ports are labeled Late-Bottled Vintage Port, Single Vintage Port, and Tawny Port. To make Port, a neutral grape alcohol is added to a wine during fermentation to stop the fermentation process while the wine still has a high sugar content and high alcohol levels. The very best vintage ports can be aged for 50 years or longer.

Sherry (SHEH-ree) is a fortified wine that has a wide range of flavors and sweetness:
- *Finos* (FEE-nohs) are dry and light.
- *Manzanillas* (mahn-zah-NEE-yahs) are very dry and very light.
- *Amontillados* (ah-MOHN-tee-YAH-dohs) are medium with a nutty flavor and are darker, sweeter and softer than the *Finos*.
- *Oloroso* (oh-loh-roh-soh), the darkest, is more full-flavored. It is also known as Cream Sherry or Golden Sherry.

Winemaking

The craft and science of growing grapes and making wine

There is a tremendous amount of teamwork in producing that bottle of delicious wine for your enjoyment. Grape growers and winemakers each play crucial roles in understanding and using various processes of nature both to grow grapes with the desired characteristics and to convert them into good wine.

The viticulturalist (grape grower) must have an intimate understanding of how grapes grow and respond to their environment. In addition, he or she must know how to grow and harvest the kind and quality of fruit desired by the winemaker.

The enologist (winemaker) uses advanced technical knowledge of the biological and chemical events that occur during wine production, along with keen judgment and skill needed to make successful crucial decisions during the winemaking process.

Snapshot of the winemaking process from the winemaker's point of view:

1. Envision the type and style of the finished wine.

2. Choose the most appropriate grape varieties for making that wine.

3. Arrange to grow or acquire the grapes which have been produced in the most appropriate climatic region and with the most appropriate vineyard management.

4. Closely follow the ripening of the grapes.

5. See that the grapes are harvested quickly at optimum ripeness.

6. Remove the juice from the grapes.

7. Manage the fermentation process.

"Wine is the mirror of the heart."
-Aeschylus

8. Clarify and stabilize the new wine.

9. Age the new wine in bulk.

10. Blend and finish the wine.

11. Bottle the wine.

12. Age the bottled wine.

13. Present the bottled wine to you at the winery or elsewhere in the marketplace.

Envisioning the type and style of wine

The winemaker has many choices in envisioning the type and style of wine. White, red, or rosé? Simple, inexpensive, generic for mass market or premium varietal wines with special aromas, bouquets, and complexities? Sweet or dry? Varietal character (flavor and/or aroma recognizable as the grape variety from which it is made) or blended from more than one grape variety.

Growing grapes for wine production ("winegrowing")

The grower wants to plant vines where the climate and soil are best for the specific grape varieties. Site selection within various macro- and microclimates and vineyard management will ultimately influence the flavors of the resulting wine.

For example, for premium white table wine production, cooler growing regions are preferred for Chardonnay, Sauvignon Blanc, Sémillon, Riesling, and Gewürztraminer grape varieties. A heavy rich soil can produce wine with grassy flavors, whereas a shallower, less fertile soil encourages fruity flavors. Likewise, more fertilization leads to "grassy" and less fertilization yields "fruity." Irrigation choices (more water vs. less), leaf canopy (heavy, dense, shady vs. open, sunny), vine density, trellis system vs. individual umbrella shaped vines, and other grower decisions dictate the characteristics of the grapes, and ultimately, the wines.

Vineyard operations include the following extremely important activities that determine yield and quality of grapes:

- selecting type of grape(s) to plant and vine density (the number of vines per acre)

- selecting vine shapes (separate vines each supported by a pole vs. widely spaced rows of vines supported by stakes and wires)

- pruning (to shape the vines and balance the crop size)

- fertilization (to grow and reproduce, vines need 17 essential elements: carbon, hydrogen, oxygen, nitrogen, phosphorus, potassium, sulfur, calcium, iron, copper, zinc, manganese, magnesium, nickel, boron, molybdenum, and chlorine)

- shoot removal (to balance leaf area and crop size)

- leaf removal (to manage photosynthesis and sugar level)

- irrigation (to manage photosynthesis and sugar level)

- protection from damaging weather conditions (e.g., frost)

- control of insect pests, powdery mildew, and weeds

- harvest

Grape ripening and the harvest

As grapes ripen they get bigger and softer, their green color fades, aromatic compounds increase, sugars increase, and both total acid concentration and acid strength decrease. The concentration of red pigments increases in the skins of red grapes.

It is important for the winemaker to closely follow the ripening process by ongoing measurements of total sugar and acid content of the grapes. During ripening, photosynthesis and storage of the resulting sugar naturally increases the sugar content of the grapes. Simultaneously, dilution through increased water storage and respiration decrease both acid content and acid strength. The concentrations of aroma components also increase as grapes ripen. The correct ripeness for harvest depends on the type and style of wine for which the grapes will be used.

The natural acidity in grapes (tartaric and malic acids) declines as grapes ripen and it is important for acid strength to decline to specific levels before harvest.

Red-wine grapes are allowed to ripen longer and are harvested at higher sugar and lower acid levels than white-wine grapes. The higher sugar levels produce wines of greater aroma and flavor intensity, varietal character, and complexity since they allow fermentation reactions to produce higher alcohol concentrations, which aid the extraction of color, flavor, and tannins.

The timing of harvest is a critical call based on a number of factors, including sugar and acid levels of the grapes, weather conditions (and forecasts), and evaluation of the soil conditions (stored water) for supporting more ripening and photosynthesis to increase sugar levels.

"Wine is bottled poetry."
–Robert Louis Stevenson

The crush and juice

After grapes are harvested, juice removal begins by (1) crushing the grapes, i.e., breaking the skins of the grape berries to allow the juice to flow out without any damage to seeds, stems, and skins, whose high concentrations of tannin could cause astringency and bitterness in the juice and wine if injured, (2) gently pressing the mixture of grapes, seeds, stems, and skins (known as "must") to extract more juice (called "free-run juice"), and (3) applying heavy pressure to the must to squeeze out more juice ("press-run juice"). The free-run juice has more sugar and less acid and tannin than press-run juice which contains less sugar and more acid and tannin.

Sulfur dioxide (SO_2) is typically added to the whole fruit or must at crushing to prevent wine spoilage. SO_2 slows the growth of potentially damaging microbes and protects the juice and wine from reactions with oxygen that could negatively affect aroma, flavor, and pigment. Often less SO_2 is needed for making red wines because their tannins assume the antioxidant function.

Chilling the must for several hours of skin contact can yield enhanced aroma and flavor in white wines.

Fermentation

In winemaking, fermentation is the conversion of grape sugar yeast enzymes of the grape sugar in the must or juice into alcohol and carbon dioxide (CO_2) in an oxygen-free environment. Winery fermentation tanks have one-way valves that allow CO_2 to escape and keep O_2 out.

Heat is also a by-product of the fermentation process. Since high temperatures can destroy wine's delicate aromas and flavors, temperature control is very important during the winemaking process. Hence, white wine juice is typically reduced to about 45° F (7°C) between pressing and the beginning of fermentation.

The juice is clarified by overnight settling, filtering, or centrifuging. Acidity level may be adjusted by adding tartaric acid. Then an active yeast is added and fermentation (conversion of grape sugar into alcohol) takes place in large stainless steel tanks (5,000 to 60,000 gallon capacity) or in barrels in humidity-controlled rooms (including caves) with temperatures of 50 to 60° F (10° to 16° C).

White wine fermentation is complete when the appropriate amount of sugar has been consumed for the style of wine that is being made. For dry wine styles such as Chardonnay, fermentation is allowed to go to completion, i.e., when all glucose molecules have been converted to alcohol. For sweeter wines such as Riesling or Gewürztraminer, the winemaker stops fermentation by deep chilling to inactivate the yeast before all glucose is converted to alcohol, leaving a residual sugar to balance the wine's acidity. The remaining cold-inactivated yeast will then be removed by filtering or centrifuging.

When alcoholic fermentation is finished, yeast cells settle out and form sediment ("lees") at the bottom of the tank. The new wine is promptly transferred off the yeast lees into a clean tank where clarification and stabilization begin. This transferring from tank to tank is called "racking."

However, to add aroma and flavor complexity and body to a white wine like Chardonnay, the winemaker may opt to allow the wine to remain in contact with the yeast for weeks or months (*"sur lie"* aging).

Another fermentation is sometimes used by winemakers to convert malic acid from the grape juice to lactic acid and CO_2. This is the malolactic fermentation (MLF) which the winemaker can initiate during alcoholic fermentation by inoculating tanks of Chardonnay with bacteria. Since lactic acid is less tart than the malic acid it replaces, the final wine has reduced acidity and can develop more complexity with aging, although MLF diminishes fruitiness.

Red wines have more intense aromas and flavors, and these are extracted (along with color and tannins) from the grapes' skins during maceration (skin contact during the alcoholic fermentation) or carbonic maceration (fermentation of uncrushed whole grapes which takes place within the cells of the berries with no need for added yeasts, resulting in intensely fruity red wines). This is the most important step in producing red wines. The tannins extracted protect red wines during longer aging periods that allow them to develop complex bouquets. The tannin level determines to a large extent how long wines will benefit from aging, creating an overall pleasant balance of tannin, acid, and fruit.

During maceration the winemaker must manage the cap (mixture of grape seeds, stems, and pulp) that rises to the top of the fermenting juice as CO_2 is produced. The cap can become thick and tightly compacted and needs to be covered with juice saturated with CO_2 to discourage the growth of vinegar bacteria and to maintain maceration throughout the juice. Winemakers can choose to pump juice from the bottom of the fermenter and spray it on the cap; or punch the cap, breaking it up and shoving it down to re-mix with the juice; or use tanks that trap the cap in the middle of the juice for "submerged cap fermentation."

Since fermentation for red wines often is complete within a few days, it is done in open-top tanks and CO_2 produced during fermentation protects the juice from oxidation. The longer the extraction goes on, the more color and tannins and varietal flavor from the skins end up in the juice.

"Wine is the most healthful and most hygienic of beverages."
–Louis Pasteur

After the winemaker ends maceration by separating the juice and pressing the solids, the free-run and press juices are kept in separate batches and fermented to dryness if all sugar has not already been consumed during maceration of the skins.

Blush or Rosé wines are made with minimal or no grape skin contact except for that occurring during the crush. The result is a pink wine where the level of pinkness is proportional to the length of time juice was in contact with the skins.

Depending on the grape variety and the style of wine being produced, fermentation temperature for red wines is from 60° to 95° F.

Clarification, stabilization, and aging

To remove particles or wine components that can react to form hazes, winemakers use racking, centrifugation, filtering and fining. Fining agents such as gelatin and egg albumen are mixed into the wine and react with specific wine components that are to be removed, forming particles that will settle out or be removed by filtration or centrifugation. Fining agents also reduce tannin content and color in red wines.

Stabilization (heat, cold, and microbial) is complete when new wine will remain clear and unchanged in aroma and bouquet in defined temperatures during specific time frames. Microbiological stability is achieved when wine will not undergo any additional fermentation or microbial growth that could spoil the wine.

While wine is being clarified and stabilized, it is also aging in bulk in a tank or barrel. The goal of bulk aging for most white wines is to preserve their characteristic aromas and not add other odors or flavors.

Red wines are deliberately exposed to air to avoid off-odors and to provide oxygen needed for normal aging in tanks and barrels. The growth of undesirable microbes is discouraged by keeping storage tanks and barrels full, or blanketing the wine with an inert gas such as nitrogen or CO_2.

Red wines more commonly are aged in oak for long periods. The winemaker's selection of type of oak (American or French) is a factor in the wine's flavor as is the amount of air exposure the wine receives during aging. Delicately flavored red wines (e.g., Pinot Noir) should be exposed to minimal amounts of air during barrel aging; whereas, more flavorful wines (e.g., Zinfandel and Cabernet Sauvignon) can benefit from more oxygen exposure.

Blending, finishing, bottling, and aging

Wines are blended to enhance their complexity, to correct defects, or to balance their sensory components.

Blending can actually occur in the vineyard where several grape varieties may be interplanted, harvested, and crushed together. Or the winemaker can blend different musts and ferment them together. Or after clarification, stabilization, and aging, the winemaker can combine nearly finished wines before bottling.

Bottle shapes and colors are based on very old traditions established in the European wine districts where wine types or styles were born. Bottles are washed and rinsed to sterilize them and filled with an inert gas, often purified nitrogen, before being filled with wine and then corked. Great care is taken to prevent oxygen or spoilage microbes into the bottles. The bottles are filled, corked, protectively capsuled, labeled, and placed in cartons to be stored upside down or on their sides for bottle aging.

Wineries store their bottled wine in the dark, with constant, cool temperatures (55° to 68° F) and no vibrations. Red wines stored at these lower, constant temperatures should attain a high degree of complexity and quality.

Premium red wines will improve in the bottle for many years. For example, Cabernet Sauvignons from the best vineyards and wineries will reach optimum drinkability about ten years after bottling and can remain delicious for another five to ten years.

Wine Bottle Labels

The wine bottle label, by law, must provide an accurate description of the wine. In addition to this basic information, there is usually a great deal more on the label.

Here is a guide to help you understand terms you'll find on wine bottle labels.

1. **Brand name**. A winery may produce multiple varieties of wines under different labels. Some are secondary lines of wines ... not necessarily inferior, but possibly with less aging. Other labels may represent a new wine available only in limited quantities.

2. **Vintage year**. If there is a date on the bottle, it refers to the year the grapes used for making the wine were harvested. In the United States, the wine label may list the vintage year if 95 percent of the wine comes from grapes crushed that year.

3. **Reserve**. This is a term used, by choice, by some vintners to indicate something special about the wine. It may be great grapes, quality barrel aging, or another unique feature.

4. **Estate bottled**. For this designation the winery either owns or controls the vineyard and is responsible for growing and crushing the grapes used in the wine, fermenting the resulting must, and finishing, aging, and bottling the wine in a continuous process.

5. **Vineyard name**. This indicates that very high-quality grapes are likely used in making this wine. Vineyard designation is purely voluntary on the part of the winery and is integral to savvy marketing.

6. **Appellation**. This is a legally protected name indicating that the grapes used are grown in a specific geographic area. By United States law, at least 75% of the grapes used in the production of this wine must come from that county, 85% from an American viticultural area, or 100% from a state.

7. **Name of the wine**. This can be (1) a grape varietal, such as Chardonnay, (2) a proprietary name created by the winery to specify a particular blend of wines, or (3) a simple generic name such as Red Table Wine.

8. **Size of the bottle and alcohol content**. The standard wine bottle is 750 ml. (25.4 oz.), a half bottle is 375 ml., and a split, or one-quarter bottle, is 187 ml.

9. **Name and address of the bottler**.

10. **Sulfites warning**. Most wines contain sulphur dioxide, a preservative that is produced by yeast or otherwise introduced by the winemaker.

11. **Message**. Many wineries use back labels to provide useful information about the wine, what flavors it embodies, foods it will pair well with, and other useful facts.

FRONT LABEL

(1)
(2)

Our Own Brand
1997

(3)
(4)

Reserve
Estate Bottled

(5)
(6)

Our Own Vineyard
The American Valley

(7)

Chardonnay

(8)

Net contents 750ml   13.5% alcohol

(9)

Vinted & bottled by Our Own Winery
Wineland, WV, USA

BACK LABEL

Vinted and Bottled by Our Own Winery, Wineland, WV, USA

(10)

Government warning: (1) According to the Surgeon General, women should not drink alcoholic beverages during pregnancy due to the risk of birth defects. (2) Consumption of alcoholic beverages impairs your ability to drive a car or operate machinery and may cause health problems. Contains sulfites.

(11)

The grapes for this wine were grown in our vineyards and vinted in our own winery by members of the same family that planted the original grape vines in 1835. We hope that you will enjoy this wine as much as we did in making it for you.

Buying Wine

For those of us who live in or near wine-producing regions, it is quite easy to visit wineries, taste different wines, and talk to knowledgeable people about wine. For those who must depend upon the label on the bottle or the advice of a sales clerk, it can be frustrating, but it does not have to be.

There are many excellent wine-buying guides that can help you become more informed about wines:

- *Dan Berger's Vintage Experiences*, is an excellent four-page weekly wine commentary that he mails or emails to subscribers.

- Hugh Johnson's *Pocket Wine Book* is an easy way to take a wine authority shopping with you in your pocket or purse.

- The *Wine Spectator* publishes the *Ultimate Guide to Buying Wine*. At nearly a thousand pages, it's not pocket-size, unless you have Very Large pockets; but it's packed with valuable information about wines available around the world.

- Robert Parker of *Wine Advocate* fame offers the extensive *Parker's Wine Buyer's Guide* (over 1600 pages).

There is also very good wine advice in such magazines as *Bon Appetit, Gourmet, Food and Wine,* and *Saveur*, but our favorite "wine" magazines are *Wine Spectator* and *Wine Enthusiast*.

In most states wine is sold through wine merchants and liquor stores, in supermarkets, some drug stores, and warehouse clubs.

Knowledgeable wine merchants can be of great help if you explain what you are looking for. Tell them your price range and try their recommendations. Usually, they can help you choose wisely, saving you money and ensuring that you buy good wines.

Supermarkets are a convenient place to shop for wine. Although the selection is often somewhat limited and you won't find rare vintage wines, you may well find good wines at a good price. If you need help in selecting your wine, bring a published wine guide with you, because you may find that store clerks will not be sufficiently knowledgeable about the store's wine inventory.

Some stores identify wines by the ratings of wine experts or judges in wine competitions. These ratings can help you find the best in various categories within specific price ranges.

Warehouse clubs often have some of the best prices for wine but a very limited selection.

There are many mail-order wine clubs as well as wineries offering to sell direct to you over the Internet. You can use a search engine to locate nearly any wine you may be looking for. Descriptions of wine attributes are often detailed enough for you to make a reasoned judgment about buying a particular wine; however, it would be prudent to buy a small enough quantity so you can taste the wine to confirm that you concur with the merchant's description before you invest in a larger quantity of the wine.

The most effective way to develop a list of favorite wines is to taste them. Some wine merchants schedule wine tastings. Wine bars present another opportunity for tasting a variety of wines and getting informed advice. Community wine tastings, often held as fundraisers, present yet another wine-education opportunity.

But, best of all is a trip to a wine-producing region. Here you can taste many different wines by many different wineries and make firsthand wine discoveries. You can get expert help from tasting-room staff and often tour wineries, sometimes meeting with winemakers to learn how they made your favorite wines. What an enjoyable and effective way to develop your wine buying skills!

A further bonus of visiting wineries is that you may find (1) specialty wines that are only sold at wineries or (2) older vintages that are no longer available in markets. Additional buying tips when you are shopping at stores, not wineries:

- Assess the wine storage temperature in the store. If the ambient temperature is very warm or hot, you may surmise that the quality of the wine may be impacted by less than ideal storage conditions.

- Examine wine bottles to assure that the wine fill level is up to the neck and hasn't leaked through a dry or faulty cork. If the wine bottle has leaked, that means air has entered it and most likely damaged the wine.

- Examine the top of the capsule that covers the cork to determine that the cork has not pushed outward from the bottle. Wines that have been exposed to high temperatures can expand in the bottle, pushing the cork against the capsule.

Storing Wine

Many red wines improve in flavor and complexity with 10 to 20 years aging. However, most white wines are meant to be enjoyed young while they possess their youth and freshness. Very few white wines need to mature, although all wine will benefit from even a few days rest before opening.

Wine is alive, so it reacts either positively or negatively to its environment. According to conventional wisdom, wine is ideally stored at a constant temperature in a clean, dark, vibration-free, humidity-controlled, odor-free place with good ventilation.

Temperature is extremely important in controlling the aging process. Wines stored at too high a temperature will age too fast and not develop the complexity that will be achieved at a slow-aging temperature.

The ideal temperature range is said to be 50° to 55° F (10° to 12° C); however, a more forgiving constant temperature range from 40° to 65° F (5° to 18° C) will be satisfactory. The key is to keep temperature constant, because rapidly fluctuating temperatures can damage wines and age them prematurely. As temperature increases and decreases, the cork may become damaged, allowing wine to seep out or (Horrors!) oxygen to enter the bottle and taint the wine.

Moderate humidity is also important to keep corks resilient, preventing them from shrinking and letting air into the bottle. Seventy percent to 75% relative humidity is ideal, with 50% being a minimum acceptable level.

Storing bottles of table wine horizontally so that wine stays in contact with the cork is also a good idea, since it is another way to preserve the integrity of the cork to keep out oxygen.

Since light can prematurely age a bottle of wine, it is logical to store wine in darkness. Obviously, wine in clear bottles is most susceptible to damage by light, but even dark-colored glass bottles can be penetrated by ultraviolet light which can ruin wine. Incandescent light is better for a cellar than fluorescent lighting.

"The temperature at which wine is served has an important impact on its taste."

Keeping your wine calm, free from constant vibration, is another factor in good wine storage, since disturbing a red wine's sediment is not beneficial to the wine. Once you have laid down a wine in storage, it should stay that way until you are ready to open it.

So, where should you store your wine? The standard household refrigerator is far from ideal with its "too cold" average temperature of 35° F. And the frequent opening and closing of the refrigerator door causes an undesirable fluctuation in temperature as well as vibrations that can loosen the cork and/or shake up the sediment in the wine. Furthermore, the refrigerator's humidity is much lower than ideal, which means the integrity of the cork can be compromised. Fortunately, there are other options. Popular storing locations include a cellar, a dark, low-activity closet, or a refrigerator designed for wine storage (wine cooler), which you can program for ideal conditions.

Serving Wine

Temperature
The temperature at which wine is served has an important impact on its taste. As a general rule, you should serve white wines at cooler temperatures.

For serving sparkling wines, an excellent temperature range is 42° to 54° F (6° to 10° C). For rosés its 48° to 54° F (9° to 12° C). For still white wines and light sherries the range should be 48° to 58° F (9° to 14° C).

For red wines, fortified wines, and dark sherries, the ideal serving temperature is a range of 57° to 68° F (13° to 30° C). You have probably heard the advice of serving red wine at room temperature, but if your room temperature is higher than 68° F, the red wine you pour may be too warm. In other words, you may need to cool it down to the ideal range.

A bottle of wine will cool 4° F for each 10 minutes in the refrigerator, and it will warm at about the same rate when removed from the refrigerator and left at room temperature (depending on the warmth of your room). If you need to chill a bottle of wine quickly, 35 minutes in the freezer will accomplish it.

If you place a bottle of red wine in your refrigerator two hours before serving, then remove and open it after an hour to let the wine breathe, it will usually reach a desirable temperature for tasting. An alternative way to allow the wine to breathe is to pour it in serving glasses and let it sit for fifteen minutes before you drink it. Breathing (aeration) can benefit a young wine although it generally does not enhance an aged wine.

White wines, particularly Champagne, require chilling. Place them in the refrigerator two hours before serving. If your room is warm, you can place the bottle half-submerged in a bucket of ice to keep it well chilled. To chill wine even faster, add water to the ice bucket. Water fills the air spaces between ice cubes so more of the bottle is in contact with the cold.

Wine bottle openers
There are many different types of wine bottle openers, but we find the following two easiest to use. One is the screw type, with two wings that remove the cork simply by pushing the wings down when the screw is embedded in the cork. The other is the waiter's screw type, which also has a knife to cut the foil around the cork.

Champagne corks are easy to remove if you simply unwire them, put a cloth over the cork and gently twist the bottle — not the cork — and ease the cork out of the bottle.

Wine glasses
Wine's appeal is not just its taste and smell, but also the visual pleasure it gives when displayed well. The shape, size

and feel of a wine glass can dramatically impact your perception of the bouquet, taste, balance, and finish of each served wine.

Some wine glasses are designed to deliver wine to the tip of your tongue and other wine glasses are designed to deliver wine to the center or back of your tongue. As you will see in the Tasting Wine chapter, these tongue locations perform very different tasting functions.

There are many styles of wine glasses. You can find a vast array of specific glasses for serving specific wines, but you can certainly do well with the following basic wine glasses:

1. *All-purpose wine glass* – Five and one-half to seven inches tall (of which the stem and base comprise about two to three inches), moderately tulip-shaped, medium-width bowl with a slight curve inward at the top of the glass to concentrate the more delicate aromas. (8 to 10 ounces)

2. *White wine glass* – Distinct tulip-shaped, medium to large bowl width, with distinct curve inward at top of glass to direct wine to the tip of your tongue. Holds in aroma for your full enjoyment ... especially the more complex whites. (8 ounces)

3. *Red wine glass* – Rounded shape with large bowl and wide straight top. The large bowl allows proper oxygenation of complex and tertiary aromas in bold red wines. The opening is tall and straight in order to direct the wine to the back of your mouth. (10 to 12 ounces)

4. *Sparkling wine flute* – Tall and thin. Tall to accommodate carbon dioxide development, keeping the bubbles from quickly dissipating and allowing your visual enjoyment of the rising-bubbles display. Thin to direct a good concentration of delicate aromas toward your nose. (7 ounces)

White wine glass

Chardonnay /
Viognier glass

Riesling
stemless glass

Chardonnay
stemless glass

Champagne
flute

Champagne
glass

Sherry glass

Port glass

Red wine glass   Pinot /   Cabernet /   Vintage Port glass
                   Nebbiolo glass   Merlot glass

Burgundy glass   Cabernet /
                   Merlot glass

*Courtesy of Riedel
The Wine Glass
Company*

5. *Aperitif glass or Cordial* – Similar in shape to the all-purpose glass but much smaller to emphasize the fruit character and not the alcohol. (2.5 ounces)

6. *Dessert wine glasses* (e.g., Port and Sherry) – Designed to emphasize the personality or character of the wine. (6 ounces)

In all wine glass styles, the stem should be of sufficient length to allow you to hold the glass by the stem away from the bowl so that the heat from your hand does not unintentionally warm the wine in your glass.

We think you will enjoy crystal, half-crystal or superior glass stemware that is clear (undecorated) and not too thick, so the clarity and color of the wine is fully observable.

A serious wine aficionado appreciates that the Riedel Company of Austria has a fine reputation for its extensive line of glasses that have specially designed rims and shapes to deliver wine to your tongue in a way that emphasizes and promotes the varying flavors and aromas of individual varietal wines.

When cleaning wine glasses, hand-wash them in lukewarm water with a small amount of soap which you thoroughly rinse off. Dry immediately. Remember that the slightest bit of soap residue will affect the wine's taste.

Store clean glasses upright on a well ventilated shelf, or hang them upside down from a wooden glass holder.

> *"Your sensory evaluation tools of sight, smell, taste, and touch all come into play when you taste wine, but your sense of smell is the most important, sensitive, and versatile sensory evaluation factor in the appreciation of wines."*

Pouring wine

It's a good idea to pour still wines toward the center of the glass to accentuate bouquet as the wine splashes on the bottom of the bowl. Sparkling wines should be poured on the side of the glass to preserve bubbles.

To control drips, twist the bottle slightly as you tilt it upwards after pouring.

Fill wine glasses from one-third to one-half full, so there is plenty of glass space remaining for swirling the wine to release its bouquet.

Tasting Wine

Your sensory evaluation tools of sight, smell, taste, and touch all come into play when you taste wine.

Sight

You can enjoy the appearance of wine in a glass as well as develop an anticipation of the taste to follow. The visual stimuli from the wine's hues, intensity, clarity, and even the bubbles in sparkling wines can be beautiful, as well as informative. For example, a very pale white wine suggests that the grapes were picked early and the wine may be low in alcohol, thin-bodied, and high in acid, presenting a "green" taste. On the other hand, dark reds are clues to intense fruit aromas and high tannin levels.

Tip your glass at a 45 degree angle and hold it up toward a light source to enjoy the wine's tantalizing color.

Swirl the wine in your glass in order to increase the surface area of the wine, releasing its aroma into your glass. You can also observe and analyze the wine's "legs" (also called "tears" or "arches") which reflect the alcohol content of the wine. The higher the alcohol level, the thinner the streams as the wine falls back down the side of the glass. Legs are entertaining to observe but are not an indicator of wine quality as was once thought.

Legs also occur in a glass of wine that has set undisturbed for a few minutes. Drops inch up the inside surface of the glass, then slowly run back down. The more alcohol in a wine, the more drops develop.

Smell

Your sense of smell is your most important, sensitive, and versatile sensory evaluation factor in the appreciation of wines. The rich, complex aroma, bouquet, and flavor of a wine are all experienced via your sense of smell.

You are obviously using your sense of smell when you put your nose into your wine glass and deeply inhale the aroma and bouquet of the wine. That sends odorous molecules to your olfactory epithelium which contains millions of nerve cells, each with one end in your nasal passage and the other end attached to your brain, which rapidly processes the incoming information and evaluates it.

But you are also using your sense of smell when you hold wine in your mouth and the aroma and bouquet stimuli reach your olfactory nerve cells through the nasal passage at the back of your mouth.

When you are tasting a glass of wine, the greater the surface area of wine exposed to air and the higher the temperature of the wine, within appropriate ranges for reds and whites, the more molecules of aroma and bouquet are released to your olfactory system. So you can see why the following wine-tasting techniques are practiced:

1. Swirling wine in your glass increases the surface area of the wine to release more volatile molecules of aroma and

bouquet for you to enjoy when you put your nose into the glass and sniff.

2. Holding wine in your mouth warms the wine.

3. Swishing wine in your mouth draws air through the wine and increases the surface area of the warmed wine.

Taste
Your sense of taste provides information about three important sensory elements of wines: sweet, sour, and bitter. You will especially appreciate a wine that has these elements well-balanced.

You have about 10,000 taste buds located on your tongue (primarily on its tip, sides, and back, with very few taste buds on the top), the roof of your mouth, the back of your epiglottis, and on your tonsils. That is why holding the wine in your mouth and swishing the wine in your mouth supplies excellent information to your various taste buds to maximize your evaluation and enjoyment of the wine.

Wine delivered to the tip of your tongue will (1) accentuate a red wine's fruit flavor and balance acidity and moderate tannins, or (2) highlight the fruit and deemphasize the naturally high acid in light fruity white wines.

On the other hand, wine delivered to the middle of your tongue will (1) harmonize the fruit, tannin, and acidity of highly tannic red wines, or (2) balance all of the components of full-bodied white wines with moderate acidity.

Touch
There are sensors in your mouth and nose which allow you to respond to the tactile stimuli in wines: viscosity, dissolved

"A jug of wine, a loaf of bread, and thou."
–Omar Khayyam

gas, temperature, astringency, heat from alcohol, and sulfur dioxide content.

When you are tasting and evaluating wines, you will find the following:

1. A wine with relatively high sugar concentration (viscosity) has more "body."

2. Young red wines with high tannin levels are astringent and puckery (a condition that usually will abate during red wine aging).

3. A wine with high alcohol content will give you a hot tactile sensation and a sweet taste.

4. Sulfur dioxide used to preserve aroma and color in wine-making should be at an imperceptible level. If your sniff of the glass of wine makes you sneeze, or if you can smell sulfur dioxide in the wine, feel free to discard that wine.

Sequence of tasting

Your sequence of tasting wines is important. For example, you should taste dry wines before sweet wines because the tartness of dry wine would be exaggerated by contrast with a sweet wine tasted first.

Here are rules-of-thumb regarding the order of tasting wines:

1. White before red
2. Dry before sweet
3. Young before old
4. Modest before fine
5. Light-bodied before full-bodied
6. Light young red before full-bodied sweet white

Wine's aromas, flavors, and nuances vs. "that tastes good"

Regardless of all of the available information about wines, the most important feature of a wine is that "it tastes good" to you.

You can swirl and sniff, direct the wine to your pertinent taste buds by using the appropriately shaped stemware, swish and analyze the aroma and bouquet, and assess the balance, complexity, and finish of your wine, but you don't have to do all of those things to thoroughly enjoy a good glass of wine. You can experience the "Wow!" affect without determining that the aroma is floral, spicy, fruity, vegetal, nutty, caramelized, etc.

You don't have to detect aromas or flavors of orange blossoms, cloves, licorice, grapefruit, lemon, blackberry, black currant, strawberry, cherry, apricot, peach, apple, pineapple, melon, banana, prune, cut green grass, bell pepper, eucalyptus, mint, green beans, asparagus, black olive, artichoke, hay, straw, tea, walnut, hazelnut, almond, honey, butterscotch, soy sauce, butter, chocolate, molasses, vanilla, smoke, and coffee. However, it can also be a lot of fun to play the sensory evaluation game as you experience a Wow!

Wine Tasting Jargon

Here is a selection of generally used terms for describing wines. There are no rules that preclude you from expressing your own descriptive adjectives, too. In fact, you may get a kick out of inventing some "off-the-wall" descriptors, which we suspect is regularly done by many wine commentators. However, they may be blessed with super-perceptive taste buds ... and you may be, too. So, don't be intimidated ... and certainly don't take it too seriously. Just have fun with it!

Acidity: Presence of natural fruit acids that give a crisp, tart, refreshing taste

Aggressive: Wine with harsh flavors, usually due to excessive tannin or acid

Aroma: Smells that originate from the grapes used to make the wine

Astringent: Harsh, drying sensation in the mouth resulting from high tannin levels; opposite of smooth

Austere: High-acid wine

Backbone: Wine with good acidity and structure

Balanced: All components of the wine harmonize; acidity, sweetness, and flavor are in pleasing relationship

Big: Wine that is full-bodied, full-flavored, and intense

Bite: Significant degree of acidity or tannin

Blend: Wine made from a mixture of different grape varieties to add complexity; or a combination of different wines that contribute different elements to the final product

Body: Ranging from light to heavy or full, the wine's viscosity ("thickness") and tactile impression on your palate; commonly full-bodied, medium-bodied, or light-bodied

Bouquet: Smells resulting from winemaking and aging

Brilliant: Appearance that is absolutely clear

Buttery: Rich, creamy flavor and texture resulting from malolactic fermentation

Character: Distinct attributes of a wine

Charmat: Bulk method for making sparkling wine via fermentation in a large vat instead of in bottles

Chewy: Rich, heavy, tannic wine that is full-bodied

Clean: Well-made wine with no off smells or off flavors

Cloudy: Hazy appearance

Cloying: Excessively sweet

Complex: Multiple layers of aromas, flavors and textures; sometimes very subtle nuances emerge, provoking the Wow! response

Corked: Tainted with moldy smells or other wine flaws related to a bad cork

Crisp: Fresh, acidic wine

Delicate: Light- to medium-body wines

Dense: Concentrated pleasant aromas desirable in young wines

Depth: Wine of complexity and intense flavors, making more than a first impression

Dry: No sweetness

Earthy: Flavors and aromas of mushroom, soil, and mineral

Elegant: Beautiful, well-balanced wine that is not necessarily full-bodied

Finish: The final impression on the palate, ranging from short to long aftertaste; flavor remaining in your mouth after swallowing or spitting out the wine; finish may be harsh, hot, soft, lingering, short, smooth, or nothing

Fino: Lightest of all sherries, usually bone dry

Firm: Texture and structure of a young, tannic red

Flabby: Soft feel and lacking acid

Flat: Low in acidity, lacking zip

Flavor: Combination of taste and smell

Fleshy: Soft, smooth texture with low tannins

Flinty: Stone- or mineral-like character

Floral: Aromas of flowers like rose, gardenia, honeysuckle, etc.

Fortified: Wine with a higher-than-normal alcohol content due to addition of brandy or spirits during winemaking

Fruity: Aromas and flavors of fruits

Grassy: Aromas and flavors of fresh cut grass or herbs

Hard: High in acidity or tannins

Harmonious: All sensory properties in balance

Heady: Wine high in alcohol content

Herbaceous: Grassy, vegetable aromas

Hollow: Lacking in middle flavors and structure; something seems to be missing between the first taste and the finish

Hot: Unbalanced, high alcohol wine that produces a burning flavor sensation

"Wine cheereth man and God." –Judges 9:13

Integrated: Wine whose flavor layers unfold, growing increasingly interesting as it breathes, with a lingering finish

Lean: Lacking mouth-filling flavors

Legs: Drops that progress up the inside surface of a glass above the wine and slowly run back down; also the viscous droplets that form and run down the glass when wine is swirled. Higher alcohol content leads to more pronounced legs. Legs are interesting to observe, but they are not an indicator of a wine's quality as was once believed.

Length: Amount of time a wine's taste and aroma are evident after it is swallowed

Malolactic Fermentation: Conversion of malic acid (hard, green apple flavor) in wine to soft, lactic acid (rich, buttery flavors)

Mature: Ready to drink

Methode Champenoise: Method of making sparkling wine via a second fermentation in a sealed bottle

Nose: Smell of a wine; aroma and bouquet

Perfumed: Delicate bouquet

Oak: Aromas and flavors imparted to wine during barrel fermentation/aging; includes vanilla, caramel, chocolate, smoke, spice, and toast

Off Dry: Slightly sweet wine

Off Flavor: Undesirable nose perceived in the mouth

Off Odor: Undesirable nose

Over-aged: Breakdown in a wine stored too long in a wooden barrel or bottle; oxidized

Oxidized: Wine ruined by contact with air; over-aged

Peak: When a wine displays its smoothest, fullest flavors

Quality: Degree of excellence of a wine regarding its complexity, harmony, and ability to cause a Wow! reaction

Rich: Intense flavors and texture

Robust: Full-bodied, intense, and vigorous

Round: Smooth flavors and textures; well-balanced

Semi-dry: Very low levels of residual sugar in wine

Simple: Wine with few characteristics that follow the initial impression; often an inexpensive young wine

Smoky: Aroma of smoke caused by aging in barrels

Smooth: Lack of astringency

Soft: Wine with low acid, tannin, and alcohol

Sour: Taste like that produced by an acid; like unripe grapes, sharp, tart, tangy

Spicy: Complementary description applicable to many fine wines (e.g., Syrah can display peppery spice and Pinot Noir can suggest cinnamon)

Spritzy: Pleasant, light sparkling sensation from a slight secondary fermentation or the addition of carbon dioxide

Stemmy: Astringent character of wine fermented too long with grape stems

Still Wine: Any wine that is not sparkling

Structure: A wine's texture, mouthfeel, and balance

Supple: Wine with well-balanced tannins and fruit characteristics

Sweet: High concentration of sugar after fermentation

Tannic: Drying, astringent, mouth-puckering sensation on the palate often associated with heavy red wines

Table Wine: In the United States, a wine under 14% alcohol can simply be labeled "table wine."

Tawny: Amber or brownish color of wine that has been aged in wood; e.g., Port

Tart: Pleasant, sour taste in young wine

Taste: Sour, bitter, and sweet are the tastes associated with wine. Other human tastes are salty and umami. (Umami is the fifth primary element of taste found in substances like monosodium glutamate, *MSG*. Identified by Kikunae Ikeda in 1907, *umami* means "delicious flavor" in Japanese.)

Terroir: Impact of soil, topography and climate on grapes and resulting wine

Thin: Lacking body and depth

Tinny: A metal taste

Toasty: Flavor of toast imparted by oak barrel fermenting

Varietal: Odor and/or aroma of a wine that can be recognized as made from a specific grape variety

Vegetal: Grassy or herbaceous aroma with bell pepper and asparagus flavors; in small amounts it adds to the complexity of the wine but is undesirable when excessive

Velvety: Wine that has smooth, silky texture with deep, rich aromas and flavors

Vinous: Wine without a specific, distinguishable aroma or bouquet

Vintage: Year that grapes were harvested and the wine made from those grapes

Woody: Off odor of wine stored too long in oak barrel

Young: Fresh, fruity, unoxidized

Zesty: Wine that is invigorating

Samples of aroma and flavor descriptors

Floral: orange blossom, rose, violet, geranium, linalool

Spicy: cloves, black pepper, anise, cinnamon, licorice, peppermint

Fruity: citrus (grapefruit, lemon); berry (blackberry, raspberry, strawberry, black currant, cassis); tree fruit (cherry, black cherry, apricot, peach, apple, plum, pear, fig); tropical fruit (pineapple, melon, banana); dried fruit (strawberry jam, raisin, prune, fig); cooked fruit (sweeter, caramelized flavors); other (artificial fruit, methyl anthranilate)

"An excellent wine has been kissed by the angels."
–Beatrice Gage

Vegetal: fresh (stemmy, cut green grass, bell pepper, eucalyptus, mint); canned, cooked (green beans, asparagus, green olive, black olive, artichoke); dried (hay, straw, tea, tobacco)

Nutty: walnut, hazelnut, almond

Caramelized: honey, butterscotch, butter, soy sauce, chocolate, molasses, cola, cocoa

Woody: phenolic (vanilla); resinous (cedar, oak); burned (smoky, burnt toast, charred, coffee)

Earthy: dusty, mushroom, musty, mildew, moldy cork

Chemical: petroleum (tar, plastic, kerosene, diesel); sulfur (rubber, hydrogen sulfide, mercaptan, garlic, skunk, cabbage, burnt match, sulfur dioxide, wet wool, wet dog); paper (filter pad, wet cardboard); pungent (ethyl acetate, acetic acid, ethanol, sulfur dioxide); other (fishy, soapy, sorbate, fusel alcohol, flinty)

Pungent: assertive, strong, distinctive

Oxidized: acetaldehyde, old or rotting fruit, vinegar

Microbiological: yeasty (leesy, flor-yeast, Brettanomyces); lactic (sauerkraut, butyric acid, sweaty, lactic acid); other (horsey, mousey)

To Your Good Health

Of course, the rule of "all things in moderation" holds true here. That being said, it is good to know that researchers have found that people who regularly drink one to three glasses of wine a day are healthier than people who drink no wine or drink more than three glasses a day.

Studies have shown that moderate wine consumption can reduce coronary heart disease incidence, lower cholesterol levels, lower glucose and insulin levels, and lower blood pressure. A Copenhagen heart study followed 130,000 people for ten years and found that those patients who averaged six glasses of wine a week had death rates 30% to 40% lower than normal.

What is wine doing? Wine works in the blood, raising high-density lipoprotein (HDL), which is commonly known as the "good" cholesterol, and lowering levels of low-density lipo-protein (LDL), the "bad" cholesterol. Red wine is especially healthy, because it has high levels of antioxidents, which prevent LDL from being oxidized. In fact, red wine contains approximately 10 times more antioxidants than other forms of alcohol. Thus, wine helps keep blood vessels clean with a beneficial effect on platelets that lasts around two days — hence, the "glass a day " mantra.

Obviously, for people who are sensitive to sulfites found in wine (higher levels in white wine than red) or who get migraine headaches from too many tannins (found mostly in red wines), it is prudent to not drink those wines.

Studies show that moderate consumption of wine (with its antioxidants and resveratrol) helps prevent certain kinds of strokes, promotes longer life, combats heart disease and cancer, reduces the level of abdominal fat, increases bone density, helps prevent ulcers, helps reduce stress which can head off health problems and help fight diseases, and can help in weight-reduction programs.

As an aside, cooking with wine can also be beneficial to your health in that you can reduce the amount of calories, sodium, fat and cholesterol dramatically when you cook with wine. Wine adds a richness to food that easily replaces high calorie ingredients. Yes, you can easily have gourmet flavors with better nutrition – a definite win-win situation.

(See a variety of "cooking with wine" books at the back of this book).

These exciting health benefits associated with drinking wine in moderation are based on numerous studies of large numbers of study groups. However, without exception, pregnant women should not drink wine ... the serious risks to the growing fetus are well-documented. For everyone else, it would certainly be advisable to ask your family physician for his or her wine consumption recommendations considering your specific state of health and lifestyle.

"A meal without wine is like a day without sunshine."
    –Anthelme Savarin

PAIRING BASICS

Your Personal Pleasure is the Goal

As we said earlier, everyone has a unique set of taste buds and olfactory nerve cells, so the perfect pairings of wines and cheeses are ultimately a matter of your personal preferences. Wine and cheese pairing is not an exact science. You should experiment extensively as you progress on an enjoyable search for **your** ultimate favorite wine and cheese pairings.

Guidelines

Since both wine and cheese are natural, living organisms whose characteristics change as they age from season to season, you actually have somewhat of a moving target as you identify cheeses and wines that you enjoy together. However, there are basic guidelines that have been developed over time which can facilitate your successful pairing experiences. Here are some basic "rules," truisms, and generally accepted principles:

- Pair red wines with hard cheeses and white wines with soft cheeses.

- The flavor of a cheese can be enhanced by a complementary wine, e.g., a sweet cheese enhances a sweet wine.

- Light style wines go well with fresh, creamy, and sweet cheeses.

- Crisp and fruity wines go well with young, tangy, and acidic cheeses.

- Most versatile wines go well with fresh, tangy, salty and acidic cheeses.

- Dessert wines go well with aged and salty cheeses.

- White wines generally are acidic and fruity, so they pair well with the saltiness in most cheeses.

- Softer, fruitier wines tend to go better with cheese than do dry wines.

- Salty or sour taste in cheese makes wine taste milder.

- Sweet or savory taste in cheese makes wine taste stronger.

- With such a large number of variables in cheeses as they age and wines as they age, it is impossible to guarantee a successful pairing every time.

- Simple cheeses pair well with light wines.

- Mild, aged cheeses pair well with older, milder wines.

- Full-flavored cheeses (e.g., creamy, washed rind) go well with medium- to full-bodied wines.

- Light cheeses go well with light wines.

"Both wine and cheese are natural, living organisms whose characteristics change as they age from season to season."

- Strong, pungent cheeses pair well with sweet wines.

- Red wines that are fruity, acidic, and low in tannins pair well with many cheeses.

- Cheese influences the flavor of wine more than vice versa.

- Some cheeses can bring out or even create bitterness in wine.

- Rich and sweet dessert wines are broadly compatible with pungent creamy cheeses and extra-strong hard cheeses. Blue cheese generally pairs well with dessert wines.

- Cheese textures that are buttery, creamy and soft pair well with wines that have similar characteristics. Cheese textures that are firm or hard match with medium-bodied and full-bodied wines.

- Creamy cheeses can exacerbate tannins, making wines taste stronger and more astringent. Wines with softer tannins or sparkling wines pair well with creamy cheeses.

- Pair a wine that does not overpower the cheese, or cheese that does not overpower the wine.

- Pair a wine and cheese according to their common area of origin. The theory is that growing conditions which impart particular characteristics ("terroir") to a region's wines similarly impact its cheeses through the vegetation on which the milk animals graze.

- Creamy cheeses pair well with sparkling wines and Champagne. The bubbles help cleanse your palate, refreshing it for the next bite.

- Fresh goat cheeses (mild, lemony, and acidic in flavor and creamy in texture) go well with crisp white wines.

- Aged sheep's milk cheeses pair well with Gewürztraminers and fruity Zinfandels.

- Aged cow's milk cheddars go well with Sherries.

- Very salty cheeses reinforce bitter and astringent qualities of some red wines, and can produce a metallic taste with more acidic wines.

- Very sweet cheeses make even well-balanced wines seem sour.

- Slightly sweet wines pair with salty cheeses better than dry wines do.

- Cold serving temperatures decrease our perception of sweetness.

Goals

- **Balance**
  Look for a combination where the wine perfectly balances the cheese, where there is no battle for taste dominance, and where the combined taste is in harmony and extremely pleasurable.
  Results ... "Voila!"

- **Enhancement**
  Look for a combination where the wine enhances the flavor of the cheese, or where the cheese enhances the flavor of the wine.
  Results ... "Yum!"

- **New surprises**
  Look for a combination where the wine and cheese

interact to produce surprising bursts of new flavor sensations. Results ... "Wow!"

More tasting suggestions

- Don't be intimidated by the jargon of wine aficionados. The myriad specialized terms associated with winemaking and tasting can be mind-numbing for a beginner. You may not care if the aroma of a wine is "vegetative with hints of asparagus and cut green grass" or "fruity with strong cherry or black currant overtones." If you want to focus solely on what tastes "good," then do it. Enjoy wine at whatever level is most satisfying to you and don't let jargon get in the way of your pleasure.

- Vary the tasting sequence by enjoying wine first before introducing the cheese, then taste cheese before introducing the wine. Since this is meant to be an enjoyable experimentation process, feel free to experiment. Sometimes, taste the cheese before tasting the wine ... and make notes of your taste sensations. Other times, taste the wine before introducing the cheese. Is the flavor sensation different in this sequence?

- When you taste cheese first, take a bite and chew it a little as it coats your palate. Then sip some wine and let the cheese and wine meld into a "cheese sauce" in your mouth.

- Have palate cleansers available during your wine and cheese pairing activity. Salt-free water crackers or baguettes serve that purpose well. Having bottled water available for palate cleansing is another good idea.

- Experiment.
  Scene 1 – Taste a cheese only and then introduce the wine.
  Scene 2 – Taste a wine only and then introduce the cheese.
  Scene 3 – Taste the cheese with a cracker or unflavored French bread or baguettes and then introduce the wine taste.
  Scene 4 – Reverse the process, tasting the wine first, and then bringing in the cheese and cracker or bread..

- Don't overwhelm your palate with too many wines or too many cheeses at one tasting. Depending on how many people are participating, three to five wines and cheeses should be either sufficient or "a bit much."

- Experiment, observe, and remember. Once you have discovered a pairing that is in contention for your "ultimate Wow!" you should write it down for future reference. And you may also want to record your not-so-great combinations so you won't repeat them.

To help you remember, we include in this book two programmed journals for your use in recording (1) your best pairings ("My Favorite Pairings" Journal) and (2) your unsatisfactory combinations ("Oops! I Won't Pair These Again" Journal).

Well, it's time for you to begin your journey. Bon voyage ... and here's to many "Wow!" experiences for you and your family and friends.

Cheese & Wine Pairing Recommendations

We have created two charts for you to use in selecting wines and cheeses to pair.

The Cheese & Wine Pairing Recommendations chart lists over 340 cheeses and provides suggested wines to serve with each of those cheeses. So, if you have selected a cheese and want a suggestion for wine to serve with it, the Cheese & Wine Pairing Recommendations chart describes some cheeses that may be particularly pleasing with that wine.

On the other hand, the Wine & Cheese Pairing Recommendations chart lists over 150 wines and provides suggestions of cheeses to serve with each of those wines. So, if you have selected a wine and want to know some cheeses that may be naturally pleasing with that wine, the Wine & Cheese Pairing Recommendations chart offers ideas to you.

You can consider these recommendations as a starting point in your quest for your Wow! experiences. Remember that the enjoyment of a specific wine with a specific cheese is a completely personal evaluation. Also, since individual wines and cheeses vary from winery to winery and from cheesemaker to cheesemaker ... and vary from year to year ... and from season to season, you have an enormous number of options in your pairings. You should never run out of potential combinations ... and therein lies your enjoyable challenge to find your Wow! pairings.

Furthermore, just because an "expert" says a specific wine pairs well with a specific cheese, it doesn't make it so for you. For example, we host many wine and cheese pairing events and as we record numerous pairing comments, we are continually amazed at the number of times that some people rate the pairing of a specific wine with a specific cheese very positively, while other people at the same event, tasting the same wine and cheese, proclaim the pairing doesn't work for them.

There is no doubt that each pairing evokes a personal response. So, as you refer to our recommendations charts for cheese and wine pairing ideas, be aware that you should also experiment and substitute similar as well as contrasting wines and cheeses. Keep in mind that your quest for the ultimate Wow! pairings is most of all to experience superb wines and cheeses and to have a lot of fun in the process.

We offer the following recommendations to give you a sampling of cheese and wine pairings that may please your tastes. They are based on one or more of the following criteria:
(1) We have personally experienced the pairings and found them ranging from pleasing to Wow!
(2) People to whom we served these pairings have found them to range from pleasing to Wow!
(3) Wine tasting experts recommended them
(4) Cheese tasting experts recommended them
(5) Winemakers recommended them
(6) Cheesemakers recommended them
(7) We have compiled analytical pairings based on the various factors in the Pairing Guidelines section of the previous chapter in this book.

Once again, the pairings we list are just a few sugestions

out of myriad potential pairings. For example, our research found more than 100 recommended cheese pairings for Cabernet Sauvignon and Pinot Noir, and in the space available, it was obviously not practical to list them all.

So please enjoy the challenge of experimentation with other wines and other cheeses of similar or contrasting genre. Who knows when you will discover a personal Wow! pairing?

Remember that as most cheeses mature and age, their flavors, aromas, textures, and firmness may change dramatically. And wines change flavors, aromas, and body as they mature and age. You will not know exactly how a wine will taste until you open a specific bottle and drink the wine. You will not know how a specific slice of cheese will taste until you experience that first bite. That's why our recommendations charts offer adjectives that commonly describe cheeses and wines at some point during their lifetimes to give you a sense of what to anticipate when you shop for cheeses and wines that you have not yet tasted.

"Cheese is milk's leap toward immortality"

-Clifton Fadiman

CHEESE	Abbaye de Belloc	WINE	
Style	firm	White	Chardonnay, Sauvignon Blanc, Pinot
Origin	Spain		Blanc, Niagara, Seyval Blanc, Rioja
Milk	sheep		Blanca, Pouilly-Fumé
Info	creamy, slightly smoky, rich, dense,	Red	Merlot, Carignan, Cabernet Sauvignon,
	caramelly, fruity, sweet, nutty		Petite Sirah, Cynthiana, Rioja, Dolcetto

CHEESE	Abertam	WINE	
Style	firm	Red	Cabernet Sauvignon, Barbera, Chianti,
Origin	Czech Republic		Landot Noir, Merlot, Sangiovese,
Milk	sheep		Torgiano
Info	robust	Dessert	Tawny Port, Icewine, Late Harvest
			Riesling

CHEESE	Aisy Cendré	WINE	
Style	semi-soft	White	Chardonnay, Roussanne, Meursault
Origin	France	Red	Burgundy, Merlot, Meritage, Barolo
Milk	cow		Cabernet Sauvignon, Beaujolais
Info	ash coat, creamy, strong, salty, tangy		Nouveau
		Dessert	Malvasia Bianca, Port, Muscat Canelli

CHEESE	Alpine Shepherd	WINE	
Style	firm	White	Rayon d'Or, Riesling, Viognier,
Origin	California		Vouvray, Magnolia, Liebfraumilch
Milk	goat	Red	Merlot, Syrah, Sangiovese, Baco Noir
Info	aged, robust, butterscotch hint	Sparkling	Champagne
		Dessert	Sherry, Muscat Canelli

CHEESE	Alverca	WINE	
Style	firm	White	Chardonnay, Sauvignon Blanc,
Origin	Portugal		Riesling, Pinot Grigio, Edelweiss
Milk	sheep or goat	Red	Beaujolais Nouveau, Pinot Noir,
Info	mild		Syrah, Zinfandel, Chambourcin
		Rosé	White Zinfandel, Blush Niagara

CHEESE	Añejo Enchilado	WINE	
Style	firm	White	Chenin Blanc, Pinot Blanc, Fumé Blanc,
Origin	Mexico		Johannisberg Riesling, Sémillon,
Milk	goat or cow		Chardonnay, Traminette
Info	full flavored, dry, salty, chili powder	Red	Rioja, Zinfandel, Petite Sirah
		Dessert	Sangria

CHEESE	Appenzeller	WINE	
Style	semi-soft	White	Riesling, Pinot Gris, Gewürztraminer,
Origin	Switzerland		Cayuga, Delaware, Grüner Veltliner,
Milk	cow		Sancerre, Aligoté, Edelweiss
Info	salty, spicy, creamy, sweet, smooth,	Red	Cabernet Sauvignon, Chianti, Dolcetto,
	fruity, tangy, dense, delicate		Bordeaux, Claret, Merlot
		Dessert	Port, Icewine

CHEESE	Ardrahan	WINE	
Style	semi-soft	White	Gewürztraminer, Riesling, Vouvray,
Origin	Ireland		Chardonnay, Chenin Blanc, Marsanne
Milk	cow	Red	Pinot Noir, Petite Sirah, Sangiovese,
Info	nutty, buttery, delicate, rich, soft,		Chianti, Carignan, Gamay Beaujolais
	pungent, creamy, smoky, complex	Dessert	Muscat

CHEESE	Asadero	WINE	
Style	firm	White	Chardonnay, Rioja Blanca, Riesling
Origin	Mexico	Red	Pinot Noir, Cabernet Sauvignon,
Milk	cow		Merlot, Sangiovese, Rioja, Tempranillo
Info	mild, sweet, buttery, smooth,	Sparkling	Crémant
	tangy	Dessert	Sangria

CHEESE	Asiago (aged)	WINE	
Style	firm	White	Gewürztraminer, Viognier, Chardonnay,
Origin	Italy		Sauvignon Blanc, Vouvray, Vignoles
Milk	cow	Red	Barolo, Baco Noir, Barbera, Rioja,
Info	tangy, salty, granular, sharp,		Merlot, Petite Sirah, Sangiovese
	extra strong with age	Dessert	Muscat, Icewine, Amagnac

CHEESE	Asiago (young)	WINE	
Style	semi-soft	White	Gewürztraminer, Riesling, Pinot Blanc,
Origin	Italy		Chenin Blanc, White Muscadine, Cayuga
Milk	cow	Red	Pinot Noir, Zinfandel, Chianti, Fredonia
Info	rich, creamy	Sparkling	Asti Spumanti
		Dessert	Malvasia Bianca, Sherry

CHEESE	Azeitão	WINE	
Style	soft	White	Chablis, Edelweiss, Fumé Blanc,
Origin	Portugal		Melody, Seyval Blanc
Milk	sheep	Red	Merlot, Grenache, Mourvèdre, Syrah,
Info	sweet, rich, creamy, delicate balance,		Tempranillo, Rioja, Dolcetto, Carignan
	thick, smooth, slightly salty, sharp	Rosé	White Grenache, Steuben

CHEESE	Baby Swiss	WINE	
Style	semi-soft	White	Chardonnay, Fumé Blanc, Viognier,
Origin	Switzerland		Cayuga, French Colombard, Villard
Milk	cow	Red	Pinot Noir, Zinfandel, Grenache,
Info	mild, nutty		Gamay Beaujolais, Dechaunac, Dolcetto
		Sparkling	Asti Spumanti

CHEESE	Banon	WINE	
Style	soft	White	Pinot Gris, Sauvignon Blanc, Riesling,
Origin	France		Aligoté, Chasselas, Sémillon, Marsanne
Milk	goat or cow or blend with sheep	Red	Pinot Noir, Barbera, Dolcetto,
Info	mild, nutty, chestnut or grape leaves	Rosé	White Zinfandel, Blush Muscadine
	wrap, woodsy, fruity	Sparkling	Champagne
		Dessert	Marsala

CHEESE	Basato	WINE	
Style	semi-soft	White	Chardonnay, Seyval, Soave
Origin	Uruguay	Red	Chianti, Cabernet Franc, Chancellor,
Milk	cow		Merlot, Kasselfest
Info	sharp	Rosé	Pink Catawba
		Dessert	Vin Santo

CHEESE	Bayley Hazen Blue	WINE	
Style	semi-soft	White	Gewürztraminer, Riesling, Rioja Blanca
Origin	Vermont	Red	Cabernet Sauvignon, Merlot,
Milk	cow		Chambourcin, Kasselfest
Info	blue, tangy, crumbly	Dessert	Muscat, Vin Santo

CHEESE	Beaufort	WINE	
Style	semi-soft	White	Chablis, Chardonnay, Riesling
Origin	France	Red	Shiraz, Cabernet Sauvignon, Pinot Noir
Milk	cow	Rosé	Steuben, White Zinfandel
Info	fruity, slightly sweet, buttery, dense,	Sparkling	Champagne
	rich, nutty	Dessert	Tokaji

CHEESE	Beaufort Alpage	WINE	
Style	hard	White	Chardonnay, Riesling, Marsanne
Origin	Switzerland	Red	Pinot Noir, Cynthiana, Maréchal Foch
Milk	cow	Rosé	White Merlot
Info	fruity, nutty, sweet, creamy, rich,	Sparkling	Blanc de Noirs
	hints of grasses and herbs	Dessert	Tokaji

CHEESE	Beaumont	WINE	
Style	semi-soft	White	Chardonnay, Riesling, Soave
Origin	France	Red	Beaujolais, Chambourcin, Muscadine
Milk	cow	Rosé	Pink Vidal
Info	mild, nutty, smooth, creamy	Sparkling	Champagne
		Dessert	Amagnac

CHEESE	Beenleigh Blue	WINE	
Style	semi-soft	White	Sauvignon Blanc, Chardonnay
Origin	England	Red	Cabernet Sauvignon, Zinfandel, Noble,
Milk	sheep	Sparkling	Blanc de Noirs
Info	blue, salty, tangy, sweet, carmelly,	Dessert	Sauternes, Sherry, Port, Muscat, Late
	slightly herbaceous		Harvest Riesling, Tokaji

CHEESE	Bel Paese	WINE	
Style	semi-soft	White	Chardonnay, Orvieto
Origin	Italy	Red	Pinot Noir, Merlot, Barbera, Chianti,
Milk	cow		Sangiovese, Landot Noir
Info	mild, sweet, buttery, smooth	Rosé	Steuben, Pink Vidal
		Sparkling	Asti Spumanti
		Dessert	Marsala

CHEESE	Bella Sorella	WINE	
Style	firm	White	Chardonnay, Edelweiss
Origin	California	Red	Pinot Noir, Merlot, Marechal Foch
Milk	cow	Rosé	Blush Muscadine
Info	sweet, subtle	Sparkling	Champagne
		Dessert	Icewine

CHEESE	Bergere Bleu	WINE	
Style	semi-soft	White	Viognier, Riesling, Niagara
Origin	New York	Red	Kasselfest, Valpolicella
Milk	sheep	Sparkling	Sparkling Soave
Info	spicy	Dessert	Banyuls

CHEESE	Berkswell	WINE	
Style	firm	White	Riesling, Gewürztraminer, Chasselas
Origin	England	Red	Pinot Noir, Rioja, Syrah, Bordeaux,
Milk	sheep		Barolo, Barbera, Alicante Bouchet
Info	rich, nutty, flowery, caramelly, fruity	Dessert	Sherry, Sauternes, Malvasia Bianca

CHEESE	Bermuda Triangle	WINE	
Style	firm	White	Sauvignon Blanc, Pinot Gris, Chablis
Origin	California	Red	Villard Noir, Kasselfest, Zinfandel
Milk	goat	Rosé	Rosé
Info	smooth, tangy, ash layer, creamy	Sparkling	Asti Spumanti
		Dessert	Vin Santo

CHEESE	Big Woods Blue	WINE	
Style	semi-soft	White	Muscadine
Origin	Minnesota	Red	Cabernet Sauvignon, Mourvèdre
Milk	sheep	Dessert	Port, Sherry
Info	salty, tangy		

CHEESE	Blarney	WINE	
Style	semi-soft	White	Chardonnay, Pinot Grigio, Marsanne
Origin	Ireland	Red	Merlot, Burgundy, Lemberger
Milk	cow	Rosé	White Merlot
Info	subtle, mild, sweet	Sparkling	Crémant
		Dessert	Ravat

CHEESE	Bleu d'Auvergne	WINE	
Style	semi-soft	White	Chardonnay, Sauvignon Blanc, Seyval,
Origin	France		Muscadine, Edelweiss, Orvieto
Milk	cow	Red	Cabernet Sauvignon, Zinfandel, Pinot
Info	salty, rich, sharp, crumbly, moist,		Noir, Alicante Bouschet
	creamy	Dessert	Port, Sherry

CHEESE	Bleu de Causses	WINE	
Style	semi-soft	White	Sauvignon Blanc, Chardonnay
Origin	France	Red	Cabernet Sauvignon, Zinfandel, Barolo,
Milk	cow		Malbec, Cynthiana, Meritus, Grenache
Info	salty, sharp, spicy	Sparkling	Champagne
		Dessert	Sauternes, Port, Madiera, Banyuls

CHEESE	Bleu de Gex	WINE	
Style	firm	White	Viognier, Delaware, Fumé Blanc
Origin	France	Red	Côtes du Rhône
Milk	cow	Sparkling	Sparkling Soave
Info	rich, mild, creamy, pungent aroma	Dessert	Port, Muscat

CHEESE	Bleu de Haut Jura	WINE	
Style	firm	White	Sauvignon Blanc, Chardonnay
Origin	France	Red	Cabernet Sauvignon, Zinfandel
Milk	cow	Rosé	Pink Catawba
Info	mild	Sparkling	Champagne
		Dessert	Sauternes

CHEESE	Blue	WINE	
Style	semi-soft to firm	White	Chardonnay
Origin	France	Red	Cabernet Sauvignon, Zinfandel, Merlot
Milk	cow	Sparkling	Champagne
Info	moldy, rich, mild to sharp, tangy	Dessert	Port, Sherry

CHEESE	Blue Brie	WINE	
Style	soft	White	Sauvignon Blanc, Chardonnay
Origin	France	Red	Cabernet Sauvignon, Zinfandel
Milk	cow	Dessert	Malvasia Bianca
Info	mild to spicy		

CHEESE	Blue Castello	WINE	
Style	soft, triple cream	White	Chenin Blanc, Sauvignon Blanc
Origin	Denmark	Red	Zinfandel, Dolcetto, Barbaresco
Milk	cow	Dessert	Port, Sherry
Info	mild, creamy, tangy		

CHEESE	Boerenhaas	WINE	
Style	firm	White	Chardonnay
Origin	Holland	Red	Syrah, Beaujolais, Grenache
Milk	cow	Sparkling	Crémant
Info	intense, aged	Dessert	Tawny Port

CHEESE	Bonbel	WINE	
Style	semi-soft	White	Gewürztraminer, Riesling
Origin	France	Red	Beaujolais, Merlot, Pinot Noir
Milk	cow	Rosé	Rosé
Info	mild, factory-made Saint-Paulin	Sparkling	Champagne
		Dessert	Icewine

CHEESE	Botana	WINE	
Style	firm	White	Kerner, Traminette
Origin	USA	Red	Petit Sirah, Amarone, Kasselfest,
Milk	goat		Malbec
Info	sharp	Dessert	Port, Hard Cider

CHEESE	Boucheron	WINE	
Style	soft	White	Gewürztraminer, Colombard, Marsanne
Origin	France	Red	Landot Noir, Beaujolais Nouveau
Milk	goat	Rosé	White Zinfandel
Info	rich, mild to tangy	Sparkling	Champagne
		Dessert	Vin Santo

CHEESE	Boulette d'Avesnes	WINE	
Style	soft	Red	Cabernet Sauvignon, Lemberger,
Origin	France		Mourvèdre, Maréchal Foch
Milk	cow		
Info	paprika, parsley, tragon, beer wash		

CHEESE	Boursault	WINE	
Style	soft, double & triple cream	White	Gewürztraminer, Riesling, Ortega
Origin	France	Red	Tempranillo, Landot Noir
Milk	cow	Rosé	Grenache Rosé
Info	very rich, mild, creamy, mellow	Sparkling	Champagne, Sparkling Soave
		Dessert	Muscat, Málaga

CHEESE	Boursin	WINE	
Style	fresh, triple cream	White	Gewürztraminer, Riesling, Sancerre,
Origin	France		Chenin Blanc, Marsanne, Pinot Gris
Milk	cow	Red	Beaujolais Nouveau
Info	creamy, rich, smooth, herbs & spices	Rosé	Pink Vidal

CHEESE	Bra	WINE	
Style	soft	Red	Barbera, Dolcetto, Gamay Beaujolais
Origin	Italy	Dessert	Port
Milk	cow		
Info	piquant, salty, very strong		

CHEESE	Brebiou	WINE	
Style	fresh	White	Chablis, Edelweiss, Fumé Blanc, Niersteiner
Origin	France		
Milk	sheep	Rosé	Blush Niagara
Info	mild		

CHEESE	Bresse Blue	WINE	
Style	soft	White	Riesling, Niagara, Seyval
Origin	France	Red	Mourvèdre
Milk	cow	Sparkling	Brut
Info	mild, buttery, spicy	Dessert	Vin Santo

CHEESE	Brick	WINE	
Style	semi-soft	White	Sauvignon Blanc, Chardonnel
Origin	Wisconsin	Red	Cabernet Sauvignon, Pinot Noir, Valpolicalla, Syrah, Merlot, Bordeaux
Milk	cow		
Info	mild to sharp, tangy, spicy, pungent aroma, sweet	Rosé	White Zinfandel, Blush Niagara, Pink Catawba

CHEESE	Brie	WINE	
Style	soft	White	Chardonnay, Viognier, Cayuga, Riesling
Origin	France	Red	Pinot Noir, Cabernet Sauvignon, Claret, Merlot, Burgundy, Bordeaux, Dolcetto
Milk	cow		
Info	creamy, mild, rich	Sparkling	Champagne
		Dessert	Sherry

CHEESE	Brie de Meaux	WINE	
Style	soft	White	Chardonnay
Origin	France	Red	Pinot Noir, Bordeaux, Burgundy, Chianti, Pinotage, Amarone, Malbec, Mouton-Rothschild, Barbera
Milk	cow		
Info	coated with spices, very fruity		
		Sparkling	Champagne

CHEESE	Brillat Savarin	WINE	
Style	soft, triple cream	White	Gewürztraminer, Riesling, Pinot Blanc
Origin	France	Red	Pinot Noir, Côtes du Rhône,
Milk	cow	Rosé	Pink Catawba
Info	mild, salty, bit sour, buttery, rich	Sparkling	Champagne, Crémant

CHEESE	Brin d'Amour	WINE	
Style	soft	White	Riesling, Chardonnay
Origin	France	Red	Cabernet Sauvignon, Syrah
Milk	sheep	Rosé	Blush Muscadine
Info	mild, sweet	Sparkling	Champagne
		Dessert	Sherry

CHEESE	Brinza	WINE	
Style	soft	White	Vignoles, Sauvignon Blanc, Riesling
Origin	Romania	Red	Merlot, Cinsault, Noble
Milk	sheep	Rosé	White Zinfandel
Info	salty, spreadable when young, crumbly with age	Sparkling	Champagne

CHEESE	Brocciu	WINE	
Style	fresh	White	Cabernet Sauvignon, Barolo, Chambourcin, Muscadine
Origin	France		
Milk	sheep or goat whey	Rosé	Rosé Rioja
Info	creamy, sharp, tangy		

CHEESE	Bruder Basil	WINE	
Style	semi-soft	White	Chardonnay, Niersteiner, Meursault, Chenin Blanc, Müeller-Thurgau
Origin	Germany		
Milk	cow	Red	Merlot, Côtes du Rhône, Zinfandel
Info	mild, smoky, smooth, rich, creamy	Rosé	Blush Muscadine
		Sparkling	Asti Spumanti

CHEESE	Brusselsekaas	WINE	
Style	soft	White	Vouvray, Gewürztraminer, Ortega
Origin	Belgium	Red	Merlot, Muscadine, Zinfandel, Gamay Beaujolais, Pinot Noir, Barbaresco
Milk	cow		
Info	smooth, salty, low-fat, no rind, strong, tangy, light spicy aroma	Sparkling	Crémant
		Dessert	Malvasia Bianca

CHEESE	Buche	WINE	
Style	semi-soft	White	Sauvignon Blanc, Pinot Gris, Chenin Blanc, Pinot Blanc
Origin	France		
Milk	goat	Red	Alicante Bouschet, Barbaresco
Info	rich, complex, creamy	Sparkling	Champagne
		Dessert	Malvasia Bianca

CHEESE	Bucheret	WINE	
Style	semi-soft	White	Sauvignon Blanc, Riesling
Origin	France	Red	Syrah, Beaujolais Nouveau, Villard Noir
Milk	goat	Sparkling	Champagne
Info	blue	Dessert	Muscat

CHEESE	Bucheron	WINE	
Style	soft	White	Chardonnay, Sauvignon Blanc
Origin	France	Red	Merlot, Dolcetto, Nebbiolo
Milk	cow	Rosé	White Zinfandel
Info	mild, tangy	Sparkling	Champagne
		Dessert	Malvasia Bianca

CHEESE	Buffalo	WINE	
Style	hard	White	Chardonnay, Sauvignon Blanc
Origin	England	Red	Merlot, Beaujolais
Milk	buffalo	Rosé	Pink Vidal
Info	mild, hint of almonds, modern	Sparkling	Champagne

CHEESE	Burgos	WINE	
Style	Fresh	White	Sauvignon Blanc, Pinot Gris
Origin	Spain	Red	Carignan, Pinot Meunier
Milk	sheep	Sparkling	Champagne
Info	smooth, very mild, slightly salty		

CHEESE	Burrini	WINE	
Style	firm	White	Chardonnay, Fumé Blanc
Origin	Italy	Red	Grüner Veltliner, Pinot Noir
Milk	cow	Sparkling	Sparkling Soave
Info	hand molded around a pat of sweet butter, mild, faint tang, spreadable	Dessert	Muscat

CHEESE	Butterkäse	WINE	
Style	semi-soft	White	Sémillon, Chardonnay
Origin	Germany	Red	Beaujolais, Pinot Noir
Milk	cow	Rosé	White Merlot
Info	mild, delicate	Sparkling	Champagne
		Dessert	Tokaji

CHEESE	Cabécou	WINE	
Style	soft	White	Pinot Grigio, Sauvignon Blanc
Origin	California	Red	Norton, Barolo, Cabernet Sauvignon
Milk	goat	Rosé	Blush Niagara
Info	rich, creamy	Sparkling	Champagne
		Dessert	Port

CHEESE	Cabécou Feuille	WINE	
Style	soft	White	Riesling, Gewürztraminer
Origin	France	Red	Pinot Noir
Milk	goat	Rosé	Pink Vidal
Info	smooth, creamy, chestnut leaf wrap	Sparkling	Blanc de Noirs
		Dessert	Madiera

CHEESE	Caboc	WINE	
Style	fresh	White	Orvieto, Chenin Blanc, Sancerre
Origin	Scotland		
Milk	cow		
Info	bland, crunchy oatmeal coating		

CHEESE	Cabrales	WINE	
Style	semi-soft	White	Chardonnay, Sauvignon Blanc, Vouvray,
Origin	Spain		Rioja Blanca
Milk	cow+goat+sheep	Red	Cabernet Sauvignon, Zinfandel, Rioja,
Info	blue, salty, powerful aroma, crumbly,		Tempranillo, Lemberger
	dense, tangy, sharp, fine texture	Dessert	Madiera, Sherry, Hard Cider, PX, Port

CHEESE	Caciocavallo	WINE	
Style	semi-soft	White	Sancerre, Vouvray
Origin	Italy	Red	Chianti, Zinfandel, Côtes du Rhône,
Milk	cow		Shiraz, Sangiovese, Merlot
Info	mellow, sweet, delicate, tangy,	Dessert	Port
	hints of anise & almonds		

CHEESE	Caciotta	WINE	
Style	semi-soft	White	Riesling, Viognier
Origin	Italy	Red	Norton, Carignan
Milk	cow+sheep	Rosé	Grenache Rosé
Info	mild, creamy, sweet, tangy, sharp	Dessert	Port
	lingering aftertaste		

CHEESE	Caerphilly	WINE	
Style	semi-soft	White	Viognier, Chardonnay, Grüner Veltliner,
Origin	Wales		Riesling, Vouvray, Gewürztraminer
Milk	cow	Red	Syrah, Cabernet Sauvignon, Mersault
Info	salty, mild, fruity, creamy, smooth,	Rosé	Pink Catawba
	moist, buttery, slightly sour, lemony	Dessert	Late Harvest Riesling

CHEESE	Cambozola	WINE	
Style	soft	White	Chardonnay, Liebfraumilch, LaCrosse,
Origin	Germany		Vouvray
Milk	cow	Red	Shiraz, Angélus, Bolduc, Beaujolais
Info	blue, creamy, mild, rich, spicy, tangy	Sparkling	Champagne
		Dessert	Tokaji, Sauternes, PX

CHEESE	Camellia	WINE	
Style	soft	White	Sauvignon Blanc, Pinot Gris, Chasselas
Origin	California	Red	Pinot Noir, Chancellor, Cynthiana,
Milk	goat		Mouton-Rothschild Bordeaux
Info	pungent, rich	Sparkling	Crémant
		Dessert	Tokaji

CHEESE	Camembert	WINE	
Style	soft	White	Viognier, Sauvignon Blanc, Chardonnay
Origin	France	Red	Merlot, Syrah, Zinfandel, Syrah, Pinot
Milk	cow		Noir, Bordeaux, Gamay Beaujolais
Info	mild, rich, buttery, creamy to	Rosé	Pink Vidal
	firm with age	Sparkling	Champagne
		Dessert	Muscato, PX

CHEESE	Cana de Cabra	WINE	
Style	semi-soft	White	Sauvignon Blanc, Pinot Gris
Origin	Spain	Red	Pinot Noir, Rioja
Milk	goat	Rosé	Rosé Rioja
Info	mild, creamy	Sparkling	Champagne
		Dessert	Sangria

CHEESE	Cana de Oveja	WINE	
Style	semi-soft	White	Sauvignon Blanc, Viognier
Origin	Spain	Red	Rioja
Milk	sheep	Rosé	Rosé Rioja
Info	rich, creamy	Sparkling	Champagne
		Dessert	Sauternes

CHEESE	Cantal	WINE	
Style	semi-soft	White	Chardonnay, Sauvignon Blanc,
Origin	France		Chenin Blanc, Blanc de Bois
Milk	cow	Red	Cabernet Sauvignon, Merlot,
Info	mild, tangy, complex, smooth,		Beaujolais, Manzanilla, Bordeaux,
	nutty, buttery		Meritage

CHEESE	Capra	WINE	
Style	soft	White	Sauvignon Blanc, Chenin Blanc,
Origin	Belgium		Magnolia
Milk	goat	Red	Dolcetto, Muscadine
Info	smooth, honey added, sweet,	Sparkling	Asti Spumanti
	tangy	Dessert	Ravat

CHEESE	Caprino	WINE	
Style	firm	White	Orvieto, Aligoté
Origin	Italy	Red	Valpolicella, Sangiovese, Marechal
Milk	cow + goat		Foch
Info	sweet	Sparkling	Asti Spumanti

CHEESE	Caram	WINE	
Style	firm	White	Chardonnay, Liebfraumilch, Niesteiner
Origin	Germany	Red	Merlot, Cynthiana, Pinot Meunier
Milk	cow	Dessert	Icewine
Info	mild, smoky, creamy		

CHEESE	Carmela	WINE	
Style	firm	White	Sauvignon Blanc, Pinot Grigio, Aurore
Origin	California	Red	Petite Sirah, Villard Noir
Milk	cow	Sparkling	Asti Spumanti
Info	aged, paprika dusted		

CHEESE	Carmody	WINE	
Style	semi-soft	White	Chardonnay, Riesling, Viognier, Condrieu
Origin	California		
Milk	cow	Red	Rioja, Pinot Noir, Tempranillo, Zinfandel
Info	salty, creamy	Sparkling	Champagne
		Dessert	Malvasia Bianca

CHEESE	Cashel Blue	WINE	
Style	semi-soft	White	Sémillon, Sancerre
Origin	Ireland	Red	Malbec, Côtes du Rhône, Barbaresco, Alicante Bouchet, Barolo
Milk	cow		
Info	rich, extra creamy, somewhat salty, mellow, sweet, slightly tangy, mild	Dessert	Tawny Port, Sherry, Madiera, Tokaji

CHEESE	Castelrosso	WINE	
Style	semi-soft	White	Chardonnay, Cayuga
Origin	Italy	Red	Merlot, Barbera, Torgiano, Cynthiana
Milk	cow	Rosé	White Zinfandel
Info	rich	Sparkling	Champagne
		Dessert	Port

CHEESE	Chabichou	WINE	
Style	soft	White	Chenin Blanc, Sancerre, Chardonnay, Sauvignon Blanc, Pouilly-Fumé, Kerner
Origin	France		
Milk	goat	Red	Cabernet Sauvignon, Zinfandel, Noble
Info	lightly sour		

CHEESE	Chalosse	WINE	
Style	semi-soft	White	Aligoté, Blanc de Bois
Origin	France	Red	Cabernet Sauvignon, Merlot, Bordeaux
Milk	goat	Rosé	Steuben
Info	rich		

CHEESE	Chaource	WINE	
Style	soft, triple cream	White	Viognier, Sancerre, Magnolia, Catawba, Chablis, Chardonnay, Traminette
Origin	France		
Milk	cow	Red	Bordeaux, Burgundy. St. Emilon
Info	sharp, creamy, smooth, dryish, mushroom scent	Rosé	Grenache Rosé
		Sparkling	Sparkling Soave

CHEESE	Chaubier	WINE	
Style	semi-soft	White	Marsanne, Chenin Blanc, Delaware
Origin	France	Red	Côtes du Rhône, Bolduc, Beaujolais
Milk	cow+goat	Rosé	White Merlot
Info	mild, creamy, nutty	Sparkling	Brut
		Dessert	Sangria

CHEESE	Chaumes	WINE	
Style	soft, triple cream	White	Chardonnay, Fumé Blanc, Albarino,
Origin	France		Chasselas, LaCrosse
Milk	cow	Red	Sangiovese, Burgundy, Bordeaux
Info	very spicy, creamy, rich, full body	Sparkling	Asti Spumanti

CHEESE	Cheddar - Mild	WINE	
Style	firm	White	Riesling, Niagara, Vignoles, Cayuga,
Origin	England		Chenin Blanc, Chardonnay, LaCrosse
Milk	cow	Red	Pinot Noir, Zinfandel, Rioja, Norton,
Info	mild		Muscadine, Petite Sirah
		Dessert	Port

CHEESE	Cheddar - Sharp	WINE	
Style	firm	White	Chenin Blanc, Sauvignon Blanc, Soave,
Origin	England		Viognier, Grüner Veltliner, Chardonnay
Milk	cow	Red	Cabernet Sauvignon, Côtes du Rhône,
Info	sharp		Merlot, Zinfandel, Nebbiolo
		Dessert	Muscat, Tawny Port, Madeira, Muscat

CHEESE	Cheshire	WINE	
Style	firm	White	Riesling, Chardonnay, Sauvignon Blanc,
Origin	England		Chenin Blanc
Milk	cow	Red	Cabernet Sauvignon, Merlot, Pinot
Info	mild, slightly salty, crumbly, sweet,		Noir, Dolcetto, Beaujolais Nouveau
	tangy, full-bodied, spicy	Dessert	Muscat

CHEESE	Chèvre	WINE	
Style	soft	White	Gewürztraminer, Sauvignon Blanc,
Origin	France		Pinot Grigio, Orvieto, Pouilly-Fumé
Milk	goat	Red	Merlot, Pinot Noir, Meritage
Info	light, creamy, tangy	Rosé	White Zinfandel, Blush Niagara
		Sparkling	Champagne

CHEESE	Chimay	WINE	
Style	semi-soft	White	Riesling, Gewürztraminer
Origin	Belgium	Red	Pinot Meunier, Petit Sirah, Zinfandel,
Milk	cow		Alicante Bouschet
Info	beer wash, nutty, mild		

CHEESE	Clisson	WINE	
Style	semi-soft	White	Gewürztraminer, Riesling, Condrieu
Origin	France	Red	Beaujolais Nouveau, Gamay Noir
Milk	goat	Rosé	White Zinfandel
Info	rich	Sparkling	Champagne
		Dessert	Sherry, Tokaji

CHEESE	Cocoa Cardona	WINE	
Style	firm	White	Gewürztraminer, Riesling, Magnolia
Origin	Wisconsin	Red	Syrah, Merlot, Meritus, Chancellor
Milk	goat		
Info	aged in cocoa		

CHEESE	Colby	WINE	
Style	semi-soft	White	Riesling, Cayuga, Vignoles, Muscadine,
Origin	Wisconsin		Magnolia, Viognier
Milk	cow	Red	Pinot Noir, Cabernet Sauvignon,
Info	mild, slightly sweet, granular		Merlot, Zinfandel, Alicante Bouschet
		Sparkling	Champagne, Brut

CHEESE	Colby Jack (Co-Jack)	WINE	
Style	semi-soft	White	Gewürztraminer, Chardonnay
Origin	Wisconsin	Red	Amarone, Fredonia, Landot Noir
Milk	cow	Sparkling	Champagne
Info	Colby + Monterey Jack, mild	Dessert	Port

CHEESE	Colorouge	WINE	
Style	soft	White	Riesling, Carlos, Sauvignon Blanc
Origin	Colorado	Red	Pinot Noir, Dechaunac, Meritage
Milk	cow	Rosé	White Zinfandel
Info	mild, creamy	Sparkling	Champagne
		Dessert	Malvasia Bianca

CHEESE	Comté	WINE	
Style	semi-soft	White	Gewürztraminer, Riesling, Sancerre
Origin	France	Red	Beaujolais, Burgundy, Merlot, Norton
Milk	cow	Rosé	Grenache Rosé
Info	mild, nutty, sweet, smooth	Sparkling	Champagne
		Dessert	Sauternes

CHEESE	Constant Bliss	WINE	
Style	soft	White	Vouvray, Sauvignon Blanc, Aurore
Origin	Vermont	Red	Pinot Noir, Merlot, Concord
Milk	cow	Rosé	Pink Catawba
Info	creamy, buttery	Sparkling	Champagne
		Dessert	Muscat

CHEESE	Coolea	WINE	
Style	firm	White	Marsanne, Verdelet, Muscadine
Origin	Holland	Red	Shiraz, Zinfandel, Gamay Beaujolais,
Milk	cow		Valpolicello, Pinot Noir, Barbaresco
Info	rich, nutty, carmelly, sweet, fruity,	Sparkling	Crémant
	mild, creamy, fresh aftertaste	Dessert	Malvasia Bianca

CHEESE	Cotija	WINE	
Style	firm	White	Chardonnay, Riesling, Rioja Blanca
Origin	Mexico	Red	Beaujolais, Mourvèdre, Noble, Rosso
Milk	goat or cow		Misto, Tempranillo
Info	salty, mellow to sharp with age,	Sparkling	Asti Spumanti
	zesty, crumbly	Dessert	Sangria, PX

CHEESE	Cotswold	WINE	
Style	firm	Red	Syrah, Dechaunac, Malbec, Mourvèdre
Origin	England	Dessert	Port
Milk	cow		
Info	rich, Double Gloucester with onions		
	& chives, crumbly		

CHEESE	Cottage Cheese	WINE	
Style	fresh	White	Riesling, Chardonnay, Sauvignon Blanc,
Origin	England		Sémillon
Milk	cow		
Info	curd cheese, mild, moist		

CHEESE	Coulommiers	WINE	
Style	soft	White	Sauvignon Blanc, Meusault, Cinsault,
Origin	France		Chardonnay
Milk	cow	Red	Bordeaux, Pinotage, Malbec,
Info	mild, tangy, extra rich		Valpolicella
		Sparkling	Champagne

CHEESE	Cream Cheese	WINE	
Style	fresh	White	Riesling, Chardonnay, Sauvignon Blanc,
Origin	Pennsylvania		Gewürztraminer, Pouilly-Fumé, Aurore
Milk	cow	Red	Beaujolais
Info	mild, tangy	Rosé	White Zinfandel
		Sparkling	Champagne

CHEESE	Crème Frâiche	WINE	
Style	fresh	White	French Colombard, Viognier, Riesling,
Origin	France		Pinot Grigio, Chenin Blanc
Milk	cow	Red	Rosso Misto, Beaujolais
Info	sweet, fruity, tangy	Sparkling	Champagne
		Dessert	Sherry, Malvasia Bianca

CHEESE	Crescenza	WINE	
Style	fresh	White	Pinot Grigio, Orvieto, Viognier, Kerner,
Origin	Italy		Sauvignon Blanc, Chasselas, Vignoles
Milk	cow	Red	Pinot Noir, Chianti
Info	smooth, creamy, rich	Dessert	Ravat

CHEESE	Crockhamdale	WINE	
Style	hard	White	Riesling, Chardonnay, Mersault
Origin	England	Red	Barbera, Cabernet Sauvignon, Merlot
Milk	sheep	Rosé	White Zinfandel
Info	mild	Sparkling	Champagne
		Dessert	PX

CHEESE	Crottin	WINE	
Style	semi-soft	White	Sauvignon Blanc, Pouilly-Fumé, Seyval,
Origin	France		Sancerre, Roussanne, Pinot Gris
Milk	goat	Red	Cabernet Franc, Beaujolais, Grenache,
Info	creamy, intense, rich, varied		Carignan
		Sparkling	Crémant

CHEESE	Crottin de Chavignol	WINE	
Style	semi-soft	White	Sauvignon Blanc, Albarino, Sancerre,
Origin	France		Catawba, Liebframilch
Milk	goat	Red	Meritus, Beaujolais, Carignan
Info	subtle, nutty, dry, creamy, salty,	Sparkling	Champagne
	mild to sharp with age	Dessert	Malvasia Bianca

CHEESE	Crozier Blue	WINE	
Style	soft	White	Magnolia, Niersteiner, Muscadine
Origin	Ireland	Red	Maréchal Foch, Bolduc, Cynthiana
Milk	sheep	Sparkling	Champagne
Info	slightly salty, mild, sweet	Dessert	Tawny Port, Sherry, Sangria

CHEESE	Damski	WINE	
Style	semi-soft	White	Chardonnay, Himmelswein, Fumé Blanc
Origin	Denmark	Red	Zinfandel, Rosso Misto, Norton,
Milk	cow		Malbec
Info	smoked, sweet	Sparkling	Blanc de Noirs

CHEESE	Danbo	WINE	
Style	semi-soft	White	Chardonnay, Colombard, Niagara
Origin	Denmark	Red	Zinfandel, Cynthiana, Pinot Meunier
Milk	cow	Rosé	White Merlot
Info	mild, swiss style, nutty, bland	Sparkling	Crémant
		Dessert	Muscat

CHEESE	Danish Blue	WINE	
Style	semi-soft	White	Chardonay, Sauvignon Blanc,
Origin	Denmark		Liebframilch
Milk	cow	Red	Cabernet Sauvignon, Zinfandel
Info	salty, mild, rich, creamy	Sparkling	Champagne
		Dessert	Port

CHEESE	Daylesford	WINE	
Style	firm	White	Chardonnay, LaCrosse, Madaline
Origin	England	Red	Merlot, Pinot Noir, Petite Sirah, Bolduc
Milk	cow	Rosé	Pink Vidal
Info	sweet, subtle	Sparkling	Champagne
		Dessert	Muscat

CHEESE	Derby	WINE	
Style	semi-firm	White	Chardonnay, Sauvignon Blanc, Chenin
Origin	England		Blanc, Symphony
Milk	cow	Red	Cabernet Sauvignon, Merlot, Rioja
Info	delicate, mild, flaky texture	Sparkling	Brut
		Dessert	Ravat

CHEESE	Dolcelatte	WINE	
Style	soft	Red	Zinfandel, Chambourcin, Muscadine,
Origin	Italy		Gamay Noir
Milk	cow	Sparkling	Champagne
Info	blue, mild, sweet	Dessert	Sauternes

CHEESE	Double Gloucester	WINE	
Style	semi-firm	White	Sancerre, Gewürztraminer, Vouvray,
Origin	England		Grüner Veltliner
Milk	cow	Red	Shiraz, Zinfandel, Alicante Bouschet
Info	slightly salty, butterscotch hints, mild,	Sparkling	Champagne
	creamy, nutty, piquant	Dessert	Tawny Port, Madiera

CHEESE	Dry Jack	WINE	
Style	hard	White	Riesling, Chardonnay, Chenin Blanc,
Origin	USA		Sancerre, Viognier, Himmelswein
Milk	cow	Red	Pinot Noir, Cabernet Sauvignon,
Info	rich, sweet, fruity, aged		Merlot, Zinfandel, Cabernet Franc
		Dessert	Late Harvest Riesling, Amagnac

CHEESE	Dubliner	WINE	
Style	firm	White	Vouvray, Seyval Blanc, Melody,
Origin	Ireland	Red	Syrah, Zinfandel, Barbaresco
Milk	cow	Rosé	White Zinfandel
Info	sweet	Sparkling	Blanc de Noirs
		Dessert	Tokaji

CHEESE	Durrus	WINE	
Style	semi-firm	White	Vouvray, Riesling, Albarino, Vignoles
Origin	Ireland	Red	Cabernet Sauvignon, Gamay Beaujolais
Milk	cow	Rosé	Grenache Rosé
Info	silky, mushroomy, sweet, fruity, rich,	Sparkling	Champagne
	creamy, smooth	Dessert	Muscat

CHEESE	Edam	WINE	
Style	semi-soft	White	Sauvignon Blanc, Riesling, Cayuga,
Origin	Holland, Switzerland		Fumé Blanc, Catawba, Viognier
Milk	cow	Red	Shiraz, Merlot, Pinot Noir, Cabernet
Info	mild, nutty, smooth, supple, mellow		Sauvignon, Valpolicella, Beaujolais
		Sparkling	Champagne

CHEESE	Emmentaler	WINE	
Style	firm	White	Vouvray, Pinot Blanc, Sémillon, Vidal
Origin	Switzerland		Blanc, Chardonnay, Gewürztraminer,
Milk	cow	Red	Shiraz, Beaujolais, Merlot, Zinfandel,
Info	strong		Cabernet Franc, Grenache, Carignan
		Dessert	Sherry

CHEESE	English Blue Cheshire	WINE	
Style	firm	White	Chardonnay, Sauvignon Blanc, Villard
Origin	England	Red	Cabernet Sauvignon, Zinfandel,
Milk	cow		Lemberger
Info	rich	Sparkling	Champagne
		Dessert	Port

CHEESE	Epoisses	WINE	
Style	soft	White	Mersault, Gewürztraminer, Chardonnay
Origin	France	Red	Cabernet Sauvignon, Baco Noir
Milk	cow	Rosé	Steuben
Info	delicate, intense, stinky, smooth,	Sparkling	Blanc de Noirs
	creamy, spicy, tangy	Dessert	Sauternes, Muscat

CHEESE	Esrom	WINE	
Style	semi-soft	Red	Burgundy, Chianti, Sangiovese,
Origin	Denmark		Chambourcin, Muscadine
Milk	cow	Sparkling	Asti Spumanti
Info	rich, spicy, slightly pungent, sweet	Dessert	Port

CHEESE	Etorki	WINE	
Style	fresh	White	Edelweiss, Verdelet, Symphony
Origin	France	Red	Beaujolais, Bolduc, Pinot Meunier
Milk	sheep	Dessert	Tawny Port
Info	mild, oily with butterfat, creamy,		
	burnt caramel flavor		

CHEESE	Everona	WINE	
Style	semi-soft	White	Chardonnay, Gewürztraminer, Pinot
Origin	Virginia		Blanc, Niagara
Milk	sheep	Red	Sangiovese, Syrah, Mouton-Rothschild
Info	rich, floral	Rosé	White Zinfandel
		Sparkling	Champagne
		Dessert	Sauternes

CHEESE	Excelsior	WINE	
Style	soft, double- or triple-cream	White	Chardonnay, Aligoté, Chablis
Origin	France	Red	Beaujolais, Chambourcin, Rosso Misto
Milk	cow	Rosé	Pink Catawba
Info	mild, very smooth, delicate	Sparkling	Champagne, Sparkling Soave
		Dessert	Malvasia Bianca

CHEESE	Explorateur	WINE	
Style	soft, triple-cream	White	Gewürztraminer, Riesling, Seyval Blanc
Origin	France	Red	Pinot Noir, Chancellor, Chianti, Bolduc
Milk	cow	Rosé	Blush Niagara
Info	rich, creamy, salty, complex	Sparkling	Champagne, Asti Spumanti
		Dessert	Muscat

CHEESE	Farmers	WINE	
Style	semi-soft	White	Riesling, Pinot Grigio, Aurore, Niagara
Origin	USA	Red	Beaujolais, Petite Sirah, Concord
Milk	cow	Rosé	Blush Muscadine
Info	mild, slightly tangy	Sparkling	Crémant
		Dessert	Muscat

CHEESE	Feta	WINE	
Style	soft	White	Riesling, Chardonnay, Sauvignon Blanc,
Origin	Greece		Pinot Gris, Viognier, Chenin Blanc
Milk	goat + sheep, or cow	Red	Gamay Beaujolais, Pinot Noir
Info	sharp, tangy, salty, creamy, rich,	Rosé	White Zinfandel
	complex	Dessert	Amagnac

CHEESE	Fiore Sardo	WINE	
Style	semi-soft	White	Pinot Grigio, Müller-Thurgau, Orvieto
Origin	Italy	Red	Sangiovese, Barbera, Torgiano, Rosso
Milk	sheep		Misto, Valpolicella
Info	sharp, crumbly, slightly salty,	Sparkling	Champagne
	long-finish, creamy	Dessert	Port

CHEESE	Fleur-de-Teche	WINE	
Style	semi-soft	White	Sauvignon Blanc, Verdelet, Villard
Origin	France	Red	Pinot Noir, Concord, Meritus
Milk	cow	Sparkling	Brut
Info	ash line	Dessert	Muscat

CHEESE	Florette	WINE	
Style	soft	White	Viognier, Chenin Blanc, Verdicchio
Origin	France	Red	Beaujolais Nouveau, Pinot Meunier
Milk	goat	Rosé	White Zinfandel
Info	delicate, creamy	Sparkling	Champagne
		Dessert	Malvasia Bianca

CHEESE	Fontal	WINE	
Style	semi-soft	White	Kerner, Verdelet, Orvieto
Origin	Italy	Red	Dolcetto, Mouton-Rothschild, Noble
Milk	cow	Rosé	White Zinfandel
Info	tender, nutty, sweet aftertaste	Sparkling	Champagne
		Dessert	Muscat

CHEESE	Fontina	WINE	
Style	semi-soft	White	Riesling, Chardonnay, Pinot Blanc
Origin	Italy, Denmark	Red	Barbaresco, Pinot Noir, Syrah, Barolo,
Milk	cow		Sangiovese, Dolcetto, Barbera
Info	mild, delicate, nutty, buttery, fruity,	Rosé	Pink Catawba
	smooth, sweet	Dessert	Sherry

CHEESE	Fougerus	WINE	
Style	soft	White	Sauvignon Blanc, Chenin Blanc, Ortega
Origin	France	Red	Pinot Noir, Nebbiolo, Valpolicella
Milk	cow	Rosé	Grenache Rosé
Info	smooth, slightly salty	Sparkling	Champagne

CHEESE	Fourme d'Ambert	WINE	
Style	semi-soft	Red	Merlot, Carignan, Côtes du Rhône,
Origin	France		Angélus
Milk	cow	Sparkling	Champagne
Info	blue, moist, mild, creamy, smooth,	Dessert	Sherry, Banyuls, Port, Sauternes
	buttery, tangy, rich		

CHEESE	Fresh Mozzarella	WINE	
Style	fresh	White	Chardonnay, Sauvignon Blanc, Pinot
Origin	Italy		Grigio, Sémillon,
Milk	cow	Red	Beaujolais Nouveau, Pinot Noir
Info	mild		

CHEESE	Fribourg	WINE	
Style	hard	White	Chenin Blanc, Traminette, Kerner
Origin	Switzerland	Red	Bordeaux, Zinfandel, Concord,
Milk	cow		Cabernet Sauvignon
Info	sharp, aged	Sparkling	Champagne
		Dessert	Vin Santo

CHEESE	Fromage Blanc	WINE	
Style	fresh	White	Riesling, Chardonnay, Sauvignon Blanc,
Origin	France		Pinot Gris, Viognier, Gewürztraminer
Milk	cow	Red	Beaujolais, Pinot Noir, Chianti,
Info	creamy, mild, nutty		Kasselfest
		Rosé	White Zinfandel

CHEESE	Gabietou	WINE	
Style	semi-soft	White	Chardonnay, Ortega, Mersault
Origin	France	Red	Pinot Noir, Noble, Chancellor
Milk	cow + sheep	Rosé	White Zinfandel
Info	rich, fruity	Sparkling	Champagne
		Dessert	Málaga

CHEESE	Gamonedo	WINE	
Style	semi-soft	White	Pinot Gris, Roussanne, Gewürztraminer
Origin	Spain	Red	Rioja, Tempranillo, Cynthiana
Milk	cow, goat or sheep	Sparkling	Champagne
Info	sharp, lightly smoked, complex, spicy, buttery, grainy, crumbly	Dessert	Hard Cider, Muscat, PX

CHEESE	Gaperon	WINE	
Style	soft	White	Himmelswein
Origin	France	Red	Zinfandel , Bolduc, Chambourcin, Mourvèdre
Milk	cow		
Info	slightly salty, with garlic & peppercorns		

CHEESE	Garazi	WINE	
Style	firm	White	Chardonnay, Pinot Blanc, Rayon d'Or
Origin	France	Red	Syrah, Burgundy, Bolduc
Milk	sheep	Rosé	White Zinfandel
Info	mild	Sparkling	Champagne
		Dessert	Ravat

CHEESE	Garden Jack	WINE	
Style	semi-soft	White	Sauvignon Blanc, Vignoles
Origin	California	Red	Mourvèdre, Malbec, Claret, Cinsault
Milk	cow		
Info	bits of tomato, onion, green pepper		

CHEESE	Garrotxa	WINE	
Style	semi-firm	White	Chardonnay, Sauvignon Blanc, Riesling, Mersault, Pinot Gris, Grüner Veltliner
Origin	Spain		
Milk	goat	Red	Rioja, Tempranillo, Baco Noir
Info	smooth, creamy, crisp, tangy, herbal, mild, hint of hazelnuts	Sparkling	Champagne
		Dessert	Sherry, Muscat

CHEESE	Gianna	WINE	
Style	firm	White	Soave, Traminette, Rousanne
Origin	Italy	Red	Torgiano, Dolcetto, Rosso Misto
Milk	cow	Sparkling	Champagne
Info	medium sharp	Dessert	Port

CHEESE	Gilboa	WINE	
Style	firm	White	Riesling, Niagara
Origin	Israel	Red	Rioja, Grenache, Concord
Milk	sheep		
Info	lemony		

CHEESE	Girollin	WINE	
Style	firm	White	Chenin Blanc, Himmelswein, Viognier,
Origin	France		Rayon d'Or
Milk	cow	Red	Burgundy, Merlot, Dechaunac
Info	tangy	Sparkling	Blanc de Noirs
		Dessert	Port

CHEESE	Gjetost	WINE	
Style	firm	White	Chardonnay, Gewürztraminer, Verdelet,
Origin	Norway		Vidal Blanc, Müller-Thurgau
Milk	goat + cow	Red	Concord, Muscadine, Maréchal Foch
Info	sweet, nutty, subtle caramel	Rosé	Blush Niagara

CHEESE	Gloucester	WINE	
Style	firm	White	Chardonnay, Sauvignon Blanc,
Origin	England	Red	Cabernet Sauvignon, Merlot, Cynthiana
Milk	cow	Rosé	White Zinfandel
Info	mild, smooth, buttery, creamy	Sparkling	Champagne
		Dessert	PX

CHEESE	Goat Cheese	WINE	
Style	fresh	White	Gewürztraminer, Sauvignon Blanc,
Origin	France		Orvioto, Pinot Grigio, Pouilly-Fumé,
Milk	goat		Sancerre, Himmelswein, Vouvray
Info	creamy, tangy, slightly grainy,	Red	Merlot, Petite Sirah
	mild, earthy	Sparkling	Champagne

CHEESE	Gorgonzola Dolce	WINE	
Style	semi-soft	White	Riesling, Chardonnay, Sauvignon Blanc,
Origin	Italy		Gewürztraminer, Blanc du Bois, Cayuga
Milk	cow	Red	Cabernet Sauvignon, Bordeaux
Info	blue, sweet, mild, creamy, salty,	Sparkling	Champagne
	buttery, sharp	Dessert	Icewine, Madeira, Muscat

CHEESE	Gorgonzola Mascarpone	WINE	
Style	soft	White	Vignoles, Fumé Blanc, Riesling
Origin	Italy	Red	Cabernet Sauvignon, Sangiovese,
Milk	cow		Barbaresco
Info	blue, sharp, spicy, crumbly	Sparkling	Champagne
		Dessert	Sherry, Port, Sauternes

CHEESE	Gouda	WINE	
Style	semi-soft	White	Riesling, Sémillon, Sauvignon Blanc
Origin	Holland	Red	Pinot Noir, Côtes du Rhône, Amarone
Milk	cow	Rosé	White Zinfandel, Steuben
Info	mild, sweet, fruity, nutty	Sparkling	Champagne
		Dessert	Sherry, Muscat

CHEESE	Graddost	WINE	
Style	semi-soft	White	Chenin Blanc, Sauvignon Blanc
Origin	Sweden	Red	Merlot, Tempranillo, Rosso Misto
Milk	cow	Rosé	Blush Niagara, White Zinfandel
Info	mild, creamy, smooth	Sparkling	Champagne
		Dessert	Late Harvest Riesling

CHEESE	Grana Padano	WINE	
Style	hard	White	Albarino, Orvieto, Madeleine Angevine
Origin	Italy	Red	Barolo, Barbaresco, Norton, Petite
Milk	cow		Sirah, Torgiano, Angélus
Info	fruity, aged, intense, complex	Sparkling	Sparkling Soave
		Dessert	Port

CHEESE	Gratte-Paille	WINE	
Style	soft, double-cream	White	Gewürztraminer, Riesling, Aligoté
Origin	France	Red	Petite Sirah, Villard Noir, Dechaunac
Milk	cow	Rosé	White Zinfandel
Info	rich	Sparkling	Champagne
		Dessert	Late Harvest Riesling

CHEESE	Graviera	WINE	
Style	firm	White	Sémillon, Carlos, Chasselas
Origin	Greece	Red	Norton, Villard Noir, Sangiovese
Milk	sheep + goat	Dessert	PX
Info	aged, rich, creamy, slightly salty, crumbly, nutty, buttery		

CHEESE	Great Hill Blue	WINE	
Style	firm	White	Niagara, Chenin Blanc
Origin	Massachusetts	Red	Angélus, Claret, Mouton-Rothschild
Milk	cow	Dessert	Port, Muscat, Late Harvest Riesling
Info	smooth, crisp, zesty, robust, pungent, balanced finish		

CHEESE	Gruyère	WINE	
Style	firm	White	Riesling, Chardonnay, Sauvignon Blanc,
Origin	Switzerland		Pinot Grigio, Sémillon, Riesling, Melody
Milk	cow	Red	Cabernet Sauvignon, Zinfandel, Chianti,
Info	slightly salty, sweet, piquant, crumbly,		Bordeaux, Sangiovese, Meritage
	nutty, spicy, complex	Rosé	Pink Catawba
		Sparkling	Champagne

CHEESE	Gubbeen	WINE	
Style	semi-soft	White	Gewürztraminer, Riesling, Vouvray
Origin	Ireland	Red	Syrah, Alicante Bouschet, Pinotage,
Milk	cow		Malbec
Info	fruity, smooth, pungent, silky, mild,	Sparkling	Champagne
	nutty, smoky, buttery	Dessert	Vin Santo

CHEESE	Habanero Jack	WINE	
Style	semi-soft	White	Meurasult, Pinot Gris, Sancerre
Origin	Wisconsin	Red	Cabernet Sauvignon, Mourvèdre,
Milk	cow		Noble
Info	salty, hot peppers		

CHEESE	Haloumi	WINE	
Style	semi-soft	White	Sémillon, Chenin Blanc, Symphony
Origin	Cyprus	Red	Beaujolais, Villard Noir, Chianti
Milk	sheep + goat	Sparkling	Champagne
Info	salty, mild, minty, crumbly, creamy,	Dessert	Malvasia Bianca
	fibrous texture		

CHEESE	Harvest Moon	WINE	
Style	semi-soft	White	Gewürztraminer, Riesling, Carlos
Origin	Colorado	Red	Pinot Meunier, Beaujolais, Muscadine
Milk	cow	Rosé	White Zinfandel
Info	mild, rich, creamy	Sparkling	Champagne
		Dessert	Sauternes

CHEESE	Havarti	WINE	
Style	semi-soft	White	Chardonnay, Chenin Blanc, Delaware
Origin	Denmark	Red	Rioja, Bordeaux, Beaujolais, Merlot
Milk	cow	Rosé	Pink Catawba
Info	mild, creamy, supple, pungent with	Sparkling	Champagne
	age	Dessert	Muscat

CHEESE	Henri	WINE	
Style	fresh	White	Sancerre, Riesling, Rayon d'Or
Origin	France	Red	Gamay Noir, Pinot Meunier
Milk	cow		
Info	tangy, creamy		

CHEESE	Hollandse Chèvre	WINE	
Style	semi-soft	White	Viognier, Vouvray, Riesling, Condrieu
Origin	Holland	Red	Kasselfest, Petite Sirah, Merlot
Milk	goat	Rosé	Blush Muscadine
Info	mild, creamy, smooth, salty	Sparkling	Champagne
		Dessert	Sauternes

CHEESE	Hoch Ybrig	WINE	
Style	semi-soft	White	Riesling, Grüner Veltliner
Origin	Switzerland	Red	Merlot, Claret, Villard Noir
Milk	cow	Rosé	White Zinfandel
Info	smooth, dense, complex, salty, nutty,	Sparkling	Blanc de Noirs
	harmonious, tangy, butterscotchy	Dessert	Tokaji, Late Harvest Riesling

CHEESE	Humboldt Fog	WINE	
Style	soft	White	Chardonnay, Sauvignon Blanc, Pinot
Origin	California		Gris, Riesling, Verdelet
Milk	goat	Red	Gamay Noir, Meritus, Rosso Misto
Info	pungent, vegetable ash, light,	Rosé	White Zinfandel
	creamy, more complex with age	Dessert	Mead

CHEESE	Hyku	WINE	
Style	semi-soft	White	Sauvignon Blanc, Pinot Gris, Edelweiss
Origin	California	Red	Zinfandel, Pinot Noir
Milk	goat	Rosé	White Zinfandel
Info	floral	Sparkling	Champagne

CHEESE	Iberico	WINE	
Style	firm	White	Rioja Blanca
Origin	Spain	Red	Grenache, Albarino, Tempranillo,
Milk	sheep + cow + goat		Zinfandel, Rioja, Meritage
Info	complex, aromatic	Dessert	PX

CHEESE	Ibores	WINE	
Style	semi-soft	White	Grüner Veltliner, Riesling, Chardonnay,
Origin	Spain		Albarino
Milk	goat	Red	Cabernet Sauvignon, Zinfandel
Info	salty, zesty, acidulous, slightly bitter,		
	paprika		

CHEESE	Irazu	WINE	
Style	firm	White	Chardonnay, Fumé Blanc
Origin	Costa Rica	Red	Merlot, Rioja, Tempranillo, Syrah,
Milk	cow		Barbaresco, Cinsault
Info	satiny texture, sharp, tangy, hints of	Sparkling	Blanc de Noirs
	lemongrass & sage		

CHEESE	Jarlsberg	WINE	
Style	firm	White	Riesling, Sémillon, Pinot Gris, Carlos
Origin	Norway	Red	Burgundy, Merlot, Zinfandel, Beaujolais
Milk	cow	Rosé	Grenache Rosé, Pink Catawba
Info	mild, creamy, slightly sweet	Sparkling	Blanc de Noirs
		Dessert	Vin Santo

CHEESE	Kaseri	WINE	
Style	firm	White	Gewürztraminer, Sylvaner, Sancerre,
Origin	Greece		Traminette, Seyval Blanc, Pinot Grigio
Milk	sheep + goat, or cow	Red	Chianti, Claret, Pinot Noir, Cabernet
Info	salty, tangy, aged, strong, buttery		Sauvignon, Angélus, Barbera
		Dessert	Port

CHEESE	Kefalograviera	WINE	
Style	hard	White	Gewürztraminer, Fumé Blanc, Kerner
Origin	Greece	Red	Claret, Pinot Noir, Cabernet Sauvignon,
Milk	sheep or sheep + goat		Mourvèdre
Info	salty, smooth, slightly nutty,	Sparkling	Champagne
	rich aroma, pungent	Dessert	Mead

CHEESE	Kefalotyri	WINE	
Style	firm	White	Pinot Grigio, Vignoles, Gewürztraminer
Origin	Greece	Red	Côtes du Rhône, Claret, Pinot Noir,
Milk	sheep		Cabernet Sauvignon, Lemberger
Info	tangy, aged, dry, slightly oily, rich,	Sparkling	Champagne
	complex, nutty, salty, sharp finish	Dessert	Muscat

CHEESE	Kikorangi	WINE	
Style	firm	Red	Meritus, Noble, Cabernet Sauvignon,
Origin	New Zealand		Barbera, Cynthiana
Milk	cow	Sparkling	Champagne
Info	strong, piquant	Dessert	Port

CHEESE	Kiku	WINE	
Style	soft	White	Sauvignon Blanc, Pinot Gris
Origin	California	Red	Pinot Noir, Fredonia, Muscadine
Milk	goat	Rosé	White Zinfandel
Info	floral	Sparkling	Champagne
		Dessert	Ravat

CHEESE	Kuminost	WINE	
Style	semi-soft	White	Kerner, Riesling
Origin	Denmark	Red	Cabernet Sauvignon, Lemberger,
Milk	cow		Grenache
Info	mild, cumin, caraway, cloves	Sparkling	Brut

CHEESE	La Peral	WINE	
Style	semi-soft	White	Viognier, Riesling, Ortega
Origin	Spain	Red	Tempranillo, Barolo, Torgiano
Milk	cow + sheep	Sparkling	Asti Spumanti
Info	blue, pungent, sharp, intense	Dessert	Sherry

CHEESE	Lancashire	WINE	
Style	semi-soft	White	Gewürztraminer, Chardonnay, Riesling,
Origin	England		Sauvignon Blanc, Grüner Veltliner
Milk	cow	Red	Cabernet Sauvignon, Merlot, Zinfandel
Info	sharp, tangy, rich, crumbly, rich,		Barbera, Syrah, Pinot Noir, Amarone,
	lemony, creamy, buttery, slightly salty		Carignan

CHEESE	Langres	WINE	
Style	semi-soft	White	Sancerre, Gewürztraminer, Sauvignon
Origin	France		Blanc
Milk	cow	Red	Villard Noir, Pinotage, Malbec,
Info	smoky, pungent, spicy, stinky		Fredonia
		Dessert	Port, Sherry, Muscat

CHEESE	Lappi	WINE	
Style	firm	White	Villard, Rivaner, Pinot Gris, Soave,
Origin	Finland		Kerner, Verdelet
Milk	cow	Red	Chancellor, Cynthiana, Kasselfest
Info	mild, sweet	Rosé	Steuben
		Dessert	Hard Cider

CHEESE	Lebbene	WINE	
Style	soft	White	Riesling, Ortega, Sémillon
Origin	Israel	Red	Petite Sirah, Tempranillo
Milk	sheep or goat	Rosé	White Zinfandel
Info	mild	Sparkling	Champagne
		Dessert	Malvasia Bianca

CHEESE	Le Chèvre Noir	WINE	
Style	firm	White	Chardonnay, Sauvignon Blanc, Carlos,
Origin	Canada		Pinot Grigio
Milk	goat	Red	Zinfandel, Syrah, Concord, Meritage,
Info	full flavor, sweet, dense		Malbec, Barolo, Cabernet Sauvignon,
			Grenache, Rioja

CHEESE	Le Roule	WINE	
Style	soft	Red	Cabernet Sauvignon, Mourvèdre, Pinot
Origin	France		Meunier
Milk	cow	Sparkling	Asti Spumanti
Info	herbs, garlic		

CHEESE	Leicester	WINE	
Style	firm	White	Chardonnay, Sauvignon Blanc, Chablis
Origin	England	Red	Cabernet Sauvignon, Gamay Noir,
Milk	cow		Meritage
Info	nutty, candy-like, grainy	Sparkling	Brut
		Dessert	Banyuls

CHEESE	Leideche Kaas	WINE	
Style	semi-soft	White	Vignoles, Niagara, Cayuga
Origin	Denmark	Red	Burgundy, Zinfandel, Mourvèdre
Milk	cow	Rosé	White Zinfandel
Info	mild, sweet	Sparkling	Champagne
		Dessert	Málaga

CHEESE	Leyden	WINE	
Style	firm	White	French Colombard, Roussanne,
Origin	Denmark		Himmelswein
Milk	cow	Red	Burgundy, Zinfandel, Syrah, Chianti,
Info	caraway seed, cumin, crumbly,		Sangiovese
	tangy, salty, spicy		

CHEESE	Liederkranz	WINE	
Style	soft	White	Gewürztraminer, Niagara, Villard
Origin	New York	Red	Cabernet Sauvignon, Zinfandel, Norton
Milk	cow	Sparkling	Champagne
Info	mild, pungent, rich, moist, velvety	Dessert	Mead, Icewine

CHEESE	Limburger	WINE	
Style	semi-soft	White	Niersteiner, Chardonnay, Mersault,
Origin	Belgium, Germany		Riesling, Gewürztraminer
Milk	cow	Red	Cabernet Sauvignon, Zinfandel,
Info	robust, stinky, sharp, slightly salty,		Malbec, Pinotage, Lemberger
	rich, tangy, creamy	Dessert	Icewine

CHEESE	Lincolnshire Poacher	WINE	
Style	semi-soft	White	Chardonnay, Niagara, Vignoles
Origin	England	Red	Merlot, Côtes du Rhône, Cabernet
Milk	cow		Sauvignon
Info	rich, bitter, sweet, long aftertaste	Dessert	Port

CHEESE	Liptauer	WINE	
Style	soft	White	Himmelswein, Niersteiner,
Origin	Hungary		Gewürztraminer
Milk	sheep + goat	Red	Cabernet Sauvignon, Burgundy,
Info	salty, hot, spicy, onion, capers,		Chambourcin, Mourvèdre
	paprika, caram		

CHEESE	Livarot	WINE	
Style	soft	White	Gewürztraminer, Grüner Veltliner, Pinot
Origin	France		Gris, Riesling, Chardonnay, Traminette
Milk	cow	Red	Pinot Noir, Cabernet Sauvignon,
Info	slightly salty, pungent, stinky, nutty,		Chianti, Burgundy, Alicante Bouschet
	assertive, smooth, creamy, spicy	Sparkling	Brut
		Dessert	Hard Cidar, Tokaji, Sherry, Malvasia

CHEESE	Lumiere	WINE	
Style	soft	White	Viognier, Sauvignon Blanc, Delaware, Chasselas, Verdelet
Origin	Georgia		
Milk	goat	Red	Fleurie, Kasselfest, Maréchal Foch
Info	grape leaf ash	Sparkling	Champagne
		Dessert	Banyuls

CHEESE	Madrigal	WINE	
Style	semi-soft	White	Müller-Thurgau, Symphony, Orvieto
Origin	France	Red	Muscadine, Lemberger
Milk	cow	Rosé	Grenache Rosé
Info	mild, nutty, sweet, smooth, creamy	Sparkling	Champagne
		Dessert	Amagnac

CHEESE	Mahón	WINE	
Style	semi-firm	White	Grüner Veltliner, Riesling, Chardonnay
Origin	Spain	Red	Pinot Noir, Barbera, Bordeaux, Rioja, Cabernet Sauvignon, Tempranillo
Milk	cow		
Info	slightly salty, fruity, sweet, bold, spicy, creamy, crumbly	Dessert	Sherry, Port

CHEESE	Majorero	WINE	
Style	semi-soft	White	Albarino, Roussanne, Soave
Origin	Spain	Red	Pinot Noir, Rioja, Baco Noir, Rosso Misto
Milk	goat		
Info	rich, cremy, delicate finish, sweet, mild	Sparkling	Crémant
		Dessert	Sherry

CHEESE	Manchego	WINE	
Style	hard	White	Chardonnay, Sauvignon Blanc, Pinot Gris, Chenin Blanc, Chasselas, Ortega
Origin	Spain		
Milk	sheep	Red	Cabernet Sauvignon, Merlot, Zinfandel, Rioja, Barbera, Tempranillo, Grenache
Info	slightly salty, mild, sweet, nutty, aged, robust, zesty	Dessert	Mead

CHEESE	Manouri	WINE	
Style	soft	White	Sauvignon Blanc, Pinot Gris, Blanc de Bois
Origin	Greece		
Milk	sheep + goat whey	Red	Chancellor, Norton, Tempranillo
Info	creamy, slightly salty, buttery, lemony finish	Sparkling	Asti Spumanti
		Dessert	Sherry

CHEESE	Maroilles	WINE	
Style	soft	White	Gewürztraminer, Riesling, Sauvignon Blanc
Origin	France		
Milk	cow	Red	Burgundy, Chianti, Sangiovese, Malbec, Pinotage, Fredonia
Info	strong, tangy , stinky, salty, very pungent	Sparkling	Champagne
		Dessert	Hard Cider, Muscat, Mead

CHEESE	Marzalino	WINE	
Style	semi-soft	White	Orvieto, Pinot Blanc, Verdelet
Origin	Italy	Red	Burgundy, Fleurie, Muscadine
Milk	sheep	Rosé	White Zinfandel
Info	delicate	Sparkling	Champagne
		Dessert	Malvasia Bianca

CHEESE	Mascarpone	WINE	
Style	fresh, double- or triple-cream	White	Melody, Viognier, Chenin Blanc,
Origin	Italy		Vouvray, Gewürztraminer,
Milk	cow	Red	Zinfandel, Beaujolais, Pinot Noir
Info	mild, slightly sweet, creamy, velvety,	Rosé	Steuben
	buttery, smooth, faintly nutty	Dessert	Marsala, Late Harvest Riesling

CHEESE	Maytag Blue	WINE	
Style	semi-soft	White	Sémillon, Riesling, Albarino, Edelweiss,
Origin	Iowa		Magnolia, Cayuga
Milk	cow	Red	Cabernet Sauvignon, Syrah, Torgiano
Info	spicy, tangy, peppery, crumbly,	Sparkling	Champagne
	pungent	Dessert	Port, Late Harvest Riesling, Madiera

CHEESE	Midnight Moon	WINE	
Style	firm	White	Sauvignon Blanc, Pinot Gris, Verdelet
Origin	Denmark	Red	Pinot Noir, Syrah, Rosso Misto
Milk	goat	Rosé	White Zinfandel
Info	tangy	Dessert	Port

CHEESE	Mimolette	WINE	
Style	firm	White	Chenin Blanc
Origin	Denmark, France	Red	Pinot Noir, Cabernet Sauvignon, Côtes
Milk	cow		du Rhône, Merlot, Beaujolais, Carignan
Info	nutty, aged, granular, sweet, fruity,	Sparkling	Champagne
	butterscotch notes	Dessert	Malvasia Bianca, Tokaji

CHEESE	Mini Babybel	WINE	
Style	semi-soft	White	Riesling, Rayon d'Or, Gewürztraminer
Origin	France	Red	Beaujolais, Merlot, Amarona
Milk	cow	Dessert	Port
Info	mild, spicy		

CHEESE	Montasio	WINE	
Style	firm	White	Pinot Grigio, Orvieto, Pinot Blanc
Origin	Italy	Red	Cabernet Sauvignon, Merlot, Pinot
Milk	sheep or cow		Noir, Nebbiolo, Bordeaux, Carignan
Info	mild, fruity, aromatic, rich, buttery,	Sparkling	Blanc de Noirs
	grassy, nutty	Dessert	Muscat

CHEESE	Montbriac	WINE	
Style	soft	White	Pinot Blanc, Grüner Veltliner
Origin	France	Red	Alicante Bouschet, Gamay Beaujolais,
Milk	cow		Barbaresco, Rosso Misto
Info	blue, mild, creamy, ash coat, gentle,	Sparkling	Champagne
	silky smooth	Dessert	Muscat

CHEESE	Montenebro	WINE	
Style	soft	White	Gewürztraminer, Riesling, Pinot Gris
Origin	Spain	Red	Grenache, Tempranillo, Albarino, Rioja
Milk	goat	Rosé	Blush Niagara, Rosé Rioja
Info	spicy, tangy, complex, slightly sharp,	Sparkling	Champagne
	rich, creamy	Dessert	Muscat, Tokaji

CHEESE	Monterey Jack	WINE	
Style	semi-soft	White	Riesling, Chenin Blanc, Sauvignon Blanc
Origin	California		Pinot Gris, Gewürztraminer, Viognier
Milk	cow	Red	Cabernet Sauvignon, Zinfandel, Pinot
Info	mild, delicate, buttery		Noir, Sangiovese, Shiraz, Barbera
		Sparkling	Champagne, Blanc de Noirs

CHEESE	Montrachet	WINE	
Style	fresh	White	Rayon d'Or, Villard, Himmelswein
Origin	France	Red	Beaujolais, Fredonia
Milk	goat		
Info	slightly salty, ash, chestnut leaves		
	wrap		

CHEESE	Morbier	WINE	
Style	semi-soft	Red	Fleurie, Pinot Noir, Merlot, Beaujolais,
Origin	France		Burgundy, Grenache, Amarone, Malbec
Milk	cow	Sparkling	Brut
Info	mild, creamy, rich, ash center layer,	Dessert	Muscat
	complex, bold		

CHEESE	Mozzarella	WINE	
Style	semi-soft	White	Chardonnay, Sauvignon Blanc, Pinot
Origin	Italy		Blanc, Sémillon, Viognier
Milk	cow	Red	Zinfandel, Chianti, Barbera, Dolcetto,
Info	mild, delicate, creamy		Nebbiolo, Beaujolais, Valpolicella
		Rosé	White Zinfandel

CHEESE	Mozzarella Bufala	WINE	
Style	fresh	White	Pinot Grigio, Chablis, Fumé Blanc,
Origin	Italy		Orvieto
Milk	buffalo + cow	Red	Chianti, Muscadine, Pinot Noir
Info	delicate, sourish		

CHEESE	Mt. Lassen	WINE	
Style	semi-soft	White	Pinot Gris, Viognier, Aligoté, Chablis
Origin	California	Red	Merlot, Amarone, Maréchal Foch
Milk	cow	Rosé	Grenache Rosé
Info	smooth, nutty	Sparkling	Asti Spumanti
		Dessert	Málaga

CHEESE	Mt. Tam	WINE	
Style	soft, triple-cream	White	Sauvignon Blanc, Pinot Grigio, Riesling
Origin	California	Red	Pinot Noir, Cabernet Sauvignon, Syrah
Milk	cow	Rosé	White Zinfandel
Info	smooth, creamy	Sparkling	Champagne, Brut
		Dessert	Malvasia Bianca

CHEESE	Münster	WINE	
Style	semi-soft when young	White	Grüner Veltliner, Gewürztraminer, Pinot
Origin	France, Germany		Gris, Riesling, Chenin Blanc, Sémillon
Milk	cow	Red	Pinot Noir, Zinfandel, Beaujolais
Info	mild, creamy, runny at peak, rich,	Rosé	White Zinfandel
	assertive, tangy	Dessert	Hard Cider, Sherry

CHEESE	Mutton Button	WINE	
Style	soft	White	Riesling, Pinot Grigio, Niagara
Origin	New York	Red	Sangiovese, Cabernet Sauvignon
Milk	sheep	Rosé	Blush Niagara
Info	delicate	Sparkling	Blanc de Noirs
		Dessert	Muscat

CHEESE	Myost	WINE	
Style	firm	White	Vignoles, Müller-Thurgau,
Origin	Norway	Red	Gamay Beaujolais, Villard Noir, Pinot
Milk	cow whey		Meunier
Info	subtle caramel	Sparkling	Champagne

CHEESE	Myzithra	WINE	
Style	hard	White	Sauvignon Blanc, Chenin Blanc, Riesling
Origin	Greece	Red	Syrah, Cabernet Sauvignon, Villard
Milk	sheep or cow whey		Noir, Meritage, Lemberger, Grenache
Info	salty, pungent, dry with age, nutty,	Sparkling	Crémant
	crumbly	Dessert	Málaga

CHEESE	Neufchâtel	WINE	
Style	fresh	White	Riesling, Sauvignon Blanc, Viognier,
Origin	France		Gewürztraminer, Sancerre, Kerner,
Milk	cow		Liebframilch, Blanc de Bois
Info	rich, sweet, salty, creamy	Red	Beaujolais

CHEESE	Nevat	WINE	
Style	soft	White	Sauvignon Blanc, Pinot Grigio, Verdelet
Origin	Spain	Red	Zinfandel, Tempranillo, Rioja
Milk	goat	Rosé	Blush Muscadine
Info	rich, creamy	Sparkling	Champagne
		Dessert	Sauternes, PX

CHEESE	Nocturne	WINE	
Style	soft	White	Merlot, Himmelswein, Niersteiner
Origin	California	Red	Fleurie, Lemberger, Muscadine
Milk	cow + goat	Rosé	Pink Vidal
Info	sweet to tart	Sparkling	Brut
		Dessert	Icewine

CHEESE	Nøkkelost	WINE	
Style	semi-soft	White	Riesling, Melody, Sauvignon Blanc
Origin	Norway	Red	Cabernet Sauvignon, Kasselfest,
Milk	cow		Maréchal Foch
Info	mild, with caraway, cumin & cloves	Sparkling	Champagne

CHEESE	Normantal	WINE	
Style	semi-soft	White	Rayon d'Or, Seyval Blanc,
Origin	France		Gewürztraminer
Milk	cow	Red	Chancellor, Fleurie, Lemberger
Info	spicy		

CHEESE	Oaxaca	WINE	
Style	semi-soft	White	Chenin Blanc, Johannesburg Riesling
Origin	Mexico	Red	Dolcetto, Sangiovese, Fredonia, Rioja
Milk	cow	Rosé	Rosé Rioja
Info	mild, sweet	Sparkling	Champagne
		Dessert	PX

CHEESE	Oka	WINE	
Style	semi-soft	White	Chardonnay, Riesling, Sémillon, Fumé
Origin	Canada		Blanc, Traminette, Gewürztraminer
Milk	cow	Red	Pinot Noir, Syrah, Zinfandel, Beaujolais
Info	mild, creamy, nutty, fruity, full flavor,	Sparkling	Champagne
	delicate subtlies, smooth	Dessert	Sangria

CHEESE	Ossau-Iraty	WINE	
Style	semi-soft	White	Pinot Blanc, Chardonnay
Origin	Spain	Red	Barbera, Syrah, Cabernet Sauvignon
Milk	sheep	Rosé	Grenache Rosé
Info	creamy, mellow, nutty, delicate, sweet,	Sparkling	Champagne
	smooth, slightly oily	Dessert	PX

CHEESE	Oszczypek	WINE	
Style	firm	White	Seyval Blanc, Niersteiner
Origin	Poland	Red	Chambourcin, Gamay Beaujolais,
Milk	sheep		Fleurie
Info	slightly salty, smoky	Sparkling	Asti Spumanti

CHEESE	Ouray	WINE	
Style	firm	White	Chardonay, Sauvignon Blanc, Niagara
Origin	New York	Red	Cabernet Sauvignon, Merlot, Pinot
Milk	cow		Noir
Info	rich	Rosé	Blush Muscadine
		Dessert	Icewine

CHEESE	Pachina	WINE	
Style	semi-soft	White	Chardonnay, Magnolia, Liebframilch
Origin	Uraguay	Red	Pinot Noir, Mourvèdre, Fleurie
Milk	cow	Sparkling	Sparkling Soave
Info	smooth, sweet	Dessert	Sauternes

CHEESE	Panache d'Aramits	WINE	
Style	hard	White	Sémillon, Carlos, Rayon d'Or
Origin	France	Red	Merlot, Sangiovese, Pinot Meunier
Milk	sheep	Rosé	White Merlot
Info	smooth, nutty	Sparkling	Champagne
		Dessert	Ravat

CHEESE	Paneer	WINE	
Style	soft	White	Sauvignon Blanc, Pinot Grigio, Riesling,
Origin	India		Edelweiss, Delaware, Chenin Blanc
Milk	cow		
Info	bland, similar to tofu		

CHEESE	Panela	WINE	
Style	fresh	White	Riesling, Chardonnay, Rioja Blanca
Origin	Mexico	Red	Beaujolais Nouveau, Grenache, Meritus
Milk	cow		
Info	mild		

CHEESE	Parm Dolce	WINE	
Style	hard	White	Pinot Blanc, Villard, Sauvignon Blanc
Origin	Uruguay	Red	Merlot, Chancellor, Petite Sirah
Milk	cow	Rosé	White Merlot
Info	rich, sweet	Sparkling	Champagne
		Dessert	Muscat

CHEESE	Parmesan	WINE	
Style	hard	White	French Colombard, Grüner Veltliner
Origin	Italy	Red	Cabernet Sauvignon, Merlot, Chianti,
Milk	cow		Barolo, Zinfandel, Shiraz, Dechaunac
Info	robust, fruity, salty, aged	Sparkling	Asti Spumanti
		Dessert	Port, Sherry, Madiera

CHEESE	Parmigiano Reggiano	WINE	
Style	hard	White	Chardonnay, Pinot Grigio, Soave
Origin	Italy	Red	Chianti, Barolo, Cabernet Sauvignon,
Milk	cow		Burgundy, Barbaresco, Meritage
Info	salty, pungent, aged, granular,	Sparkling	Champagne
	crumbly, subtle, complex	Dessert	Tawny Port

CHEESE	Pau Saut Maueu	WINE	
Style	semi-soft	White	Riesling, Carlos, Madeline Angevine
Origin	Spain	Red	Barolo, Chambourcin, Fleurie
Milk	goat	Sparkling	Champagne
Info	smooth, pungent	Dessert	Mead, Madiera, Vin Santo

CHEESE	Pave d'Affinois	WINE	
Style	soft, double-cream	White	Sauvignon Blanc, Sancerre, Vouvray
Origin	France	Red	Barbaresco, Rosso Misto, Fleurie
Milk	cow	Rosé	Rosé Rioja
Info	rich, strong	Sparkling	Crémant
		Dessert	Port

CHEESE	Pecorino	WINE	
Style	firm	White	Orvieto, Viognier, Pouilly-Fumé
Origin	Italy	Red	Chianti, Pinot Noir, Torgiano, Cabernet
Milk	sheep		Sauvignon, Zinfandel, Muscadine
Info	mild, slightly lemony, salty	Dessert	Port

CHEESE	Pecorino Ginepro	WINE	
Style	firm	White	Soave
Origin	Italy	Red	Cabernet Sauvignon, Shiraz, Chianti,
Milk	sheep		Amarone, Barolo
Info	salty, balsamic vinegar bath		

CHEESE	Pecorino Romano	WINE	
Style	hard	White	Gewürztraminer, Riesling, Vignoles
Origin	Italy	Red	Chianti, Shiraz, Cabernet Sauvignon,
Milk	sheep		Barbera, Merlot, Sangiovese, Amarone
Info	salty, sharp, dry, slightly spicy,	Dessert	Marsala, Tawny Port
	peppery, tangy, robust with age		

CHEESE	Pepato	WINE	
Style	hard	White	Chenin Blanc, Riesling, Sémillon,
Origin	Italy		Himmelswein, Traminette
Milk	sheep	Red	Cabernet Sauvignon, Mourvèdre,
Info	piquant, rich, spicy, with black		Dolcetto, Pinotage, Syrah, Zinfandel
	peppercorns	Dessert	Hard Cider

CHEESE	Pepper Jack	WINE	
Style	semi-soft	White	Chardonnay, Sauvignon Blanc, Riesling
Origin	California	Red	Pinot Noir, Zinfandel, Claret, Bolduc
Milk	cow	Dessert	Hard Cider
Info	zesty, spicy		

CHEESE	Père Joseph	WINE	
Style	semi-soft	White	Chardonnay, Carlos, Liebframilch
Origin	Belgium	Red	Pinot Noir, Syrah, Cabernet Sauvignon,
Milk	cow	Rosé	Grenache Rosé
Info	mild, creamy, satiny, aromatic,	Sparkling	Sparkling Soave
	slightly sharp, salty	Dessert	Sherry

CHEESE	Petit Basque (aka P'tit Basque)	WINE	
Style	semi-soft	White	Gewürztraminer, Viognier, Riesling
Origin	France	Red	Cabernet Sauvignon, Shiraz, Zinfandel
Milk	sheep	Rosé	Pink Catawba
Info	mild, aromatic, dry texture, earthy,	Sparkling	Champagne
	nutty	Dessert	Sauternes

CHEESE	Petit-Suisse	WINE	
Style	fresh, double-cream	White	Sauvignon Blanc, Pinot Grigio, Carlos,
Origin	France		Magnolia
Milk	cow	Red	Muscadine, Gamay Beaujolais, Villard
Info	sweet & sour, bland, watery		Noir

CHEESE	Piave	WINE	
Style	hard	White	Fumé Blanc, Villard, Vignoles
Origin	Italy	Red	Pinot Noir, Grenache, Dolcetto
Milk	cow	Rosé	Blush Muscadine
Info	intense, full body	Sparkling	Champagne
		Dessert	Vin Santo

CHEESE	Picodon	WINE	
Style	soft	White	Villard, Rayon d'Or, Chasselas
Origin	France	Rosé	White Zinfandel
Milk	goat		
Info	sour, milky, ripe		

CHEESE	Picon	WINE	
Style	semi-soft	Red	Beaujolais, Tempranillo, Concord, Rioja
Origin	Spain	Dessert	Mead, Malvasia Bianca
Milk	sheep		
Info	blue, pungent, maple leaf wrap		

CHEESE	Pierce Point	WINE	
Style	soft	White	Sauvignon Blanc, Riesling, Carlos
Origin	California	Red	Pinot Noir, Meritus, Kasselfest
Milk	cow	Sparkling	Blanc de Noirs
Info	muscat-based sweet wine wash	Dessert	Muscat

CHEESE	Pierre Robert	WINE	
Style	soft, triple-cream	White	Pinot Blanc, Gewürztraminer, Viognier,
Origin	France		Chardonnay, Pinot Gris, Riesling
Milk	cow	Red	Cabernet Sauvignon, Zinfandel
Info	mild, rich, buttery, tangy	Sparkling	Champagne
		Dessert	Ravat

CHEESE	Pio Vecchio	WINE	
Style	hard	Red	Cabernet Sauvignon, Zinfandel, Syrah,
Origin	Italy		Sangiovese, Torgiano, Chambourcin
Milk	cow		
Info	salty, tangy		

CHEESE	Pleasant Ridge Reserve	WINE	
Style	hard	White	Chardonnay, Verdelet, Aurore, Chablis
Origin	Wisconsin	Red	Merlot, Noble, Bolduc, Chianti
Milk	cow	Sparkling	Champagne
Info	subtle		

CHEESE	Podhalanski	WINE	
Style	firm	White	Villard, Ortetga, Melody
Origin	Poland	Red	Concord, Noble, Kasselfest, Pinotage
Milk	cow + sheep	Rosé	White Merlot
Info	creamy, lightly smoked	Sparkling	Champagne
		Dessert	Port

CHEESE	Point Reyes Blue	WINE	
Style	semi-soft	White	Chardonnay, Cayuga, Colombard
Origin	California	Red	Cabernet Sauvignon, Merlot, Amarone
Milk	cow	Sparkling	Champagne
Info	creamy, full flavor	Dessert	Sherry, Port, Amagnac

CHEESE	Pont L'Eveque	WINE	
Style	soft	White	Sauvignon Blanc, Pinot Blanc, Riesling
Origin	France	Red	Chianti, Sangiovese, Bordeaux, Pinot
Milk	cow		Noir, Burgundy, Meritage
Info	mild, sweet, creamy, tangy, rich,	Sparkling	Champagne, Sparkling Soave
	delicate, pungent	Dessert	Port

CHEESE	Port-Salut	WINE	
Style	semi-soft	White	Chardonnay, Vignoles, Aurore, Melody
Origin	Denmark, France	Red	Pinot Noir, Cabernet Sauvignon, Syrah,
Milk	cow		Merlot, Burgundy
Info	mild, creamy, sweet, smooth, velvety	Sparkling	Champagne
		Dessert	Sherry

CHEESE	Postel	WINE	
Style	firm	White	Sauvignon Blanc, Chardonnay, Chablis
Origin	Belgium	Red	Pinot Noir, Petite` Sirah, Cabernet
Milk	cow		Sauvignon, Lemberger
Info	mild, rich, nutty, slightly salty	Sparkling	Asti Spumanti
		Dessert	Port

CHEESE	Poudre Puff	WINE	
Style	soft, double-cream	White	Sauvignon Blanc, Pinot Gris, Traminette
Origin	Colorado	Red	Pinot Noir, Merlot, Beaujolais
Milk	cow	Dessert	Icewine
Info	silky, tangy		

CHEESE	Pouligny-St. Pierre	WINE	
Style	soft, double-cream	White	Albarino, Sancerre, Chardonnay,
Origin	France		Sauvignon Blanc, Chenin Blanc, Riesling
Milk	goat	Red	Cabernet Sauvignon, Zinfandel, Malbec
Info	creamy, slightly sour, nutty, tangy	Rosé	Rosé
		Sparkling	Champagne

CHEESE	Provolone	WINE	
Style	semi-soft	White	Chardonnay, Orvieto, Delaware, Pinot
Origin	Italy		Blanc, Roussanne
Milk	cow	Red	Barolo, Chianti, Sangiovese, Pinot Noir,
Info	sweet, mild, smooth		Cabernet Sauvignon, Baco Noir
		Sparkling	Blanc de Noirs

CHEESE	Quark	WINE	
Style	fresh	White	Pinot Grigio, Orvieto, Sancerre,
Origin	Germany & Austria		Verdelet, Niersteiner
Milk	cow		
Info	lemony taste, smooth, mild,		
	faintly tangy		

CHEESE	Queso Blanco	WINE	
Style	fresh	White	Vidal Blanc, Orvieto
Origin	Mexico	Red	Rioja, Tempranillo
Milk	cow	Rosé	
Info	mild	Sparkling	
		Dessert	

CHEESE	Queso Cabrero	WINE	
Style	soft	Red	Chancellor, Rioja, Meritage
Origin	Mexico	Dessert	Port, PX
Milk	goat		
Info	dipped in red wine		

CHEESE	Queso Fresco	WINE	
Style	fresh	White	Orvieto, Riesling
Origin	Mexico	Red	Rioja, Tempranillo
Milk	goat or cow		
Info	mild, salty, young feta, granular, crumbly, milky		

CHEESE	Rabacal	WINE	
Style	soft	White	Melody, Vidal Blanc, Riesling
Origin	Portugal	Red	Pinot Meunier, Mouton-Rothschild
Milk	sheep or goat	Rosé	Blush Niagara
Info	mild	Sparkling	Champagne
		Dessert	Ravat

CHEESE	Raclette	WINE	
Style	firm	White	Chenin Blanc, Chardonnay, Riesling
Origin	France	Red	Beaujolais, Burgundy, Merlot, Pinot Noir, Syrah, Sangiovese, Grenache
Milk	cow		
Info	sweet, fruity, creamy, buttery	Sparkling	Sparkling Soave
		Dessert	Sherry

CHEESE	Raschera	WINE	
Style	soft	White	Chenin Blanc, Riesling, Viognier
Origin	Italy	Red	Beaujolais, Concord, Villard Noir
Milk	cow	Rosé	Grenache Rosé
Info	subtle, delicate, nutty	Sparkling	Champagne
		Dessert	Malvasia Bianca

CHEESE	Rauchkase	WINE	
Style	firm	White	Chardonnay, Symphony, Niersteiner
Origin	Germany	Red	Merlot, Dechaunac, Pinot Meunier
Milk	cow	Rosé	Rosé
Info	mild, smoky	Sparkling	Champagne
		Dessert	Muscat

CHEESE	Reblochon	WINE	
Style	soft	White	Gewürztraminer, Riesling, Chardonnay
Origin	France	Red	Carignan, Beaujolais, Angélus, Pinot
Milk	cow		Noir, Bordeaux, Pinotage
Info	rich, nutty, creamy, complex, smooth,	Sparkling	Champagne
	strong herbal aroma, fruity	Dessert	Sherry

CHEESE	Red Hawk	WINE	
Style	soft, triple-cream	White	Gewürztraminer, Riesling, Pinot Gris
Origin	California	Red	Zinfandel, Pinot Meunier, Cinsault
Milk	cow	Rosé	White Merlot
Info	salty, full flavor, washed rind	Sparkling	Asti Spumanti, Sparkling Soave
		Dessert	Malvasia Bianca

CHEESE	Reggianito	WINE	
Style	hard	White	Viognier, Müller-Thurgau, Symphony
Origin	Argentina	Red	Cabernet Sauvignon, Chianti, Barolo
Milk	cow	Sparkling	Champagne
Info	smooth, complex, rich, grainy	Dessert	Tawny Port

CHEESE	Ricotta	WINE	
Style	fresh	White	Chardonay, Sauvignon Blanc, Frascati,
Origin	Italy		Soave, Viognier, Fumé Blanc, Sémillon,
Milk	cow or sheep		Seyval, Roussanne
Info	bland, slightly sweet, moist, grainy,		
	faint vanilla aroma		

CHEESE	Ricotta Salata	WINE	
Style	firm	White	Riesling, Pinot Gris, Delaware
Origin	Italy	Red	Pinot Noir, Cabernet Sauvignon,
Milk	sheep		Merlot, Fleurie, Cinsault
Info	mild, nutty, sweet, pungent	Sparkling	Champagne
		Dessert	Amagnac, PX

CHEESE	Ridder	WINE	
Style	firm	White	Chardonnay, LaCrosse, Riesling
Origin	Norway	Red	Syrah, Pinot Noir, Burgundy, Pinotage
Milk	cow	Rosé	Pink Vidal
Info	rich, mild, buttery	Sparkling	Champagne
		Dessert	Icewine

CHEESE	Robiola Lombardia	WINE	
Style	soft	White	Gewürztraminer, Riesling, Chenin Blanc
Origin	Italy	Red	Cabernet Sauvignon, Chianti, Syrah,
Milk	cow, goat, or sheep, or blend		Burgundy, Barolo, Barbaresco
Info	robust, rich, sharp, aged, creamy,	Sparkling	Champagne
	buttery, supple, pungent, tangy	Dessert	Muscat

CHEESE	Robiola Piemonte	WINE	
Style	fresh	White	Gewürztraminer, Riesling, Chardonnel
Origin	Italy	Red	Cabernet Sauvignon, Chianti, Syrah,
Milk	cow		Burgundy, Barolo
Info	soft, ultra creamy, full flavor,	Sparkling	Champagne
	slightly sweet, citrusy aroma	Dessert	Muscat

CHEESE	Roccolo	WINE	
Style	soft	White	Sauvignon Blanc, Sémillon, Orvieto,
Origin	Italy		Pinot Grigio, Condrieu
Milk	cow	Red	Pinot Noir, Sangiovese, Dolcetto
Info	salty, complex	Dessert	Port

CHEESE	Rochefort Montagne	WINE	
Style	semi-soft	White	Chardonnay, Pinot Grigio, LaCrosse
Origin	France	Red	Syrah, Pinot Noir, Maréchal Foch
Milk	cow	Rosé	White Merlot
Info	rich	Sparkling	Crémant
		Dessert	Ravat

CHEESE	Romano Vacchino	WINE	
Style	hard	Red	Sangiovese, Zinfandel, Merlot, Fleurie,
Origin	Italy		Cabernet Sauvignon
Milk	cow	Rosé	White Zinfandel
Info	robust, sharp, nutty, aged	Sparkling	Champagne
		Dessert	Madiera

CHEESE	Roncal	WINE	
Style	firm	White	Sauvignon Blanc, Chardonnay, Pouilly-
Origin	Spain		Fumé, Madeleine Angevine, Albarino
Milk	sheep	Red	Pinot Noir, Syrah, Angélus, Merlot,
Info	sweet, rustic, smooth, dense, nutty,		Sangiovese, Zinfandel, Tempranillo
	piquant, olivey flavor	Dessert	Sherry

CHEESE	Roomano	WINE	
Style	hard	Red	Cabernet Sauvignon, Zinfandel, Merlot,
Origin	Netherlands		Syrah, Bordeaux, Carignan
Milk	cow		
Info	spicy yet sweet, fruity, caramel &		
	butterscotch notes		

CHEESE	Roquefort	WINE	
Style	semi-soft	White	Chardonay, Sauvignon Blanc. Pinot Gris
Origin	France	Red	Cabernet Sauvignon, Zinfandel, Syrah,
Milk	sheep		Barbera, Banyuls, Fleurie
Info	blue, salty, rich, sharp, spicy	Sparkling	Champagne
		Dessert	Port, Muscat, Sauternes, Madiera

CHEESE	Rougette	WINE	
Style	soft, triple-cream	White	Liebframilch, Müller-Thurgau,
Origin	Germany		Niersteiner
Milk	cow	Red	Pinot Meunier, Beaujolais
Info	robust	Sparkling	Crémant, Sparkling Soave
		Dessert	Port

CHEESE	Saga Blue	WINE	
Style	soft	White	Aurore, Colombard, Marsanne,
Origin	Denmark		Vouvray
Milk	cow	Red	Pinot Noir, Muscadine, Rosso Misto
Info	creamy	Dessert	Tokaji, Sauternes, PX, Late Harvest
			Riesling

CHEESE	Saint-André	WINE	
Style	soft, triple-cream	White	Gewürztraminer, Riesling, Seyval Blanc,
Origin	France		Catawba, Viognier, Sémillon, Delaware
Milk	cow	Red	Bordeaux, Pinot Noir, Chianti, Claret
Info	slightly salty, mild, creamy, rich,	Sparkling	Brut
	buttery	Dessert	Muscat

CHEESE	Saint Marcellin	WINE	
Style	soft	White	Meursault, Aligoté, Viognier, Sancerre,
Origin	France		Soave, Roussanne, Sémillon
Milk	cow or goat	Red	Syrah, Gamay Noir
Info	slightly salty, rich, fruity, nutty, mild,	Sparkling	Champagne
	intensely creamy, complex	Dessert	Malvasia Bianca

CHEESE	Saint Maure	WINE	
Style	soft	White	Albarino, Sancerre, Sauvignon Blanc,
Origin	France		Chardonnay, Chenin Blanc, Fumé Blanc,
Milk	goat		Aligoté, Marsanne, Vidal Blanc
Info	ash coated, crumbly, tangy, creamy,	Red	Chancellor, Meritage, Cinsault
	nutty	Dessert	Sauternes

CHEESE	Saint Nectaire	WINE	
Style	semi-soft	White	Sauvignon Blanc, Viognier, Rioja Blanca
Origin	France	Red	Beaujolais, Pinot Noir, Merlot, Syrah
Milk	cow	Rosé	Pink Catawba
Info	mild, rich, slightly salty, fruity,	Sparkling	Champagne
	buttery, grassy, pungent	Dessert	Mead

CHEESE	Saint Paulin	WINE	
Style	semi-soft	White	Chardonnay, Melody, Sauvignon Blanc
Origin	France	Red	Syrah, Pinot Noir, Kasselfest
Milk	cow	Rosé	Pink Vidal
Info	mild, creamy, bland	Sparkling	Champagne
		Dessert	Sauternes

CHEESE	Salers	WINE	
Style	hard	White	Sauvignon Blanc, Pinot Gris, Sémillon,
Origin	France		Vignoles, Symphony, Chenin Blanc
Milk	cow	Red	Zinfandel, Syrah, Bolduc
Info	smooth, mild, tangy, complex,	Sparkling	Champagne
	buttery	Dessert	PX

CHEESE	Sally Jackson's Sheep	WINE	
Style	firm	White	Sancerre, Riesling, Chardonnay,
Origin	Washington		Albarino, Grüner Veltliner, Aligoté
Milk	sheep	Red	Sangiovese , Carignan, Petite Sirah
Info	chestnut leaves wrap	Rosé	White Zinfandel
		Dessert	Sherry

CHEESE	Samsø	WINE	
Style	semi-soft	White	Vidal Blanc, Müller-Thurgau, Villard
Origin	Denmark	Red	Pinot Meunier, Merlot, Gamay Noir
Milk	cow	Rosé	White Merlot
Info	mild, nutty, sweet, pungent with age	Sparkling	Champagne
		Dessert	Muscat

CHEESE	San Andreas	WINE	
Style	semi-soft	White	Chardonnay, Sauvignon Blanc,
Origin	California		Symphony, Blanc de Bois
Milk	sheep	Red	Cabernet Sauvignon, Merlot, Chianti
Info	mild, creamy	Sparkling	Champagne
		Dessert	Ravat

CHEESE	San Simon	WINE	
Style	firm	White	Rioja Blanca, Madeleine Angevine,
Origin	Spain		Catawba, Symphony
Milk	cow	Red	Merlot, Rioja , Noble
Info	smoked, creamy, buttery	Sparkling	Champagne

CHEESE	Sapsago	WINE	
Style	hard	White	Gewürztraminer, Albarino
Origin	Switzerland	Red	Cabernet Sauvignon, Chancellor,
Milk	cow		Norton, Grüner Veltliner
Info	sharp, clover-like, strong, spicy,	Sparkling	Crémant
	with powdered herbs, pale green hue		

CHEESE	Sardo	WINE	
Style	hard	White	Kerner, Gewürztraminer, Chardonnay
Origin	Eqypt	Red	Malbec, Merlot, Concord, Lemberger,
Milk	sheep		Bolduc
Info	robust, sharp	Sparkling	Brut
		Dessert	Sangria

CHEESE	Scamorza	WINE	
Style	semi-soft	White	Soave, Himmelswein
Origin	Italy	Red	Cabernet Sauvignon, Chianti, Côtes du
Milk	cow		Rhône, Syrah, Sangiovese
Info	salty, strong	Dessert	PX

CHEESE	Schloss	WINE	
Style	soft	White	Niersteiner, Chardonnay
Origin	Austria	Red	Cabernet Sauvignon, Merlot, Fleurie
Milk	cow	Sparkling	Champagne
Info	tangy, stinky	Dessert	Port, Sherry

CHEESE	Sebastian	WINE	
Style	firm	White	Chardonnay, Müller-Thurgau,
Origin	Germany		Niersteiner
Milk	cow	Red	Merlot, Bolduc, Pinotage
Info	mild	Sparkling	Brut
		Dessert	Muscat

CHEESE	Selles-sur-Cher	WINE	
Style	soft	White	Albarino, Sauvignon Blanc, Sancerre,
Origin	France		Riesling, Blanc de Bois, Delaware
Milk	goat	Rosé	White Merlot
Info	sweet, nutty, creamy, flaky, ash & salt coat	Dessert	Ravat

CHEESE	Serena	WINE	
Style	firm	White	Sauvignon Blanc, Pinot Grigio, Chenin
Origin	Spain		Blanc, Gewürztraminer, Riesling
Milk	cow	Red	Pinot Noir, Cabernet Sauvignon,
Info	rich, nutty, bold, crumbly, tangy		Shiraz, Merlot, Landot Noir, Norton
		Sparkling	Champagne

CHEESE	Serpa	WINE	
Style	soft	White	Riesling, Symphony, Ortega
Origin	Portugal	Red	Grenache, Landot Noir, Bordeaux
Milk	sheep	Rosé	Blush Niagara
Info	floral, full flavor, sharp, peppery, soft, buttery, sweet	Sparkling	Champagne
		Dessert	Port, Malvasia Bianca

CHEESE	Shepherd's Wheel	WINE	
Style	soft	White	Aurore, Niagara, Riesling
Origin	New York	Red	Cabernet Sauvignon, Syrah, Merlot,
Milk	sheep		St. Emilion
Info	mild, creamy, slightly tangy	Sparkling	Champagne
		Dessert	Sangria

CHEESE	Shropshire Blue	WINE	
Style	firm	Red	Pinot Noir, Côtes du Rhône, Pinotage,
Origin	England		Zinfandel, Shiraz
Milk	cow	Dessert	Sherry, Madiera, Sauternes, Tawny
Info	creamy, rich, crumbly, slightly tannic,		Port
	sharp, strong, dark orange color		

CHEESE	Smoked Gouda	WINE	
Style	firm	White	Chardonnay, Delaware, Villard
Origin	Holland	Red	Dolcetto, Gamay Noir, Pinot Meunier
Milk	cow		
Info	smoky		

CHEESE	Sonoma Jack	WINE	
Style	firm	White	Sauvignon Blanc, Gewürztraminer,
Origin	California		Blanc de Bois, Müller-Thurgau
Milk	cow	Red	Alicante Bouschet, Barbaresco, Merlot
Info	sweet	Rosé	White Zinfandel
		Dessert	Sauternes, Ravat

CHEESE	Sottocenere	WINE	
Style	semi-soft	White	Johannesberg Riesling, Symphony,
Origin	Italy		LaCrosse
Milk	cow	Red	Claret, Cabernet Sauvignon, Landot
Info	aged in ash		Noir, Gamay Beaujolais
		Sparkling	Champagne

CHEESE	Spenwood	WINE	
Style	hard	White	Pinot Gris, Albarino, Gewürztraminer,
Origin	England		Cayuga, Delaware, Vouvray, Pinot Blanc
Milk	goat	Red	Pinot Noir, Bordeaux, Rioja,
Info	rich, nutty, tangy, creamy, sweet,		Merlot, Côtes du Rhône, Sangiovese
	caramel flavor, complex	Sparkling	Brut

CHEESE	Stilton	WINE	
Style	semi-soft	White	Chardonnay, Sauvignon Blanc, Catawba
Origin	England	Red	Cabernet Sauvignon, Zinfandel, Meritus
Milk	cow	Sparkling	Champagne
Info	blue, rich, creamy, fruity, mellow,	Dessert	Port, Madiera, Icewine, Tawny Port
	salty, velvety, buttery, strong, tangy		

CHEESE	Stracchino	WINE	
Style	soft	Red	Dolcetto, Barbera, Barolo, Chianti,
Origin	Italy		Merlot, Cynthiana, Norton
Milk	cow		
Info	mild, stinky, gentle, creamy		

CHEESE	Swiss, American	WINE	
Style	firm	White	Riesling, Viognier, Sauvignon Blanc,
Origin	USA		Gewürztraminer, Pinot Gris, Vidal Blanc
Milk	cow	Red	Pinot Noir, Grenache, Carignan,
Info	mild, smooth to sharp		Merlot, Fredonia, Traminette
		Rosé	White Zinfandel

CHEESE	Taleggio	WINE	
Style	soft	White	Chardonnay, Gewürztraminer, Vouvray,
Origin	Italy		Pinot Grigio, Sauvignon Blanc
Milk	cow	Red	Pinot Noir, Merlot, Barbera, Barolo,
Info	slightly salty, creamy, full flavor,		Chianti, Syrah, Sangiovese
	sweet, buttery, intense with age, fruity	Dessert	Muscat

CHEESE	Taupiniere	WINE	
Style	soft	White	Sauvignon Blanc, Riesling, Sancerre
Origin	France	Red	Pinot Noir, Zinfandel, Lemberger
Milk	goat	Sparkling	Champagne
Info	nutty, tangy	Dessert	Port

CHEESE	Teleme	WINE	
Style	soft	White	Sauvignon Blanc, Riesling, Cayuga,
Origin	California	Red	Pinot Noir, Chancellor, Zinfandel
Milk	cow	Rosé	White Zinfandel
Info	mild, tangy, creamy, fruity	Sparkling	Crémant
		Dessert	Muscat

CHEESE	Testouri	WINE	
Style	semi-soft	White	Vignoles, Sauvignon Blanc, Muscadine
Origin	Eqypt	Red	Malbec, Noble, Merlot, Zinfandel
Milk	sheep or goat		
Info	salty		

CHEESE	Tête de Moine	WINE	
Style	firm	White	Viognier, Chardonnay, Pinot Grigio,
Origin	Switzerland		Sauvignon Blanc, Sancerre
Milk	cow	Red	Burgundy, Merlot, Gamay Beaujolais
Info	sweet, tangy, pungent, delicate,	Sparkling	Champagne
	creamy, intense, nutty	Dessert	Mead

CHEESE	Tetilla	WINE	
Style	soft	White	Sauvignon Blanc, Chardonnay, Müller-
Origin	Spain		Thurgau
Milk	cow	Red	Beaujolais, Pinot Noir, Merlot
Info	mild, creamy, salty, tangy, buttery,	Sparkling	Champagne
	tart	Dessert	Sherry, PX

CHEESE	Ticklemore	WINE	
Style	firm	White	Viognier, Riesling , Albarino
Origin	England	Red	Dolcetto, Beaujolais, Rioja, Pinot Noir,
Milk	goat	Sparkling	Champagne
Info	tangy, creamy, medium body, dry, crumbly	Dessert	Port

CHEESE	Tillamook Cheddar	WINE	
Style	firm	White	Gewürztraminer, Marsanne, Riesling
Origin	Oregon	Red	Beaujolais, Grenache, Gamay Noir,
Milk	cow		Pinotage, Lemberger
Info	medium to vintage extra sharp	Rosé	Blush Niagara

CHEESE	Tilsit	WINE	
Style	firm	White	Delaware, Liebfraumilch, Niersteiner
Origin	Germany	Red	Cabernet Sauvignon, Chianti, Burgundy,
Milk	cow		Meritage, Fleurie
Info	intense, buttery, spicy, creamy	Sparkling	Brut
		Dessert	Port

CHEESE	Tintern	WINE	
Style	semi-soft	Red	Shiraz, Cynthiana, Fredonia, Kasselfest,
Origin	Wales		Mourvèdre
Milk	cow + (sheep or goat)	Dessert	Port
Info	creamy with shallots & chives, green wax cover		

CHEESE	Toma	WINE	
Style	soft	White	Chardonnay, Viognier, LaCrosse
Origin	Italy	Red	Bordeaux, Burgundy, Dolcetto, Merlot
Milk	cow	Rosé	White Zinfandel
Info	mild, custard-like interior, gentle sweet & sour	Sparkling	Champagne
		Dessert	Malvasia Bianca

CHEESE	Tome d'Aquitaine au Sauternes	WINE	
Style	semi-soft	White	Riesling, Chardonnay, Gewürztraminer
Origin	France	Sparkling	Champagne
Milk	goat	Dessert	Sherry
Info	Muscadet wash		

CHEESE	Tome des Recollets	WINE	
Style	semi-soft	White	Riesling, Rayon d'Or, Gewürztraminer
Origin	France	Red	Bordeaux, Zinfandel, Landot Noir
Milk	cow + goat	Sparkling	Champagne
Info	Sauterne wash + peppercorns	Dessert	Port, Sauternes

CHEESE	Tomini	WINE	
Style	soft	White	Soave, Chablis, Muscadine
Origin	Italy	Red	Concord, Meritage, Côtes du Rhône
Milk	cow + (sheep or goat)	Rosé	Pink Vidal
Info	delicate, creamy, slightly salty	Sparkling	Champagne
		Dessert	Port

CHEESE	Tomme Crayeuse	WINE	
Style	soft	White	Rayon d'Or, Chardonnay, Fumé Blanc
Origin	France	Red	Merlot, Cynthiana, Gamay Noir
Milk	cow	Rosé	Grenache Rosé
Info	rich, creamy, buttery	Sparkling	Champagne
		Dessert	Malvasia Bianca

CHEESE	Tomme de Savoie	WINE	
Style	semi-soft	White	Riesling, Chardonnay, Sauvignon Blanc,
Origin	France		Pinot Gris, Riesling, Chasselas,
Milk	cow	Red	Pinot Noir, Cabernet Sauvignon, Syrah,
Info	mild, sweet, citrus tangy, nutty, salty,		Merlot, Gamay Beaujolais, Amarone
	robust, smooth	Sparkling	Champagne

CHEESE	Toscanello	WINE	
Style	firm	White	Vouvray, Orvieto, Ortega, Chenin Blanc
Origin	Italy	Red	Petite Sirah, Torgiano, Concord
Milk	sheep	Rosé	Blush Niagara
Info	sweet	Sparkling	Asti Spumanti
		Dessert	Icewine

CHEESE	Touloumi	WINE	
Style	semi-soft	White	Villard, Chardonnay, Niagara, Cayuga
Origin	Greece	Red	Chancellor, Zinfandel, Dechaunac,
Milk	goat		Chambourcin
Info	mild, creamy, tangy, nutty	Sparkling	Brut
		Dessert	Port

CHEESE	Ubriaco	WINE	
Style	hard	White	Sauvignon Blanc, Blanc de Bois, Vidal
Origin	Italy		Blanc, Madeleine Angevine, Orvieto
Milk	cow	Red	Pinot Noir, Baco Noir, Merlot
Info	mild, fruity, sweet	Rosé	White Zinfandel
		Dessert	Sauternes

CHEESE	Urgelia	WINE	
Style	semi-soft	White	Traminette, Chardonnay, Niagara
Origin	Spain	Red	St. Emilion, Tempranillo, Rioja, Merlot
Milk	cow	Dessert	PX
Info	mild, stinky, creamy		

CHEESE	Vacherin Mont d'Or	WINE	
Style	soft	White	Meursault
Origin	France	Red	Cabernet Sauvignon, Burgundy, Chianti
Milk	cow	Rosé	
Info	nutty, spreadable, complex	Sparkling	
		Dessert	

CHEESE	Vadenost	WINE	
Style	semi-soft	White	Chardonnay, St. Emilion, Riesling
Origin	Sweden	Red	Cabernet Sauvignon, Merlot, Cynthiana
Milk	cow	Dessert	Port
Info	full body, slightly grassy		

CHEESE	Vaesterbottenost	WINE	
Style	hard	White	Meursault, Villard, LaCrosse
Origin	Sweden	Red	Pinot Noir, Chambourcin, Fredonia,
Milk	cow		Fleurie
Info	pungent, bitter	Dessert	Mead

CHEESE	Valdeon	WINE	
Style	semi-soft	White	Gewürztraminer, Riesling, Edelweiss
Origin	Spain	Red	Rioja, Barbera, Cabernet Sauvignon,
Milk	blend		Barolo
Info	blue, pungent, sweet, tangy, spicy, sycamore leaf wrap, complex, intense	Dessert	Tawny Port, Muscat

CHEESE	Valençay	WINE	
Style	soft	White	Chardonnay, Sauvignon Blanc, Chablis, Sancerre, Chenin Blanc, Albarino
Origin	France		
Milk	goat	Red	Cabernet Sauvignon, Merlot, Malbec
Info	creamy, intense, delicate, tangy, smooth, rich, lemony	Sparkling	Crémant
		Dessert	Mead

CHEESE	Vermont Shepherd	WINE	
Style	soft	White	Riesling, Viognier, Chardonnay
Origin	Vermont	Red	Pinot Noir, Zinfandel, Syrah
Milk	sheep	Rosé	Rosé
Info	smooth, creamy, dense, elegant, complex, aromatic, rich, nutty	Sparkling	Champagne, Blanc de Noirs
		Dessert	Port

CHEESE	Vidalia Onion Jack	WINE	
Style	semi-soft	White	Pinot Blanc, Müller-Thurgau
Origin	California	Red	Mourvèdre, Norton, Dechaunac,
Milk	cow		Cinsault
Info	onion flavor		

CHEESE	Vignerons	WINE	
Style	firm	White	Riesling, Chardonnay, Gewürztraminer
Origin	Switzerland	Red	Beaujolais, Pinot Noir, Zinfandel
Milk	cow		
Info	satiny, nutty, sweet		

CHEESE	Wasabi Disk	WINE	
Style	soft	White	Sauvignon Blanc, Pinot Grigio, Niagara
Origin	Massachussetts	Red	Malbec, Fleurie, Mourvèdre, Merlot
Milk	goat	Sparkling	Champagne
Info	hot, wasabi + chives		

CHEESE	Wabash Cannonball	WINE	
Style	semi-soft	White	Sauvignon Blanc, Grüner Veltliner,
Origin	Indiana		Johannesberg Riesling
Milk	goat	Red	Zinfandel, Chancellor, Meritus
Info	gentle, creamy, slightly acidic	Sparkling	Blanc de Noirs

CHEESE	Wensleydale	WINE	
Style	firm	White	Chardonnay, Gewürztraminer, Aligoté
Origin	England	Red	Cabernet Sauvignon, Merlot, Pinot
Milk	sheep or cow		Noir, Burgundy, , Barbaresco
Info	mild, slightly salty, smooth, creamy,	Sparkling	Champagne
	fragrant, sweet	Dessert	Tokaji

CHEESE	Zamorano	WINE	
Style	hard	White	Riesling, Albarino, Liebfraumilch
Origin	Spain	Red	Rioja, Tempranillo, Zinfandel, Pinot
Milk	sheep		Noir, Carignan, Burgundy
Info	aged, creamy, nutty, slightly caramel,	Sparkling	Champagne
	buttery, salty, tart	Dessert	Sherry, Sangria

CHEESE		WINE	
Style		White	
Origin		Red	
Milk		Rosé	
Info		Sparkling	
		Dessert	

CHEESE		WINE	
Style		White	
Origin		Red	
Milk		Rosé	
Info		Sparkling	
		Dessert	

Wine & Cheese Pairing Recommendations

Here is our Wine & Cheese Pairing Recommendations chart which lists over 150 wines and provides suggestions of cheeses to serve with each of those wines. If you have selected a wine and want ideas of some cheeses that may be particularly pleasing with that wine, the Wine & Cheese Pairing Recommendations chart offers suggestions.

On the other hand, the Cheese & Wine Pairing Recommendations chart earlier in this book lists over 340 cheeses and provides suggestions for wines to serve with each of those cheeses.

As we indicated previously, you can consider these recommendations as a starting point in your quest for your Wow! pairing experiences and that the enjoyment of a specific wine with a specific cheese is a completely personal evaluation. Furthermore, since individual wines and cheeses vary from winery to winery, from cheesemaker to cheesemaker, from year to year, and from season to season, you have an enormous number of options in your pairing experimentations. You should never run out of potential combinations ... and therein lies your enjoyable challenge to find your Wow! pairings.

Remember, just because an "expert" says a specific wine pairs well with a specific cheese, it may not click for you. For example, we host many wine and cheese pairing events and as we record numerous pairing comments, we are continually amazed at the number of times that some people rate the pairing of a specific wine with a specific cheese very positively, while other people at the same event, tasting the same wine and cheese, proclaim the pairing doesn't work for them.

There is no doubt that each pairing evokes a personal response. So, as you refer to our recommendations charts for cheese and wine pairing ideas, be aware that you should also experiment and substitute similar as well as contrasting wines and cheeses. Keep in mind that your quest for the ultimate Wow! pairings is most of all to experience superb wines and cheeses and to have a lot of fun in the process.

We offer the following recommendations to give you a sampling of wine and cheese pairings that may please your tastes. They are based on one or more of the following criteria:

1. We have personally experienced the pairings and found them ranging from pleasing to Wow!

2. People we served these pairings have found them to range from pleasing to Wow!

3. Wine tasting experts recommended them

4. Cheese tasting experts recommended them

5. Winemakers recommended them

6. Cheesemakers recommended them

7. We have compiled analytical pairings based on the various factors in the Pairing Guidelines section of the previous chapter in this book.

Once again, the pairings we list are just a few suggestions out of myriad potential pairings. For example, our research found more than 100 recommended cheese pairings for Cabernet Sauvignon and Pinot Noir, and in the space available, it was obviously not practical to list them all.

So please enjoy the challenge of experimenting with other wines and other cheeses of similar or contrasting genre. Who knows when you will discover a personal Wow! pairing?

Remember that wines change flavors, aromas, and body as they mature and age. And as most cheeses mature and age, their flavors, aromas, textures, and firmness may change dramatically. You will not know exactly how a wine will taste until you open a specific bottle and drink the wine. You will not know how a specific slice of cheese will taste until you experience that first bite. That's why our recommendations charts offer adjectives that commonly describe wines and cheeses at some point during their lifetimes to give you a sense of what to anticipate when you shop for wines and cheeses that you have not yet tasted.

"Wine is bottled poetry."

–Robert Louis Stevenson

WHITE WINES

"Wine maketh glad the heart of man."

—Book of Psalms 104:15

WINE	Albarino	CHEESE	
Characteristics:		Soft	Brie, Selles-sur-Cher, Montenebro, Pouligny-St. Pierce, Valençay
Light, dry, fruity, rich, creamy, fragrant		Semi-soft	Crottin de Chavigne, Majorero
		Firm	Brin d'Amour, Iberico, Ticklemore, Roncal, Gloucester,
		Hard	Spenwood, Zamarano, St. Maure

WINE	Aligoté	CHEESE	
Characteristics:		Soft	Excelsior, Banon, Pierre Robert
Light, dry, fruity		Semi-soft	Appenzeller, Mt. Tam, Chalosse
		Firm	Sally Jackson's Sheep, Gruyère, Caprino, Wensleydale
		Hard	St. Maure
		Blue	Blue Brie

WINE	Aurore	CHEESE	
Characteristics:		Fresh	Cream Cheese
Light, sweet to dry, smooth, fruity		Soft	Cabécou, Constant Bliss, Teleme
		Semi-soft	Monterey Jack, Port Salut, Farmers
		Firm	Jarlsberg, Gouda, Carmela, Ouray
		Hard	Pleasant Ridge Reserve
		Blue	Saga Blue

WINE	Blanc de Bois	CHEESE	
Characteristics:		Fresh	Neufchâtel, Crescenza
Light, semi-dry to dry, fruity, spicy		Soft	Selles-sur-Cher, Cabécou, Manouri
		Semi-soft	San Andreas, Cantal, Graddost
		Firm	Serena, Sonoma Jack, Mild Cheddar
		Hard	Ubriaco
		Blue	Gorgonzola Dolce

WINE	Carlos	CHEESE	
Characteristics:		Fresh	Petit-Suisse
Light, semi-dry to sweet, fruity		Soft	Chèvre, Colorouge, Pierce Point
		Semi-soft	Père Joseph, Harvest Moon, Pau Saut Maueu
		Firm	Graviera, Jarlsberg, Le Chèvre Noir
		Hard	Panache d'Aramits

WINE	Catawba	CHEESE	
Characteristics:		Fresh	Ricotta, Cream Cheese
Medium, semi-dry, fruity		Soft	St. André, Chaource, Chèvre, Crottin
		Semi-soft	Comté, Edam, Port Salut
		Firm	American Swiss, San Simon, Raclette
		Hard	Dry Jack
		Blue	Stilton

WINE	Cayuga	CHEESE	
Characteristics:		Fresh	Crescenza
Delicate, crisp, semi-dry, fruity		Soft	Brie, Camembert, Teleme
		Semi-soft	Asiago, Castelrosso, Fontina, Havarti
		Firm	Cheddar, Emmentaler, Gouda, Colby
		Hard	Dry Jack, Spenwood
		Blue	Maytag Blue, Point Reyes Blue

WINE	Chablis	CHEESE	
Characteristics:		Fresh	Brebiou, Mozzarella Bufala
Light, semi-dry, smooth, crisp		Soft	Tomini, Excelsion, Azeitão, Chaource
		Semi-soft	Beaufort, Mt. Lassen, Rochefort Montagne,
		Firm	Podhalanski, Valençay, Jarlsberg
		Hard	Grana Padano

WINE	Chardonel	CHEESE	
Characteristics:		Fresh	Robiola Piemonte, Mascarpone
Bold, full-bodied, dry, fruity, floral, soft,		Soft	Epoisses, Brie, Valençay
creamy, rich		Semi-soft	Brick, Cantal, Blarney
		Firm	Brin d'Amour, Gruyère, Serena, Rauchkase
		Hard	St. Maure

WINE	Chardonnay (unoaked)	CHEESE	
Characteristics:		Fresh	Cottage Cheese, Fromage Blanc
Light to medium, semi-dry to dry, wide range of		Soft	Bucheron, Asiago, Vermont Shepherd
fruity flavor		Semi-soft	Caerphilly, Fontina, Bel Paese, Oka
		Firm	Mild Cheddar, Cotija, Caram, Gruyère
		Hard	Beaufort Alpage, Manchego, Dry Jack
		Blue	Cambozola, Cabrales, Roquefort

WINE	Chardonnay (oaked)	CHEESE	
Characteristics:		Soft	Vermont Shepherd, Camembert, Feta, Humboldt Fog, Chabichou, Tetilla
Bold, semi-dry, buttery, creamy, vanilla,		Semi-soft	Beaufort, Ibores, St. Paulin, Idiazábal
complex		Firm	Mahón, Garroxta, Cheshire, Gjetost
		Hard	Parmigiano Reggiano, Crockhamdale
		Blue	Stilton, Danish Blue, Cambozola

WINE	Chasselas	CHEESE	
Characteristics:		Fresh	Crescenza
Light to medium, dry, fruity		Soft	Banon, Lumiere, Chaumes, Picodon
		Semi-soft	Tomme de Savoie, Caerphilly, Havarti
		Firm	Raclette, Postel, Graviera, Garroxta
		Hard	Ubriaco, Manchego
		Blue	Blue Brie

WINE Chenin Blanc (unoaked)	CHEESE	
Characteristics:	Fresh	Boursin, Ricotta, Mascarpone
Light to medium, slightly sweet to dry,	Soft	Capra, Florette, Paneer, Chabichou
fresh, fruity, delicate, crisp	Semi-soft	Ardrahan, Derby, Graddost, Cantal
	Firm	Serena, Sharp Cheddar, Garazi
	Hard	Myzithra, Dry Jack, St. Maure
	Blue	Blue Brie

WINE Chenin Blanc (oaked)	CHEESE	
Characteristics:	Soft	Camembert, Chaorce, Banon, Teleme
Bold, sweet to dry, buttery	Semi-soft	Buche, Monterey Jack, Bruder Basil
	Firm	Raclette, Cheshire, Crottin
	Hard	Fribourg, Salers, Manchego
	Blue	Blue Castello

WINE Cinsault	CHEESE	
Characteristics:	Fresh	Goat Cheese
Delicate, light, dry, floral, fruity, creamy,	Soft	Humboldt Fog, Nocturne, Red Hawk
rich, honey, low tannin	Semi-soft	Carmody, Garden Jack
	Firm	Ricotta Salada, Alpine Shepherd
	Hard	St. Maure

WINE Colombard / French Colombard	CHEESE	
Characteristics:	Fresh	Crème Fraiche
Light, semi-dry to dry, fruity, floral, crisp	Soft	Boucheron, Cabécou Feuille
	Semi-soft	Baby Swiss, Danbo, Monterey Jack
	Firm	Gruyère, Leyden, Port Salut
	Hard	Parmesan Dolce
	Blue	Saga Blue, Pt. Reyes Blue

WINE Delaware	CHEESE	
Characteristics:	Fresh	Ricotta
Light to medium, semi-dry, fruity, fragrant,	Soft	Paneer, Lumier, St. André
rich	Semi-soft	Appenzeller, Provolone, Chaubier
	Firm	Tilsit, Garroxta, Smoked Gouda
	Hard	Spenwood, Pleasant Ridge Reserve
	Blue	Bleu de Gex

WINE Edelweiss	CHEESE	
Characteristics:	Fresh	Brebious, Etorki
Light, sweet, fruity, fragrant	Soft	Azeitão, Banon, Vermont Shepherd
	Semi-soft	Hyku, Farmers, Butterkäse
	Firm	Alverca, Ricotta Salada, Bella Sorella
	Hard	Beaufort Alpage, Zamarano
	Blue	Valdeon, Maytag Blue

WINE Fumé Blanc	CHEESE	
Characteristics:	Fresh	Mozzarella Bufala, Ricotta, Brebiou
Medium body, crisp, dry, fruity, vegetal,	Soft	Reblochon, Chaumes, Azeitão
oaky, floral, honey	Semi-soft	Damski, Edam, Comté, Baby Swiss
	Firm	Añejo Enchilado, Dubliner, Raclette
	Hard	Grana Padano, Kefalograviera, Piave
	Blue	Bleu de Gex, Gorgonzola

WINE Gewürztraminer	CHEESE	
Characteristics:	Fresh	Cream Cheese, Robiola Piemonte
Medium body, sweet to dry, fruity, floral, spicy,	Soft	Chèvre, Tallegio, Pierre Robert
intense, crisp	Semi-soft	Chimay, Langres, Lancashire, Clisson
	Firm	Dubliner, Double Gloucester, Kasseri
	Hard	Pecorino Romano, Spenwood
	Blue	Bayley Hazen Blue, Gorgonzola Dolce

WINE Grüner Veltliner	CHEESE	
Characteristics:	Soft	Vacherin Mont d'Or, Liverot, St. André
Medium to full body, dry, velvety, floral, spice,	Semi-soft	Münster, Lancashire, Ibores, Hoch
pepper, pear, citrus, versatile		Ybrig, Wabash Cannonball, Fontina
	Firm	Mahón, Sally Jackson's Sheep, Gjetost
	Hard	Parmasan Dolce
	Blue	Blue Brie

WINE Himmelswein	CHEESE	
Characteristics:	Fresh	Goat Cheese, Montrachet
Light, semi-dry, fruity	Soft	Gaperon, Liptauer, Humboldt Fog,
		Nocturne
	Semi-soft	Pepper Jack, Scamorza, Damski
	Firm	Leyden, Girollin
	Hard	Pepato, Dry Jack, Pecorino Romano

WINE Johannisberg Riesling	CHEESE	
Characteristics:	Fresh	Robiola Piemonte, Brocciu
Light, sweet to dry, fruity, floral	Soft	Pierre Robert, Vacherin, Serra
	Semi-soft	Sottocenere, Vadenost, Fontina, Asiago
	Firm	Serena, Ridder, Emmentaler, Mahón
	Hard	Zamarano
	Blue	Gorgonzola Mascarpone

WINE Kerner	CHEESE	
Characteristics:	Fresh	Neufchâtel, Crescenza
Full bodied, sweet, fruity, flowery	Soft	Chabichou, Chèvre, Pierre Robert
	Semi-soft	Lappi, Kuminost, Fontal, Hyku
	Firm	Mild Cheddar, Bermuda Triangle,
		Botana, Swiss, Cotija, Boerenkaas
	Hard	Fribourg, Sardo, Kefalograviera

WINE	LaCrosse	CHEESE	
Characteristics:		Fresh	Crème Fraiche
Bold, dry, elegant		Soft	Camelia, Chaumes, Toma
		Semi-soft	Sottocenere, Rochefort Montagne
		Firm	Ridder, Daylesford, Leicester
		Hard	Vaesterbottenost, Myzithra
		Blue	Danish Blue

WINE	Liebfraumilch	CHEESE	
Characteristics:		Fresh	Neufchâtel
Light to medium body, semi-dry, fruity		Soft	Rougette, St. André, Crottin
		Semi-soft	Pachina, Père Joseph, Havarti
		Firm	Alpine Shepherd, Caram, Postel, Tilsit
		Hard	Zamarano
		Blue	Cambozola

WINE	Madeleine Angevine	CHEESE	
Characteristics:		Soft	Teleme, Rabaçal, Serra
Delicate, dry, crisp, fruity, clean		Semi-soft	Pau Saut Mauer, Appenzeller
		Firm	San Simon, Roncal, Gruyère
		Hard	Ubriaco, Grana Padano, St. Maure

WINE	Magnolia	CHEESE	
Characteristics:		Fresh	Petit-Suisse
Medium body, sweet, fruity, smooth		Soft	Chaource, Capra
		Semi-soft	Colby, Farmers, Pachina, Provolone
		Firm	Cacao Cardona, Tillamook Cheddar
		Hard	Crockhamdale
		Blue	Crozier Blue, Maytag Blue

WINE	Marsanne	CHEESE	
Characteristics:		Fresh	Boursin
Light to bold body, semi-dry, fruity, soft,		Soft	Boucheron, Banon, Brie
complex, rich		Semi-soft	Blarney, Chaubier, Ardrahan
		Firm	Valençay, Coolea, Emmentaler
		Hard	Beaufort Alpage, St. Maure
		Blue	Saga Blue

WINE	Melody	CHEESE	
Characteristics:		Fresh	Mascarpone
Light, delicate, semi-dry, floral		Soft	Azeitão, Pierre Robert, Rabaçal
		Semi-soft	Port Salut, Nøkkelost, St. Paulin
		Firm	Podhalanski, Dubliner, Gruyère
		Hard	Salers
		Blue	Blue Brie

145

WINE Meursault	CHEESE	
Characteristics:	Soft	Coulommiers, Epoisses, Reblochon, St. Marcellin, Vacherin Mont d'Or
Bold, dry, rich, buttery, nutty	Semi-soft	Caerphilly, Habanero Jack, Gabietou
	Firm	Garroxta, Cheshire, Sharp Cheddar, Emmantaler
	Hard	Crockhamdale, Vaesterbottenost

WINE Müller-Thurgau	CHEESE	
Characteristics:	Fresh	Crescenza
Light, delicate, dry, fruity, mild, soft,	Soft	Tetilla, Rougette, Cabécou
aromatic, low acidity	Semi-soft	Fiore Sardo, Samsø, Madrigal
	Firm	Lappi, Gjetost, Sebastian, Rauchkase, Tête de Moine, Sonoma Jack
	Hard	Reggianito, Dry Jack

WINE Muscadine (white)	CHEESE	
Characteristics:	Fresh	Petit-Suisse
Light, delicate, semi-dry, fruity	Soft	Teleme, Brie, Colorouge, Tomini
	Semi-soft	Münster, Graddost, Colby, Blarney
	Firm	Kasseri, Asiago, Ricotta Salada
	Hard	Grana Padano, Pecorino Romano
	Blue	Big Woods Blue, Bleu d'Auvergne

WINE Niagara	CHEESE	
Characteristics:	Fresh	Cream Cheese
Medium body, sweet to semi-dry, fruity, floral	Soft	Shepherd's Wheel, Mutton Button
	Semi-soft	Danbo, Touloumi, Tomme de Savoie
	Firm	Wensleydale, Abbaye de Belloc, Ouray
	Hard	Wasabi Disk, Pleasant Ridge Reserve
	Blue	Great Hill Blue, Bergere Blue

WINE Niersteiner	CHEESE	
Characteristics:	Fresh	Quark, Brebiou
Medium body, semi-dry, soft, crisp, fruity	Soft	Liptauer, Nocturne, Schloss, Rougette
	Semi-soft	Limburger, Butterkäse, Bruder Basil
	Firm	Caram, Oszczypek, Sebastian, Tilsit
	Hard	Ubriaco
	Blue	Crozier Blue

WINE Ortega	CHEESE	
Characteristics:	Soft	Lebbeen, Boursault, Montenebro, Serpa, Fougerus
Medium body, semi-dry, crisp, fruity	Semi-soft	Idiazábal, Ganonado, Harvest Moon
	Firm	Mahón, Podhalanski, Toscanello
	Hard	Manchego, Zamorano
	Blue	La Peral, Bresse Blue

WINE	Orvieto	CHEESE	
Characteristics:		Fresh	Goat Cheese, Quark
Light, delicate, dry		Soft	Raschera, Roccolo, Tallegio
		Semi-soft	Fontal, Madrigal, Marzalino
		Firm	Montasio, Pecorino, Toscanello, Caprino
		Hard	Ubriaco, Parmesan, Grana Padano

WINE	Pinot Blanc	CHEESE	
Characteristics:		Fresh	Crescenza, Ricotta
Light, dry, fruity, floral		Soft	Pierre Robert, Teleme, Chèvre, Pont L'Eveque, Montbriac, Brillat Savarin
		Semi-soft	Ossau-Iraty, Everona, Mozzarella
		Firm	Garazi, Montasio, Vidalia Onion Jack
		Hard	Spenwood, Parmesan Dolce

WINE	Pinot Grigio	CHEESE	
Characteristics:		Fresh	Boursin, Fromage Blanc, Quark
Crisp, light and dry		Soft	Camellia, Rocollo, Nevat, Camembert
		Semi-soft	Buche, Mt. Lassen, San Andreas Sardo, Cana de Cabra, Ossau-Iraty
		Firm	Serena, Swiss
		Hard	Spenwood, Sapsago

WINE	Pinot Gris	CHEESE	
Characteristics:		Fresh	Neufchâtel, Fromage Blanc, Oka
Heavy, full-bodied, sweet, rich, smooth,		Soft	Liverot, Camellia, Feta, Rocollo, Nevat
fairly flamboyant		Semi-soft	St. Nectaire, Buche, Mt. Lassen, Fiore Sardo, Blarney
		Firm	Garrotxa, Kefalotyri, Serena, Gruyère
		Hard	Le Chèvre Noir, Ubriaco, Salers

WINE	Pouilly-Fumé	CHEESE	
Characteristics:		Fresh	Goat Cheese
Light, dry, fruity		Soft	Chabichou, Camembert, Chèvre
		Semi-soft	Crottin, Monterey Jack, Panela
		Firm	Abbaye de Belloc, Berkswell, Roncal, Cheshire
		Hard	St. Maure

WINE	Rayon D'Or	CHEESE	
Characteristics:		Fresh	Montrachet, Henri
Light, dry, smooth, herbal		Soft	Vacherin, Tomme Crayeuse, Picodon
		Semi-soft	Tome des Recollets, Normantal
		Firm	Garazi, Girollin, Alpine Shepherd
		Hard	Panache d'Aramits
		Blue	Bleu de Haut Jura

WINE	Riesling	CHEESE	
Characteristics:		Fresh	Henri, Neufchâtel
Light, sweet to medium-dry, fruity, crisp, floral, complex		Soft	Epoisses, Brie, Vacherin, Boursault
		Semi-soft	Durrus, Hoch Ybrig, Ibores, Chimay
		Firm	Serena, Gouda, Cotija, Boerenkaas
		Hard	Pepato, Beaufort Alpage, Pepato
		Blue	Bucheret, Maytag Blue, Bresse Blue

WINE	Rioja Blanca	CHEESE	
Characteristics:		Fresh	Panela
Light, semi-dry		Soft	Pont L'Eveque, Reblochon, Azeitão
		Semi-soft	Cabrales, Cana de Cabra, San Simon
		Firm	Abbaye de Belloc, Asadero, Cotija
		Hard	Sap Sago
		Blue	Bayley Hazen Blue

WINE	Roussanne	CHEESE	
Characteristics:		Fresh	Goat Cheese, Crème Frâiche, Ricotta
Light to medium body, semi-dry, fruity, floral, great finesse		Soft	Chabichou, Crottin, St. Marcelin
		Semi-soft	Gamenado, Aisy Cendré, Provolone
		Firm	Jarlsberg, Wensleydale, Leyden

WINE	Sancerre	CHEESE	
Characteristics:		Fresh	Quark, Henri, Boursin, Neufchâtel
Light, delicate, semi-dry to dry, fruity, vegetative		Soft	Pouligny St.Pierre, Valençay, Taupinere
		Semi-soft	Crottin, Comté, Langres
		Firm	Double Gloucester, Jarlsberg, Gouda
		Hard	St. Maure, Grana Padano, Dry Jack
		Blue	Cashel Blue

WINE	Sauvignon Blanc (unoaked)	CHEESE	
Characteristics:		Fresh	Petit-Suisse, Cottage Cheese, Ricotta
Light, sweet to dry, crisp, fruity, acidic		Soft	Selles-sur-Cher, Capra, Constant Bliss
		Semi-soft	Cana de Oveja, Brick, Cantal, Derby
		Firm	Sonoma Jack, Berkswell, Idiazábal
		Hard	Manchego, Salers
		Blue	Blue d'Averge, Bleu de Haut Jura

WINE	Sauvignon Blanc (oaked) / Fumé Blanc	CHEESE	
Characteristics:		Fresh	Goat Cheese
Medium to bold body, sweet to dry, slightly smoky		Soft	Boucheron, Teleme, Taupinere, Feta
		Semi-soft	Vadenost, St. Nectaire, Fleur-de-Teche
		Firm	Abbaye de Belloc, Garrotxa, Cheddar
		Hard	Ubriaco, Myzithra
		Blue	Bucheret, Stilton, Blue Castello

WINE Sémillon	CHEESE	
Characteristics:	Fresh	Cottage Cheese, Cream Cheese
Light to medium body, sweet to dry, fruity,	Soft	Banon, Rocollo, Lebbeen, Pierce Point
floral, nutty, creamy	Semi-soft	Panela, Tomme de Savoie, Butterkäse
	Firm	Graviera, Cheddar, Gouda, Gruyère
	Hard	Panache d'Aramits, Salers, Pepato
	Blue	Maytag Blue

WINE Seyval Blanc	CHEESE	
Characteristics:	Fresh	Ricotta, Fromage Blanc, Crescenza
Light, semi-dry, crisp, citrus, spicy, nutty,	Soft	Pave Affinois, Explorateur, St. André
fruity	Semi-soft	Fiore Sardo, Normanthal, Basato
	Firm	Dubliner, Kasseri, Abbaye de Belloc
	Hard	Dry Jack, St. Maure
	Blue	Bresse Blue

WINE Soave	CHEESE	
Characteristics:	Fresh	Ricotta
Light, dry, smooth, nutty, floral	Soft	Crottin, Tomini, St. Marcellin
	Semi-soft	Beaumont, Scamorza, Comté, Bassato
	Firm	Ganna, Lappi, Pecorino Ginepro
	Hard	Parmigiano Reggiano, Zamarano
	Blue	English Blue Cheshire

WINE Symphony	CHEESE	
Characteristics:	Fresh	Etorki
Light, dry, fruity	Soft	Coulommiers, Chèvre, Serpa
	Semi-soft	Derby, Haloumi, San Andreas
	Firm	San Simon, Sonoma Jack, Rauchkase
	Hard	Reggianito, Salers
	Blue	Blue Brie

WINE Traminette	CHEESE	
Characteristics:	Soft	Poudre Puff, Brie, Chaource, Livarot
Medium body, dry, spicy, floral	Semi-soft	Urgelia, Port Salut, Oka, Mozzarella
	Firm	Añejo Enchilado, Botana, Kasseri
	Hard	Kefalograviera, Pepato, Fribourg
	Blue	Bleu de Gex

WINE Verdelet	CHEESE	
Characteristics:	Fresh	Etorki, Quark
Light, delicate, dry, flinty	Soft	Florette, Humboldt Fog, Nevat
	Semi-soft	Fontal, Marzalino, Fleur de Teche
	Firm	Asiago, Midnight Moon, Ganna, Lappi
	Hard	Crockhamdale, Pleasant Ridge Reserve

WINE	Verdicchio	CHEESE	
Characteristics:		Fresh	
Light, delicate, dry		Soft	Florette, Taupiniere, Pierre Robert
		Semi-soft	Carmody, Clisson, Tome d'Aquitaine
		Firm	Gjetost, Emmentaler, Serena, Cheddar
		Hard	Beaufort Alpage, Dry Jack
		Blue	Pt. Reyes Blue

WINE	Vidal Blanc	CHEESE	
Characteristics:		Fresh	Queso Blanco, Cream Cheese
Light, semi-dry, fruity, floral		Soft	Rabaçal, Chèvre, Chabichou, Feta
		Semi-soft	Graddost, Münster, Samsø, Lumiere
		Firm	Fontinella, Jarlsberg, Raclette
		Hard	Ubriaco, Reggianito, St. Maure

WINE	Vignoles	CHEESE	
Characteristics:		Fresh	Crescenza
Full body, sweet to semi-dry, fruity, floral		Soft	Epoisses, Teleme
		Semi-soft	Port Salut, Monterey Jack, Caciotta
		Firm	Myost, Asiago, Kefalotyri, Cheddar
		Hard	Piave, Pecorino Romano, Salers
		Blue	Gorgonzola

WINE	Villard	CHEESE	
Characteristics:		Fresh	Montrachet
Light, dry, fruity		Soft	Toma, Picodon, Liederkranz
		Semi-soft	Touloumi, Samsø, Fleur-de-Teche
		Firm	Lappi, Smoked Gouda, Podhalanski
		Hard	Parmesan Dolce, Vaesterbottenost
		Blue	English Blue Cheshire

WINE	Viognier	CHEESE	
Characteristics:		Fresh	Mascarpone
Light to medium body, sweet to semi-dry,		Soft	Vermont Shepherd, Pierre Robert
fruity, floral, spicy, vanilla, rich, complex		Semi-soft	Caerphilly, Hollandse Chèvre, La Peral
		Firm	Sonoma Jack, Ticklemore, Swiss
		Hard	Dry Jack, Reggianito
		Blue	Bergere Blue, Pt. Reyes Blue

WINE	Vouvray	CHEESE	
Characteristics:		Fresh	Goat Cheese, Mascarpone
Light to full body, sweet to dry, fruity		Soft	Constant Bliss, Epoisses
		Semi-soft	Durrus, Caerphilly, Carmody
		Firm	Tête de Moine, Double Gloucester
		Hard	St. Maure, Gubbeen, Spenwood
		Blue	Roquefort, Saga Blue, Gorgonzola

RED WINES

"Man has yet to find a better companion to cheese than wine."
—Pierre Androuet

WINE Alicante Bouschet	CHEESE	
Characteristics:	Soft	Montbriac, Banon, Livarot
Bold, dry, fruity, smooth, rich, spicy,	Semi-soft	Buche, Chimay, Colby, Gubbeen
earthy	Firm	Berkswell, Double Gloucester, Sonoma Jack
	Hard	Piave, Parmesan, Manchego
	Blue	Bleu d'Auverge, Cashel Blue

WINE Amarone	CHEESE	
Characteristics:	Soft	Vacherin Mont d'Or, Camembert
Bold, dry, fruity, powerful, hearty	Semi-soft	Münster, Beaufort, Lancashire, Mt. Lassen, Morbier, Tomme de Savoie
	Firm	Pecorino Ginepro, Botana, Cheddar
	Hard	Pecorino Romano, Reggiano
	Blue	Pt. Reyes Blue

WINE Angélus	CHEESE	
Characteristics:	Soft	Reblochon, Pave d'Affinois
Bold, sweet, fruity, layered	Semi-soft	Idiazábal, Petit Basque, Fourme d'Ambert, Oaxaca, Leideche Kaas
	Firm	Kasseri, Roncal, Sonoma Jack
	Hard	Grana Padano, Piave, Parmesan
	Blue	Cambozola, Great Hill Blue

WINE Baco Noire	CHEESE	
Characteristics:	Soft	Camembert, Cabécou Feuille, Azeitão
Medium body, dry, fruity, rich, complex	Semi-soft	Fontina, Havarti, Provolone
	Firm	Alpine Shepherd, Abbaye de Belloc, Garrotxa, Asiago
	Hard	Ubriaco, Pecorino Romano
	Blue	Roquefort

WINE Barbaresco	CHEESE	
Characteristics:	Soft	Fougerus, Toma, Montbriac
Medium body, dry, rich	Semi-soft	Ibores, Buche, Petit Basque, Buche
	Firm	Coolea, Gruyère, Dubliner, Ridder
	Hard	Manchego, Parmigiano Reggiano
	Blue	Gorgonzola Mascarpone

WINE Barbera	CHEESE	
Characteristics:	Soft	Banon, Stracchino, Camembert
Bold, dry, rich, robust, fruity, medium tannins	Semi-soft	Fontina, Bel Paese, Castelrosso, Fiore Sardo, Ossay-Iraty, Lancashire
	Firm	Gouda, Kikorangi, Asiago, Kasseri
	Hard	Crockhamdale, Manchego, Dry Jack
	Blue	Valdeon

WINE	Barolo	CHEESE	
Characteristics:		Fresh	Brocciu, Robiolo Piemonte
Bold, dry, rich, fruity, floral, thick, complex		Soft	Robiolo Lombardia, Taleggio,
		Semi-soft	Münster, Provolone, Fontina
		Firm	Roncal, Berkswell, Asiago, Parmesan
		Hard	Pecorino, Parmigiano Reggiano
		Blue	Bleu de Causses, Le Peral, Cashel Blue

WINE	Beaujolais	CHEESE	
Characteristics:		Fresh	Boursin, Neufchâtel, Fromage Blanc
Light to bold, semi-dry to dry, fruity, aromatic,		Soft	Reblochon, Excelsior, Poudre Puff
soft tannins		Semi-soft	Bonbel, Morbier, Cantal, Havarti
		Firm	Tillamook Cheddar, Cotija, Mimolette
		Hard	Spenwood, Beaufort Alpage
		Blue	Picon, Cambozola

WINE	Beaujolais Nouveau	CHEESE	
Characteristics:		Fresh	Crème Fraiche, Mascarpone
Light to medium, semi-dry, fruity		Soft	Brie, Florette, Banon, Boucheron
		Semi-soft	Chaubier, Clisson, Münster, Beaumont
		Firm	Garazi, Jarlsberg, Raclette
		Blue	Bucheret

WINE	Bolduc	CHEESE	
Characteristics:		Fresh	Etorki
Bold, semi-dry, fruity, pepper		Soft	Epoisses, Gaperon, Explorateur
		Semi-soft	St. Nectaire, Aisy Cendré, Chaubier
		Firm	Daylesford, Raclette, Sonoma Jack
		Hard	Sardo, Pepper Jack, Salers
		Blue	Crozier Blue, Cambozola

WINE	Bordeaux	CHEESE	
Characteristics:		Soft	Pierre Robert, Reblochon, Livarot
Medium body, dry, smooth, spicy,		Semi-soft	Havarti, Morbier, Brick, Cantal
complex, strong tannins		Firm	Mimolette, Gruyère, Cheddar
		Hard	Fribourg, Manchego, Asiago
		Blue	Gorgonzola

WINE	Burgundy	CHEESE	
Characteristics:		Fresh	Robiola Piemonte
Medium to bold, semi-dry, fruity, velvety,		Soft	Brie de Meaux, Liptaur, Maroilles
refined, medium tannins		Semi-soft	Blarney, Esrom, Leideche Kaas
		Firm	Garazi, Girollin, Leyden, Raclette
		Hard	Zamorano, Parmesan Regianno
		Blue	Blue Castello

WINE	Cabernet Franc		
Characteristics:		CHEESE	
Medium to bold, fruity, rich, robust		Soft	St. Marcellin, Brie, Brin d'Amour
		Semi-soft	Crottin, Edam, Havarti, Oka, Brick
		Firm	Coolea, Cheshire, Emmentaler, Ouray
		Hard	Le Chèvre Noir, Dry Jack, Manchego
		Blue	Big Woods Blue

WINE	Cabernet Sauvignon		
Characteristics:		CHEESE	
Medium to bold, semi-dry to dry,		Soft	Boulette d'Avesnes, Epoisses, Brie,
very complex, strong tannins, ages extremely			Vacherin Mont d'Or, Mt. Tam, Schloss
well, fruity undertones		Semi-soft	Durrus, Scamorza, Nøkkelost, Colby
		Firm	Strong Cheddar, Mahón, Serena
		Hard	Roomano, Spenwood, Crockhamdale
		Blue	Beenleigh Blue, Pt. Reyes Blue, Stilton

WINE	Carignane / Carignan		
Characteristics:		CHEESE	
Medium to bold, dry, toasty, peppery, fruity,		Soft	Chèvre, Reblochon, Kiku, Azeitão
spicy, rich, high tannins		Semi-soft	Père Joseph, Andrahan, Crottin
		Firm	Asiago, Berkswell, Montasio, Gouda,
			Mimolette, Abbaye de Belloc
		Hard	Parmesan, Zamorona
		Blue	Fourme d'Ambert

WINE	Chambourcin		
Characteristics:		CHEESE	
Medium, dry, fruity, rich, coffee, complex		Fresh	Brocciu
		Soft	Excelsior, Gaperon, Liptauer, Chèvre
		Semi-soft	Touloumi, Esrom, Beaumont
		Firm	Alverca, Oszczypek, Raclette
		Hard	Pio Vecchio, Vaesterbottenost
		Blue	Bayley Hazen Blue, Dolcelatte

WINE	Chancellor		
Characteristics:		CHEESE	
Light to bold, dry, spicy, thin to robust		Soft	Teleme, Queso Cabrero, Manouri
		Semi-soft	Gabietou, Basato, Wabash Cannonball
		Firm	Boerenkaas, Gloucester, Lappi
		Hard	Parm Dolce, Sap Sago, St. Maure
		Blue	

WINE	Chianti		
Characteristics:		CHEESE	
Bold, dry, fruity, velvety, strong tannins		Fresh	Robiola Piemonte, Mozzarella Bufala
		Soft	Pont L'Eveque, Ardrahan, Maroilles,
			Explorateur, Vacherin Mont d'Or
		Semi-soft	Caciocavallo, Fontina, Basato, Esrom
		Firm	Pecorino Ginepro, Kasseri, Gruyère
		Hard	Pecorino Romano, Reggianito

WINE	Claret	CHEESE	
Characteristics:		Soft	Brie, St. André
Full body, dry, fruity, soft tannins		Semi-soft	Appenzeller, Sottocenere, Garden Jack, Hoch Ybrig
		Firm	Gouda, Kefalotyri, Gruyère, Kasseri
		Hard	Kefalograviera, Pepper Jack
		Blue	Great Hill Blue

WINE	Concord	CHEESE	
Characteristics:		Soft	Raschera, Constant Bliss, Tomini
Light, semi-dry, fruity, crsip		Semi-soft	Comté, Beaumont, Fleur de Teche
		Firm	Toscanello, Gilboa, Podhadanski, Gjetost
		Hard	Myzithra, Fribourg, Sardo
		Blue	Picon

WINE	Côtes du Rhône	CHEESE	
Characteristics:		Soft	Tomini, Brie de Meaux, Brillat Savarin
Medium to bold, semi-dry to dry, fruity		Semi-soft	Caciocavallo, Chaubier, Bruder Basil, St. Nectaire, Scamorza, Petit Basque
		Firm	Mimolette, Strong Cheddar, Cheshire
		Hard	Spenwood, Romano Vacchino
		Blue	Shropshire Blue, Cashel Blue

WINE	Cynthiana	CHEESE	
Characteristics:		Soft	Camellia, Tomme Crayeuse, Stracchino
Bold, dry, floral		Semi-soft	Provolone, Tintern, Danbo, Vadenost, Kastelrosso
		Firm	Caram, Lappi, Abbaye de Belloc
		Hard	Beaufort Alpage, Pecorino Romano
		Blue	Crozier Blue

WINE	Dechaunac	CHEESE	
Characteristics:		Soft	Colorouge, Mutton Button, Gratte-Paille
Light, semi-dry to dry, nutty, vegetative		Semi-soft	Baby Swiss, Touloumi, Vidalia Onion Jack
		Firm	Jarlsberg, Girollin, Rauchkase
		Hard	Parmesan

WINE	Dolcetto	CHEESE	
Characteristics:		Soft	Azeitão, Banon, Capra, Brie, Roccolo
Light to medium, dry, fruity, soft		Semi-soft	Fontina, Appenzeller, Fontal, Oaxaca
		Firm	Ganna, Smoked Gouda, Ticklemore, Abbaye de Belloc
		Hard	Pepato, Piave
		Blue	Gorgonzola

WINE Fleurie	CHEESE	
Characteristics:	Soft	Schloss, Teleme, Lumiere, Nocturne
Light, slightly sweet, fruity, floral, spicy,	Semi-soft	Morbier, Marzalino, Pau Saut Maueu
smooth, velvety	Firm	Tilsit, Oszczytek, Ricotta Salada
	Hard	Piave, Vaesterbottenost, Romano Vacchino
	Blue	Roquefort

WINE Fredonia	CHEESE	
Characteristics:	Fresh	Montrachet
Medium body, semi-dry, fruity, floral, fresh	Soft	Kiku, Cabécou, Maroilles
	Semi-soft	Ossau-Iraty, Tintern, Oxaca, Langres
	Firm	Mild Cheddar, Co-Jack, Gruyère
	Hard	Fribourg
	Blue	Blue Brie

WINE Gamay Beaujolais	CHEESE	
Characteristics:	Fresh	Petit Suisse
Light to medium, semi-dry, fruity, fragrant	Soft	Camembert, Feta, Taleggio
	Semi-soft	Fontina, Ardrahan, Durrus, Baby Swiss
	Firm	Tête de Moine, Myost, Postel, Gouda
	Hard	Pio Vecchio, Pepato, Parmesan
	Blue	Montbriac, Dolcelatte

WINE Gamay Noir	CHEESE	
Characteristics:	Fresh	Henri
Light to medium, semi-dry to dry, fruity	Soft	St. Marcellin, Humboldt Fog, Brie
	Semi-soft	Samsø, Clisson, Cana de Oveja
	Firm	Tillamook Cheddar, Leicester
	Hard	Ubriaco
	Blue	Fourme d'Ambert

WINE Grenache	CHEESE	
Characteristics:	Fresh	Panela
Medium body, sweet, powerful, medium tannins,	Soft	Montenebro, Chaource, Serpa
very fragrant, strong fruity overtones	Semi-soft	Crottin, Morbier, Baby Swiss, Urgelia
	Firm	Iberico, Asiago, Roncal, Emmentaler
	Hard	Manchego, Piave, Dry Jack, Myzithra
	Blue	Pt. Reyes Blue

WINE Kasselfest	CHEESE	
Characteristics:	Fresh	Fromage Blanc
Medium body, sweet, fruity	Soft	Pierce Point, Pierre Robert, Lumiere
	Semi-soft	Hollandse Chèvre, St. Paulin, Tintern
	Firm	Botana, Lappi, Podhalanski
	Hard	Beaufort Alpage, Crockhamdale
	Blue	Bayley Hazen Blue, Bergere Blue

WINE Landot Noir	CHEESE	
Characteristics:	Soft	Boucheron, Boursault, Serpa
Bold, dry, fruity	Semi-soft	Normanthal, Tome des Recollets, Co-Jack, Bel Paese, Sottocenere
	Firm	Tête de Moine, Serena, Abertam
	Hard	Dry Jack, Ubriaco
	Blue	Blue Castello

WINE Lemberger	CHEESE	
Characteristics:	Soft	Boulette d'Avesnes, Nocturne, Taupinere
Bold, dry, fruity, rich, spicy, mild tannins	Semi-soft	Kuminost, Madrigal, Limburger
	Firm	Tillamook Cheddar, Postel, Kefalotyri
	Hard	Sardo, Pecorino Romano, Myzithra
	Blue	Cabrales, English Blue Cheshire

WINE Malbec	CHEESE	
Characteristics:	Soft	Valençay, Coulommier, Wasabi Disk
Medium body, dry, fruity, peppery, buttery, dense, tannic	Semi-soft	Gubbeen, Langres, Morbier, Garden Jack, Testouri, Limburger
	Firm	Mimolette, Botana, Cotswold
	Hard	Le Chèvre Noir, Sardo
	Blue	Bleu de Causses, Cashel Blue

WINE Maréchal Foch	CHEESE	
Characteristics:	Fresh	Henri
Light to bold, semi-dry to dry, fruity, smooth	Soft	Rabaçal, Boulette d'Avesnes, Lumiere
	Semi-soft	Nøkkelost, Mt. Lassen, Comté, Edam
	Firm	Asiago, Bella Sorella, Caprino, Schloss
	Hard	Spenwood, Beaufort Alpage
	Blue	Crozier Blue

WINE Meritage	CHEESE	
Characteristics:	Soft	Tomini, St. André, Pierre Robert
Medium body, dry, fruity	Semi-soft	Ossau-Iraty, Cantal, Aisy Cendré
	Firm	Iberico, Mahón, Leicester, Gruyère
	Hard	Manchego, Parmigiano Reggiano, Le Chèvre Noir, Myzithra
	Blue	Pt. Reyes Blue

WINE Meritus	CHEESE	
Characteristics:	Fresh	Panela
Bold, dry, fruity, complex	Soft	Humboldt Fog, Valençay, Pierce Point
	Semi-soft	Wabash Cannonball, Fleur de Teche
	Firm	Kikoranji, Cocao Cardona, Kefalotyri
	Hard	Pleasant Ridge Reserve, Dry Jack
	Blue	Stilton

WINE	Merlot	CHEESE	
Characteristics:		Fresh	Goat Cheese
Light to bold, dry, fruity, soft,		Soft	Camembert, Brie, Liverot, Valençay
medium tannins, rich, velvety,		Semi-soft	Caerphilly, Ibores, Hoch Ybrig, Brick
complex nuances		Firm	Montasio, Roncal, Dubliner, Colby
		Hard	Romano, Spenwood, Parm Dolce
		Blue	Gorgonzola Dolce, Pt. Reyes Blue

WINE	Mourvèdre	CHEESE	
Characteristics:		Soft	Liptauer, Gaperon, Le Roule
Bold, dry, fruity, rich, cinnamon, aromatic,		Semi-soft	Leideche Kaas, Vidalia Onion Jack,
tannic			Blarney, Habanero Jack, Garden Jack
		Firm	Cotswold, Cotija
		Hard	Pepato, Kefalograviera
		Blue	Bresse Blue, Big Woods Blue

WINE	Mouton-Rothschild Bordeaux	CHEESE	
Characteristics:		Soft	Rabaçal, Camellia, Brie de Meaux
Bold, dry, fruity, powerful, rich		Semi-soft	Everona, Hollandse Chèvre, Fontal
		Firm	Dubliner, Sebastian, Abbaye de Belloc
		Hard	Fribourg, Manchego
		Blue	Great Hill Blue

WINE	Muscadine	CHEESE	
Characteristics:		Fresh	Mozzarella Bufala, Brocciu
Light, delicate, sweet to semi-dry, fruity		Soft	Kiku, Colorouge, Florette, Capra
		Semi-soft	Madrigal, Esrom, Marzalino
		Firm	Mild Cheddar, Pecorino, Gjetost
		Hard	Parm Dolce, Beaufort Alpage
		Blue	Dolcelatte, Saga Blue

WINE	Nebbiolo	CHEESE	
Characteristics:		Soft	Fougerus, Robiolla, Constant Bliss
Bold, dry, herbal, high tannins, fruity, spicy,		Semi-soft	Fontina, Ibores, Mozzarella, Baby Bel
very fragrant		Firm	Asiago, Berkswell, Montasio, Ouray
		Hard	Pecorino Romano, Piave
		Blue	Gorgonzola Dolce

WINE	Noble	CHEESE	
Characteristics:		Soft	Chèvre, Chabichou, Nevat
Bold, sweet to dry, robust		Semi-soft	Durrus, Fontal, Gabietou, Habanero
			Jack, Ossau-Iraty
		Firm	San Simon, Cotija, Kikoranji
		Hard	Pleasant Ridge Reserve, Spenwood
		Blue	Beenleigh Blue

WINE	Norton	CHEESE	
Characteristics:		Soft	Caciodtta, Lieberkranz, Manouri
Bold, dry, fruity, rich, spicy		Semi-soft	Morbier, Damski, Vidalia Onion Jack
		Firm	Asiago, Serena, Graviera, Cheddar
		Hard	Grana Padano, Sap Sago, Dry Jack

WINE	Petite Sirah	CHEESE	
Characteristics:		Fresh	Goat Cheese
Light to bold, dry, fruity, intense,		Soft	Ardrahan, Gratte-Paille, Lebbeen
peppery overtones		Semi-soft	Chimay, Farmers, Hollandese Chèvre
		Firm	Añejo Enchilado, Botana, Carmela, Toscanello
		Hard	Parm Dolce

WINE	Pinot Meunier	CHEESE	
Characteristics:		Fresh	Etorki
Light, delicate, dry, fruity, subtle spice,		Soft	Red Hawk, Rabaçal, Florette, Le Roule
floral		Semi-soft	Chimay, Butterkäse, Danbo, Vadenost
		Firm	Caram, Rauchkase, Harvest Moon
		Hard	Panache d'Aramits
		Blue	Blue Brie

WINE	Pinot Noir	CHEESE	
Characteristics:		Fresh	Fromage Blanc, Mozzarella Bufala
Light to medium, dry, fruity, velvety, layers		Soft	Azeitão, Vermont Shepherd, Mt. Tam
of aromas, complex, smooth, soft to medium		Semi-soft	Port Salut, Bonbel, Beaufort, Edam
tannins		Firm	Mahón, Berkswell, Asiago, Boerenkaas
		Hard	Spenwood, Ubriaco, Beaufort Alpage
		Blue	Shropshire Blue, Saga Blue

WINE	Pinotage	CHEESE	
Characteristics:		Soft	Reblochon, Mariolles, Brie de Meaux, Epoisses, Vacherin, Coulommiers
Bold, dry, fruity, peppery		Semi-soft	Münster, Langres, Morbier, Limburger
		Firm	Ridder, Sebastian, Podhalanski, Ouray
		Hard	Spenwood, Pepato, Tillamook Cheddar
		Blue	Montbriac

WINE	Rioja	CHEESE	
Characteristics:		Fresh	Queso Blanco, Queso Fresco
Bold, sweet, fruity, rich, medium tannins		Soft	Azeitão, Montenebro, Queso Cabrero
		Semi-soft	Ibores, Caerphilly, Cana de Cabra
		Firm	Mahón, Berkswell, Iberico, Cheddar
		Hard	Spenwood, Le Chèvre Noir,
		Blue	Cabrales, Valdeon, Picon

WINE Rosso Misto	CHEESE	
Characteristics:	Fresh	Crème Fraiche
Medium body, dry, fruity	Soft	Humboldt Fog, Pave d'Affinois, Brie
	Semi-soft	Graddost, Damski, Fiore Sardo
	Firm	Cotija, Ganna, Midnight Moon
	Hard	Ubriaco, Crockhamdale, Manchego
	Blue	Montbriac, Saga Blue

WINE Saint Emilion Bordeaux	CHEESE	
Characteristics:	Soft	Brie, Camembert, Pierre Robert,
Bold, semi-dry, fruity		Vermont Shepherd, Reblochon
	Semi-soft	Cantal, Comté, Ossau-Iraty
	Firm	Cotswold, Dubliner, Garazi, Roncal
	Hard	Pio Vecchio
	Blue	Roquefort

WINE Sangiovese	CHEESE	
Characteristics:	Soft	Maroilles, Chaumes, Mutton Button
Medium to bold, semi-dry to dry, fruity,	Semi-soft	Bel Paese, Caciocavallo, Everona,
floral, high acidity		Fiore Sardo, Monterey Jack, Oka
	Firm	Roncal, Gruyère, Raclette, Caprino
	Hard	Peccorino Romano, Romano Vacchino
	Blue	Gorgonzola Mascarpone

WINE Syrah / Shiraz	CHEESE	
Characteristics:	Soft	Mt. Tam, Vermont Shepherd, Brie
Light to bold, dry, fruity, spicy complexity,	Semi-soft	Beaufort, St. Nectaire, Ibores, Edam,
intense, peppery, robust, earthy, tannic		Ossau-Iraty, Fontina, Caerphilly
	Firm	Double Gloucester, Berkswell, Serena
	Hard	Le Chèvre Noir, Parmesan, Pepato
	Blue	Cambozola, Bucheret, Maytag Blue

WINE Tempranillo	CHEESE	
Characteristics:	Fresh	Queso Blanco, Queso Fresco
Medium to bold, dry, rich, complex, fruity,	Soft	Boursault, Lebbeen, Nevat, Manouri
medium tannins	Semi-soft	Canc de Oveja, Graddost, Carmody
	Firm	Garrotxa, Mahón, Urgelia, Cotija
	Hard	Manchego, Zamarano
	Blue	Cabrales, La Peral, Picon

WINE Torgiano	CHEESE	
Characteristics:	Semi-soft	Castelrosso, Fiore Sardo, Asiago
Bold, dry, fruity, intense	Firm	Pecorino, Abertam, Ganna, Cheshire,
		Toscanello
	Hard	Piave, Grana Padano, Pio Vecchio
	Blue	La Peral, Pt. Reyes Blue, Maytag Blue

WINE Valpolicella	CHEESE	
Characteristics:	Soft	Pouligny-St. Pierre, Fougerus, Brie, Taleggio, Coulommiers, Brie
Light to medium, sweet, fruity, acidic, rich, fragrant, robust	Semi-soft	Fiore Sardo, Brick, Mozzarella, Edam
	Firm	Cheshire, Emmentaler, Wensleydale
	Hard	Kefalograveria, Grana Padano
	Blue	Bergere Blue

WINE Villard Noir	CHEESE	
Characteristics:	Fresh	Petit Suisse
Light to medium, sweet to dry, fruity	Soft	Gratte-Paille, Raschera, Hoch Ybrig
	Semi-soft	Langres, Haloumi,
	Firm	Graviera, Myost, Bermuda Triangle
	Hard	Myzithra
	Blue	Bucheret

WINE Zinfandel	CHEESE	
Characteristics:	Soft	Pierre Robert, Vermont Shepherd, Camembert, Mt. Tam, Chabichou
Medium to bold, dry, peppery, spicy, fruity, soft	Semi-soft	Wabash Cannonball, Münster, Chimay
	Firm	Coolea, Dubliner, Asiago, Cheddar
	Hard	Zamarano, Pio Vecchio, Dry Jack
	Blue	Beenleigh Blue, Stilton, Danish Blue

WINE	CHEESE
Characteristics:	Fresh
	Soft
	Semi-soft
	Firm
	Hard
	Blue

WINE	CHEESE
Characteristics:	Fresh
	Soft
	Semi-soft
	Firm
	Hard
	Blue

WINE	CHEESE
Characteristics:	Fresh
	Soft
	Semi-soft
	Firm
	Hard
	Blue

ROSÉ WINES

"If God forbade drinking,
would He have made wine so good?"

—Cardinal Richeleu

WINE	Blush Muscadine	CHEESE	
Characteristics:		Soft	Banon, Nevat, Explorateur
Light, delicate, sweet to semi-dry, fruity		Semi-soft	Farmers, Hollandse Chèvre, Bruder Basil
		Firm	Ouray, Bella Sorella
		Hard	Piave

WINE	Blush Niagara	CHEESE	
Characteristics:		Fresh	Brebiou
Light, sweet to semi-dry, fruity		Soft	Mutton Button, Montenebro, Rabaçal, Shepherds Wheel, Chèvre
		Semi-soft	Graddost, Brick
		Firm	Alverca, Tillamook Cheddar, Gjetost
		Hard	Manchego

WINE	Grenache Rosé	CHEESE	
Characteristics:		Soft	Azeitão, Chaource, Boursault, Pierre Robert, Rachera, Fourgerus
Medium body, sweet to dry, fruity		Semi-soft	Ossau-Iraty, Bonbel, Caciotta, Comté, Durrus
		Firm	Jarlsberg, Bermuda Triangle

WINE	Pink Catawba	CHEESE	
Characteristics:		Soft	Brie, Cabécou, Excelsior, Constant Bliss, Brillat Savarin,
Light, delicate, sweet, crisp, fruity		Semi-soft	Havarti, Basato, Petit Basque, Brick, Fontina, St. Nectaire
		Firm	Gruyère, Jarlsberg, Raclette

WINE	Pink Vidal	CHEESE	
Characteristics:		Fresh	Brebiou, Boursin
Light, semi-dry, crisp, fruity		Soft	Camembert, Nocturne, Tomini
		Semi-soft	Bel Paese, Beaumont, Durrus, St. Paulin
		Firm	Daylesford, Ridder

WINE	Rosé	CHEESE	
Characteristics:		Soft	St. André, Montenebro
Light, sweet, fruity		Semi-soft	Basato
		Firm	Sharp Cheddar, Botano
		Hard	Romano Vacchino

WINE Rosé Rioja	CHEESE	
Characteristics:	Fresh	Brocciu
Light, semi-dry, fruity	Soft	Pave d'Affinois, Montenebro
	Semi-soft	Oaxaca, Cana de Cabra
	Firm	Roncal

WINE Steuben	CHEESE	
Characteristics:	Fresh	Mascarpone
Light, semi-dry, fruity, spicy, nutty	Soft	Azeitão, Cabécou Feuille, Epoisses
	Semi-soft	Beaufort, Chalosse, Bel Paese
	Firm	Lappi, Gouda
	Hard	
	Blue	

WINE White Merlot	CHEESE	
Characteristics:	Fresh	Cream Cheese
Medium body, semi-dry, fruity, spicy	Soft	Selles-sur-Cher, Red Hawk, Banon
	Semi-soft	Butterkäse, Samsø, Blarney, Chaubier
	Firm	Podhalanski, Abbaye de Belloc
	Hard	Parm Dolce, Beaufort Alpage, Panache d'Aramits

WINE White Zinfandel	CHEESE	
Characteristics:	Soft	Banon, Feta, Humboldt Fog, Mt. Tam
Light, dry, fruity spicy	Semi-soft	Gaddost, Münster, Rochefort Montague, Brick
	Firm	Alverca, Gouda, Midnight Moon, Sally Jackson's Sheep, Asiago
	Hard	Ubriaco

WINE	CHEESE	
Characteristics:	Fresh	
	Soft	
	Semi-soft	
	Firm	
	Hard	
	Blue	

WINE	CHEESE	
Characteristics:	Fresh	
	Soft	
	Semi-soft	
	Firm	
	Hard	
	Blue	

DESSERT WINES

"Good wine is a good familar creature if it be well used."

—William Shakespeare

WINE Commandaria	CHEESE	
Characteristics:	Soft	Paneer, Pierre Robert
Bold, sweet, fruity, cloudy	Firm	Lappi

WINE Banyuls	CHEESE	
Characteristics:	Soft	Cabicou, Lumiere
Bold, sweet, spicy	Semi-soft	Fourme d'Ambert
	Firm	Liedcester
	Blue	Gorgonzola, Bleu de Gex, Bleu de Causses

WINE Hard Cider	CHEESE	
Characteristics:	Soft	Livarot, Maroilles
Bold, sweet, fruity	Semi-soft	Gamonedo, Münster
	Firm	Lappi, Botana
	Hard	Pepper Jack, Pepato
	Blue	Cabrales

WINE Icewine / Eiswein	CHEESE	
Characteristics:	Soft	Nocturne, Liederkranz
Bold, sweet, fruity, nutty, smooth	Semi-soft	Appenzeller, Bonbel, Limburger
	Firm	Ouray, Abertam, Bella Sorella, Caram, Asiago
	Hard	Parmesan
	Blue	Gorgonzola Dolce, Stilton, Cabrales

WINE Late Harvest Riesling	CHEESE	
Characteristics:	Fresh	Mascarpone
Bold, sweet, fruity	Soft	Gratte-Paille, Poudre Puff
	Semi-soft	Butterkäse, Caerphilly
	Firm	Abertam, Cheddar, Asiago
	Hard	Parmesan
	Blue	Roquefort, Saga Blue, Maytag Blue

WINE Madeira	CHEESE	
Characteristics:	Soft	Rabaçal
Bold, sweet to dry, toasty, nutty	Semi-soft	Pau Saut Maueu
	Firm	Sharp Cheddar, Double Gloucester, Asiago
	Hard	Romano Vacchino
	Blue	Bleu d'Auverge, Shropshire Blue

WINE Málaga	CHEESE	
Characteristics:	Soft	Boursault, Feta
Bold, sweet, silky	Semi-soft	Mt. Lassen, Gabietou, Leideche Kass
	Firm	Dubliner, Wensleydale
	Hard	Myzithra, Parmesan
	Blue	Gorgonzola, Maytag Blue

WINE Malvasia Bianca	CHEESE	
Characteristics:	Fresh	Crème Fraiche
Bold, sweet, fruity, complex	Soft	Mt. Tam, Raschera, Florette, Serpa
	Semi-soft	Aisy Cendré, Buche, Carmody
	Firm	Abertam, Boerenkaas, Mimolette
	Hard	Parmesan, Myzithra
	Blue	Roquefort, Picon, Pt. Reyes Blue

WINE Marsala	CHEESE	
Characteristics:	Fresh	Mascarpone
Bold, sweet, fruity	Soft	Banon
	Semi-soft	Bel Paese
	Firm	Cheddar, Ricotta Salada
	Hard	Pecorino Romano, Parmesan
	Blue	Gorgonzala, Roquefort

WINE Mead	CHEESE	
Characteristics:	Soft	Maroilles, Valençay, Liederkranz
Light, sweet, fruity, aromatic, honey	Semi-soft	St. Nectaire, Pau Saut Maueu
	Firm	Tête de Moine
	Hard	Kefalograviera, Vaesterbottenost
	Blue	Humboldt Fog, Picon

WINE Muscat / Muscat Canelli	CHEESE	
Characteristics:	Soft	Epoisses, Taleggio, Montenebro,
Medium body, very dry to sweet, intensly		Maroilles, Camembert
fruity and floral	Semi-soft	Ardrahan, Langres, Farmers, Morbier
	Firm	Asiago, Garrotxa, Cheddar
	Hard	Dry Jack
	Blue	Bucheret, Bayley Hazen Blue

WINE Pedro Ximenez / PX	CHEESE	
Characteristics:	Soft	Tetilla, Nevat, Queso Cabrero
Bold, sweet, buttery, fruity	Semi-soft	Ossau-Iraty, Oaxaca, Urgelia
	Firm	Cotija, Ricotta Salata, Iberico, Graviera
	Hard	Crockhamdale, Salers
	Blue	Saga Blue, Cabrales, Cambozola

WINE	Port	CHEESE	
Characteristics:		Soft	Queso Cabrero, Serpa, Schloss
Bold, sweet, fruity		Semi-soft	Langres, Caerphilly, Ossau-Iraty
		Firm	Colby, Cotswold, Asiago, Swiss
		Hard	Grana Padano, Parmesan
		Blue	Fourme d'Ambert, Stilton, Pt. Reyes Blue, Great Hill Blue

WINE	Ravat	CHEESE	
Characteristics:		Fresh	Crescenza
Light, crisp, semi-dry, fruity		Soft	Pierre Robert, Rabaçal, Capra
		Semi-soft	San Andreas, Rochefort Montague
		Firm	Sonoma Jack, Vermont Shepherd
		Hard	Panache d'Aramits
		Blue	Roquefort, Blue Brie, Blue Castello

WINE	Sangria	CHEESE	
Characteristics:		Soft	Shepherd's Wheel, Cabécou Feuille
Medium body, semi-dry, fruity, spicy		Semi-soft	Oka, Chaubier
		Firm	Añejo Enchilato, Asadero, Cotija
		Hard	Sardo, Zamarano
		Blue	Crozier Blue, Cashell Blue

WINE	Sauternes	CHEESE	
Characteristics:		Fresh	Mascarpone
Bold, sweet, fruity, honey, smooth, creamy		Soft	Epoisses, Hollandse Chèvre, Nevat
		Semi-soft	Sottocenere, Comté, Cana de Oveja
		Firm	Sonoma Jack, Serena, Tilsit, Postel
		Hard	St. Maure, Ubriaco, Pachina
		Blue	Beenleigh Blue, Roquefort, Saga Blue

WINE	Sherry	CHEESE	
Characteristics:		Fresh	Crème Frâiche
Bold, sweet to dry, fruity		Soft	Brie, Manouri, Schloss, Tetila
		Semi-soft	Tome d'Aquitain, Clisson, Majorero
		Firm	Alpine Shepherd, Berkswell, Mahón
		Hard	Dry Jack, Zamarano
		Blue	La Peral, Pt. Reyes Blue, Cabrales

WINE	Tawny Port	CHEESE	
Characteristics:		Fresh	Etorki
Bold, sweet, nutty, caramel, buttery		Soft	Mt. Tam, Pouligny-St. Pierre, Le Roule
		Semi-soft	Valderon, Durrus, Idiazábal
		Firm	Gouda, Gloucester, Montasio, Ouray
		Hard	Pecorino Romano, Myzithra
		Blue	Stilton, Crozier Blue, Shropshire Blue

WINE Tokaji / Tokay	CHEESE	
Characteristics:	Soft	Liverot, Montenebro, Camellia
Bold, sweet, fruity, balanced	Semi-soft	Beaufort, Hoch Ybrig, Clisson
	Firm	Mimolette, Dubliner, Wensleydale
	Hard	Beaufort Alpage
	Blue	Beenleigh Blue, Cashel Blue, Saga Blue

WINE Vin Santo	CHEESE	
Characteristics:	Soft	Boucheron
Bold, sweet to dry, smooth, intense	Semi-soft	Pau Saut Maueu, Dubbeen, Basato
	Firm	Boerenkaas, Jarlsberg, Bermuda Triangle
	Hard	Fribourg, Piave
	Blue	Bayley Hazen Blue, Bresse Blue

WINE	CHEESE
Characteristics:	Fresh
	Soft
	Semi-soft
	Firm
	Hard
	Blue

WINE	CHEESE
Characteristics:	Fresh
	Soft
	Semi-soft
	Firm
	Hard
	Blue

WINE	CHEESE
Characteristics:	Fresh
	Soft
	Semi-soft
	Firm
	Hard
	Blue

WINE	CHEESE
Characteristics:	Fresh
	Soft
	Semi-soft
	Firm
	Hard
	Blue

CHAMPAGNE & SPARKLING WINES

"In water one sees one's own face; but in wine, one beholds the heart of another."

—French Proverb

WINE Asti Spumanti	CHEESE	
Characteristics:	Soft	Camembert, Chaumes, Manouri, Capra
Light to bold, crisp, doux to sec,	Semi-soft	Esrom, Baby Swiss, Bel Paese
fruity, slightly sparkling	Firm	Cotija, Carmela, Oszczypek
	Hard	Parmesan
	Blue	La Peral

WINE Blanc de Blancs	CHEESE	
Characteristics:	Soft	Pierre Robert, Brie, Tomini
Light, extra-dry to brut, made from	Semi-soft	Chalosse, Blarney, Durrus
Chardonnay grapes	Firm	Alverca, Dubliner, Vignerons
	Hard	Crockhamdale
	Blue	Danish Blue

WINE Blanc de Noirs	CHEESE	
Characteristics:	Soft	Epoisses, Pierce Point, Mutton
Light, extra-dry to brut, made from red or		Button, Pierre Robert
black grapes, usually Pinot Noir & Pinot	Semi-soft	Provolone, Damski, Ibores, Beaufort
Meunier	Firm	Montasio, Dubliner, Jarlsberg
	Hard	Serena, Beaufort Alpage
	Blue	Bleu de Gex, Beenleigh blue

WINE Champagne	CHEESE	
Characteristics:	Fresh	Mascarpone, Cream Cheese
Light, extra-dry to natural brut, crisp	Soft	Chèvre, Vacherin, Camembert, Brie
	Semi-soft	Buche, Clisson, Colby, Edam
	Firm	Garrotxa, Cheddar, Alpine Shepherd
	Hard	Pleasant Ridge Reserve, Dry Jack
	Blue	Gorgonzola Dolce, Stilton, Roquefort

WINE Crémant	CHEESE	
Characteristics:	Fresh	Mascarpone
Light, extra-dry, fruity	Soft	Brillat Savarin, Camellia, Rougette
	Semi-soft	Majero, Crottin, Danbo, Farmers
	Firm	Asadero, Bella Sorella, Coolea
	Hard	Sardo, Myzithra, Sap Sago
	Blue	Blue Castello

WINE Prosecco	CHEESE	
Characteristics:	Soft	Shepherd's Wheel, Kiku, Brie
Light, demi-sec to sec, gentle, aromas of	Semi-soft	Majorero, Lincolnshire Poacher
almonds, apples, and pears	Firm	Ridder, Pecorino, Jarlsberg
	Hard	Parm Dolce

WINE Sparkling Brut	CHEESE	
Characteristics:	Soft	Nocturne, Camembert, Mt. Tam,
Light, brut, fruity		St. André, Chaumes, Pierre Robert
	Semi-soft	Edam, Fleur de Teche, Morbier
	Firm	Serena, Colby
	Hard	Spenwood
	Blue	Bresse Blue

WINE Sparkling Shiraz	CHEESE	
Characteristics:	Soft	Pave d'Affinois, Brie, Pierre Robert
Light, demi-sec to extra-dry, fruity,	Semi-soft	Bel Paese, Baby Swiss, Hollandse
floral, deep red to black		Chèvre
	Firm	Ouray, Montasio
	Hard	Beaufort Alpage
	Blue	Bayley Hazen Blue

WINE Sparkling Soave	CHEESE	
Characteristics:	Soft	Boursault, Rougette, Chaource,
Light, doux to sec, fruity,		Excelsior, Explorateur, St. André
	Semi-soft	Pachina, Père Joseph, Blarney
	Firm	Sebastian, Raclette
	Hard	Grana Padano
	Blue	Bergere Blue, Pt. Reyes Blue

WINE	CHEESE
Characteristics:	Fresh
	Soft
	Semi-soft
	Firm
	Hard
	Blue

WINE	CHEESE
Characteristics:	Fresh
	Soft
	Semi-soft
	Firm
	Hard
	Blue

WINE	CHEESE
Characteristics:	Fresh
	Soft
	Semi-soft
	Firm
	Hard
	Blue

"My Favorite Pairings" Journal

The major theme of your quest for perfect pairings is to **experiment, observe,** and **remember**. Once you have discovered a pairing that is in contention for your "ultimate Wow!" you should write it down for future reference. It's a good idea to keep a journal record of all your successful pairings so you can repeat them for yourself and your guests.

By the way, you may also want to record your not-so-great combinations that you don't want to repeat.

To help you remember your experiments and observations, we include in this book the following two programmed journals for you to use to record the pertinent details about (1) your best pairings ("My Favorite Pairings" Journal) and (2) your unsatisfactory combinations ("Oops! I Won't Pair These Again" Journal).

Cheese: _____ Wine: _____
Manufacturer: _____ Winery: _____
Appellation: _____
☐ Soft   ☐ Creamy   Vintage: _____
☐ Semi-soft ☐ Crumbly   Cost: _____
☐ Firm   ☐ Young   ☐ White
☐ Hard   ☐ Aged   ☐ Red   ☐ Dessert
☐ Salt brined ☐ Blue   ☐ Rosé   ☐ Sparkling
☐ Triple cream ☐ Fresh
Nose (Aroma & Bouquet): _____
Milk: ☐ Cow ☐ Goat ☐ Sheep
Comments: _____ Flavor: _____
_____ Balance: _____
_____ Finish: _____
Date: By: Comments:

Cheese: _____ Wine: _____
Manufacturer: _____ Winery: _____
Appellation: _____
☐ Soft   ☐ Creamy   Vintage: _____
☐ Semi-soft ☐ Crumbly   Cost: _____
☐ Firm   ☐ Young   ☐ White
☐ Hard   ☐ Aged   ☐ Red   ☐ Dessert
☐ Salt brined ☐ Blue   ☐ Rosé   ☐ Sparkling
☐ Triple cream ☐ Fresh
Nose (Aroma & Bouquet): _____
Milk: ☐ Cow ☐ Goat ☐ Sheep
Comments: _____ Flavor: _____
_____ Balance: _____
_____ Finish: _____
Date: By: Comments:

Cheese: _____ Wine: _____
Manufacturer: _____ Winery: _____
Appellation: _____
☐ Soft   ☐ Creamy   Vintage: _____
☐ Semi-soft ☐ Crumbly   Cost: _____
☐ Firm   ☐ Young   ☐ White
☐ Hard   ☐ Aged   ☐ Red   ☐ Dessert
☐ Salt brined ☐ Blue   ☐ Rosé   ☐ Sparkling
☐ Triple cream ☐ Fresh
Nose (Aroma & Bouquet): _____
Milk: ☐ Cow ☐ Goat ☐ Sheep
Comments: _____ Flavor: _____
_____ Balance: _____
_____ Finish: _____
Date: By: Comments:

Cheese: _____

Manufacturer: _____

☐ Soft ☐ Creamy
☐ Semi-soft ☐ Crumbly
☐ Firm ☐ Young
☐ Hard ☐ Aged
☐ Salt brined ☐ Blue
☐ Triple cream ☐ Fresh

Milk: ☐ Cow ☐ Goat ☐ Sheep

Comments: _____
_____
_____

Date: By:

Wine: _____

Winery: _____

Appellation: _____

Vintage: _____

Cost: _____

☐ White
☐ Red ☐ Dessert
☐ Rosé ☐ Sparkling

Nose (Aroma & Bouquet): _____
_____

Flavor: _____

Balance: _____

Finish: _____

Comments:

Cheese: _____

Manufacturer: _____

☐ Soft ☐ Creamy
☐ Semi-soft ☐ Crumbly
☐ Firm ☐ Young
☐ Hard ☐ Aged
☐ Salt brined ☐ Blue
☐ Triple cream ☐ Fresh

Milk: ☐ Cow ☐ Goat ☐ Sheep

Comments: _____
_____
_____

Date: By:

Wine: _____

Winery: _____

Appellation: _____

Vintage: _____

Cost: _____

☐ White
☐ Red ☐ Dessert
☐ Rosé ☐ Sparkling

Nose (Aroma & Bouquet): _____
_____

Flavor: _____

Balance: _____

Finish: _____

Comments:

Cheese: _____

Manufacturer: _____

☐ Soft ☐ Creamy
☐ Semi-soft ☐ Crumbly
☐ Firm ☐ Young
☐ Hard ☐ Aged
☐ Salt brined ☐ Blue
☐ Triple cream ☐ Fresh

Milk: ☐ Cow ☐ Goat ☐ Sheep

Comments: _____
_____
_____

Date: By:

Wine: _____

Winery: _____

Appellation: _____

Vintage: _____

Cost: _____

☐ White
☐ Red ☐ Dessert
☐ Rosé ☐ Sparkling

Nose (Aroma & Bouquet): _____
_____

Flavor: _____

Balance: _____

Finish: _____

Comments:

Cheese: _____
Manufacturer: _____

☐ Soft ☐ Creamy
☐ Semi-soft ☐ Crumbly
☐ Firm ☐ Young
☐ Hard ☐ Aged
☐ Salt brined ☐ Blue
☐ Triple cream ☐ Fresh

Milk: ☐ Cow ☐ Goat ☐ Sheep

Comments: _____
_____
_____
Date: By:

Wine: _____
Winery: _____
Appellation: _____
Vintage: _____
Cost: _____
☐ White
☐ Red ☐ Dessert
☐ Rosé ☐ Sparkling

Nose (Aroma & Bouquet): _____

Flavor: _____
Balance: _____
Finish: _____
Comments:

Cheese: _____
Manufacturer: _____

☐ Soft ☐ Creamy
☐ Semi-soft ☐ Crumbly
☐ Firm ☐ Young
☐ Hard ☐ Aged
☐ Salt brined ☐ Blue
☐ Triple cream ☐ Fresh

Milk: ☐ Cow ☐ Goat ☐ Sheep

Comments: _____
_____
_____
Date: By:

Wine: _____
Winery: _____
Appellation: _____
Vintage: _____
Cost: _____
☐ White
☐ Red ☐ Dessert
☐ Rosé ☐ Sparkling

Nose (Aroma & Bouquet): _____

Flavor: _____
Balance: _____
Finish: _____
Comments:

Cheese: _____
Manufacturer: _____

☐ Soft ☐ Creamy
☐ Semi-soft ☐ Crumbly
☐ Firm ☐ Young
☐ Hard ☐ Aged
☐ Salt brined ☐ Blue
☐ Triple cream ☐ Fresh

Milk: ☐ Cow ☐ Goat ☐ Sheep

Comments: _____
_____
_____
Date: By:

Wine: _____
Winery: _____
Appellation: _____
Vintage: _____
Cost: _____
☐ White
☐ Red ☐ Dessert
☐ Rosé ☐ Sparkling

Nose (Aroma & Bouquet): _____

Flavor: _____
Balance: _____
Finish: _____
Comments:

Cheese: _____
Manufacturer: _____

☐ Soft   ☐ Creamy
☐ Semi-soft   ☐ Crumbly
☐ Firm   ☐ Young
☐ Hard   ☐ Aged
☐ Salt brined ☐ Blue
☐ Triple cream ☐ Fresh

Milk: ☐ Cow   ☐ Goat   ☐ Sheep

Comments: _____
_____
_____

Date: By:

Wine: _____
Winery: _____
Appellation: _____
Vintage: _____
Cost: _____
☐ White
☐ Red   ☐ Dessert
☐ Rosé   ☐ Sparkling

Nose (Aroma & Bouquet): _____
_____
Flavor: _____
Balance: _____
Finish: _____
Comments:

Cheese: _____
Manufacturer: _____

☐ Soft   ☐ Creamy
☐ Semi-soft   ☐ Crumbly
☐ Firm   ☐ Young
☐ Hard   ☐ Aged
☐ Salt brined ☐ Blue
☐ Triple cream ☐ Fresh

Milk: ☐ Cow   ☐ Goat   ☐ Sheep

Comments: _____
_____
_____

Date: By:

Wine: _____
Winery: _____
Appellation: _____
Vintage: _____
Cost: _____
☐ White
☐ Red   ☐ Dessert
☐ Rosé   ☐ Sparkling

Nose (Aroma & Bouquet): _____
_____
Flavor: _____
Balance: _____
Finish: _____
Comments:

Cheese: _____
Manufacturer: _____

☐ Soft   ☐ Creamy
☐ Semi-soft   ☐ Crumbly
☐ Firm   ☐ Young
☐ Hard   ☐ Aged
☐ Salt brined ☐ Blue
☐ Triple cream ☐ Fresh

Milk: ☐ Cow   ☐ Goat   ☐ Sheep

Comments: _____
_____
_____

Date: By:

Wine: _____
Winery: _____
Appellation: _____
Vintage: _____
Cost: _____
☐ White
☐ Red   ☐ Dessert
☐ Rosé   ☐ Sparkling

Nose (Aroma & Bouquet): _____
_____
Flavor: _____
Balance: _____
Finish: _____
Comments:

Cheese: _____ Wine: _____
Manufacturer: _____ Winery: _____
                                  Appellation: _____
☐ Soft   ☐ Creamy   Vintage: _____
☐ Semi-soft   ☐ Crumbly   Cost: _____
☐ Firm   ☐ Young
☐ Hard   ☐ Aged   ☐ White
☐ Salt brined   ☐ Blue   ☐ Red   ☐ Dessert
☐ Triple cream ☐ Fresh   ☐ Rosé   ☐ Sparkling

Milk: ☐ Cow   ☐ Goat   ☐ Sheep   Nose (Aroma & Bouquet): _____
                                  _____
Comments: _____   Flavor: _____
_____   Balance: _____
_____   Finish: _____
Date: By: Comments:

Cheese: _____ Wine: _____
Manufacturer: _____ Winery: _____
                                  Appellation: _____
☐ Soft   ☐ Creamy   Vintage: _____
☐ Semi-soft   ☐ Crumbly   Cost: _____
☐ Firm   ☐ Young
☐ Hard   ☐ Aged   ☐ White
☐ Salt brined   ☐ Blue   ☐ Red   ☐ Dessert
☐ Triple cream ☐ Fresh   ☐ Rosé   ☐ Sparkling

Milk: ☐ Cow   ☐ Goat   ☐ Sheep   Nose (Aroma & Bouquet): _____
                                  _____
Comments: _____   Flavor: _____
_____   Balance: _____
_____   Finish: _____
Date: By: Comments:

Cheese: _____ Wine: _____
Manufacturer: _____ Winery: _____
                                  Appellation: _____
☐ Soft   ☐ Creamy   Vintage: _____
☐ Semi-soft   ☐ Crumbly   Cost: _____
☐ Firm   ☐ Young
☐ Hard   ☐ Aged   ☐ White
☐ Salt brined   ☐ Blue   ☐ Red   ☐ Dessert
☐ Triple cream ☐ Fresh   ☐ Rosé   ☐ Sparkling

Milk: ☐ Cow   ☐ Goat   ☐ Sheep   Nose (Aroma & Bouquet): _____
                                  _____
Comments: _____   Flavor: _____
_____   Balance: _____
_____   Finish: _____
Date: By: Comments:

Cheese: _____
Manufacturer: _____

- ☐ Soft
- ☐ Semi-soft
- ☐ Firm
- ☐ Hard
- ☐ Salt brined
- ☐ Triple cream

- ☐ Creamy
- ☐ Crumbly
- ☐ Young
- ☐ Aged
- ☐ Blue
- ☐ Fresh

Milk: ☐ Cow   ☐ Goat   ☐ Sheep

Comments: _____
_____
_____

Date: _____   By: _____

Wine: _____
Winery: _____
Appellation: _____
Vintage: _____
Cost: _____

- ☐ White
- ☐ Red
- ☐ Rosé

- ☐ Dessert
- ☐ Sparkling

Nose (Aroma & Bouquet): _____

Flavor: _____
Balance: _____
Finish: _____
Comments: _____

Cheese: _____
Manufacturer: _____

- ☐ Soft
- ☐ Semi-soft
- ☐ Firm
- ☐ Hard
- ☐ Salt brined
- ☐ Triple cream

- ☐ Creamy
- ☐ Crumbly
- ☐ Young
- ☐ Aged
- ☐ Blue
- ☐ Fresh

Milk: ☐ Cow   ☐ Goat   ☐ Sheep

Comments: _____
_____
_____

Date: _____   By: _____

Wine: _____
Winery: _____
Appellation: _____
Vintage: _____
Cost: _____

- ☐ White
- ☐ Red
- ☐ Rosé

- ☐ Dessert
- ☐ Sparkling

Nose (Aroma & Bouquet): _____

Flavor: _____
Balance: _____
Finish: _____
Comments: _____

Cheese: _____
Manufacturer: _____

- ☐ Soft
- ☐ Semi-soft
- ☐ Firm
- ☐ Hard
- ☐ Salt brined
- ☐ Triple cream

- ☐ Creamy
- ☐ Crumbly
- ☐ Young
- ☐ Aged
- ☐ Blue
- ☐ Fresh

Milk: ☐ Cow   ☐ Goat   ☐ Sheep

Comments: _____
_____
_____

Date: _____   By: _____

Wine: _____
Winery: _____
Appellation: _____
Vintage: _____
Cost: _____

- ☐ White
- ☐ Red
- ☐ Rosé

- ☐ Dessert
- ☐ Sparkling

Nose (Aroma & Bouquet): _____

Flavor: _____
Balance: _____
Finish: _____
Comments: _____

Cheese: _____ Wine: _____
Manufacturer: _____ Winery: _____
                                     Appellation: _____
☐ Soft   ☐ Creamy   Vintage: _____
☐ Semi-soft   ☐ Crumbly   Cost: _____
☐ Firm   ☐ Young   ☐ White
☐ Hard   ☐ Aged   ☐ Red   ☐ Dessert
☐ Salt brined   ☐ Blue   ☐ Rosé   ☐ Sparkling
☐ Triple cream ☐ Fresh
                                     Nose (Aroma & Bouquet): _____
Milk: ☐ Cow ☐ Goat ☐ Sheep   _____

Comments: _____ Flavor: _____
_____ Balance: _____
_____ Finish: _____
 Date: By: Comments:

Cheese: _____ Wine: _____
Manufacturer: _____ Winery: _____
                                     Appellation: _____
☐ Soft   ☐ Creamy   Vintage: _____
☐ Semi-soft   ☐ Crumbly   Cost: _____
☐ Firm   ☐ Young   ☐ White
☐ Hard   ☐ Aged   ☐ Red   ☐ Dessert
☐ Salt brined   ☐ Blue   ☐ Rosé   ☐ Sparkling
☐ Triple cream ☐ Fresh
                                     Nose (Aroma & Bouquet): _____
Milk: ☐ Cow ☐ Goat ☐ Sheep   _____

Comments: _____ Flavor: _____
_____ Balance: _____
_____ Finish: _____
 Date: By: Comments:

Cheese: _____ Wine: _____
Manufacturer: _____ Winery: _____
                                     Appellation: _____
☐ Soft   ☐ Creamy   Vintage: _____
☐ Semi-soft   ☐ Crumbly   Cost: _____
☐ Firm   ☐ Young   ☐ White
☐ Hard   ☐ Aged   ☐ Red   ☐ Dessert
☐ Salt brined   ☐ Blue   ☐ Rosé   ☐ Sparkling
☐ Triple cream ☐ Fresh
                                     Nose (Aroma & Bouquet): _____
Milk: ☐ Cow ☐ Goat ☐ Sheep   _____

Comments: _____ Flavor: _____
_____ Balance: _____
_____ Finish: _____
 Date: By: Comments:

Cheese: _____ Wine: _____
Manufacturer: _____ Winery: _____
                                 Appellation: _____
☐ Soft   ☐ Creamy   Vintage: _____
☐ Semi-soft   ☐ Crumbly   Cost: _____
☐ Firm   ☐ Young   ☐ White
☐ Hard   ☐ Aged   ☐ Red   ☐ Dessert
☐ Salt brined   ☐ Blue   ☐ Rosé   ☐ Sparkling
☐ Triple cream ☐ Fresh
                                 Nose (Aroma & Bouquet): _____
Milk: ☐ Cow ☐ Goat ☐ Sheep   _____

Comments: _____   Flavor: _____
_____   Balance: _____
_____   Finish: _____
Date: _____ By: ____   Comments:

Cheese: _____ Wine: _____
Manufacturer: _____ Winery: _____
                                 Appellation: _____
☐ Soft   ☐ Creamy   Vintage: _____
☐ Semi-soft   ☐ Crumbly   Cost: _____
☐ Firm   ☐ Young   ☐ White
☐ Hard   ☐ Aged   ☐ Red   ☐ Dessert
☐ Salt brined   ☐ Blue   ☐ Rosé   ☐ Sparkling
☐ Triple cream ☐ Fresh
                                 Nose (Aroma & Bouquet): _____
Milk: ☐ Cow ☐ Goat ☐ Sheep   _____

Comments: _____   Flavor: _____
_____   Balance: _____
_____   Finish: _____
Date: _____ By: ____   Comments:

Cheese: _____ Wine: _____
Manufacturer: _____ Winery: _____
                                 Appellation: _____
☐ Soft   ☐ Creamy   Vintage: _____
☐ Semi-soft   ☐ Crumbly   Cost: _____
☐ Firm   ☐ Young   ☐ White
☐ Hard   ☐ Aged   ☐ Red   ☐ Dessert
☐ Salt brined   ☐ Blue   ☐ Rosé   ☐ Sparkling
☐ Triple cream ☐ Fresh
                                 Nose (Aroma & Bouquet): _____
Milk: ☐ Cow ☐ Goat ☐ Sheep   _____

Comments: _____   Flavor: _____
_____   Balance: _____
_____   Finish: _____
Date: _____ By: ____   Comments:

Cheese: _____
Manufacturer: _____

☐ Soft ☐ Creamy
☐ Semi-soft ☐ Crumbly
☐ Firm ☐ Young
☐ Hard ☐ Aged
☐ Salt brined ☐ Blue
☐ Triple cream ☐ Fresh

Milk: ☐ Cow ☐ Goat ☐ Sheep

Comments: _____
_____
_____
Date: By:

Wine: _____
Winery: _____
Appellation: _____
Vintage: _____
Cost: _____
☐ White
☐ Red ☐ Dessert
☐ Rosé ☐ Sparkling

Nose (Aroma & Bouquet): _____
_____
Flavor: _____
Balance: _____
Finish: _____
Comments:

Cheese: _____
Manufacturer: _____

☐ Soft ☐ Creamy
☐ Semi-soft ☐ Crumbly
☐ Firm ☐ Young
☐ Hard ☐ Aged
☐ Salt brined ☐ Blue
☐ Triple cream ☐ Fresh

Milk: ☐ Cow ☐ Goat ☐ Sheep

Comments: _____
_____
_____
Date: By:

Wine: _____
Winery: _____
Appellation: _____
Vintage: _____
Cost: _____
☐ White
☐ Red ☐ Dessert
☐ Rosé ☐ Sparkling

Nose (Aroma & Bouquet): _____
_____
Flavor: _____
Balance: _____
Finish: _____
Comments:

Cheese: _____
Manufacturer: _____

☐ Soft ☐ Creamy
☐ Semi-soft ☐ Crumbly
☐ Firm ☐ Young
☐ Hard ☐ Aged
☐ Salt brined ☐ Blue
☐ Triple cream ☐ Fresh

Milk: ☐ Cow ☐ Goat ☐ Sheep

Comments: _____
_____
_____
Date: By:

Wine: _____
Winery: _____
Appellation: _____
Vintage: _____
Cost: _____
☐ White
☐ Red ☐ Dessert
☐ Rosé ☐ Sparkling

Nose (Aroma & Bouquet): _____
_____
Flavor: _____
Balance: _____
Finish: _____
Comments:

Cheese: _____ Wine: _____
Manufacturer: _____ Winery: _____
                                 Appellation: _____
☐ Soft   ☐ Creamy   Vintage: _____
☐ Semi-soft   ☐ Crumbly   Cost: _____
☐ Firm   ☐ Young
☐ Hard   ☐ Aged   ☐ White
☐ Salt brined ☐ Blue   ☐ Red   ☐ Dessert
☐ Triple cream ☐ Fresh   ☐ Rosé   ☐ Sparkling

Milk: ☐ Cow ☐ Goat ☐ Sheep   Nose (Aroma & Bouquet): _____

Comments: _____   Flavor: _____
_____ Balance: _____
_____ Finish: _____
Date: By: Comments:

Cheese: _____ Wine: _____
Manufacturer: _____ Winery: _____
                                 Appellation: _____
☐ Soft   ☐ Creamy   Vintage: _____
☐ Semi-soft   ☐ Crumbly   Cost: _____
☐ Firm   ☐ Young
☐ Hard   ☐ Aged   ☐ White
☐ Salt brined ☐ Blue   ☐ Red   ☐ Dessert
☐ Triple cream ☐ Fresh   ☐ Rosé   ☐ Sparkling

Milk: ☐ Cow ☐ Goat ☐ Sheep   Nose (Aroma & Bouquet): _____

Comments: _____   Flavor: _____
_____ Balance: _____
_____ Finish: _____
Date: By: Comments:

Cheese: _____ Wine: _____
Manufacturer: _____ Winery: _____
                                 Appellation: _____
☐ Soft   ☐ Creamy   Vintage: _____
☐ Semi-soft   ☐ Crumbly   Cost: _____
☐ Firm   ☐ Young
☐ Hard   ☐ Aged   ☐ White
☐ Salt brined ☐ Blue   ☐ Red   ☐ Dessert
☐ Triple cream ☐ Fresh   ☐ Rosé   ☐ Sparkling

Milk: ☐ Cow ☐ Goat ☐ Sheep   Nose (Aroma & Bouquet): _____

Comments: _____   Flavor: _____
_____ Balance: _____
_____ Finish: _____
Date: By: Comments:

Cheese: _____ Wine: _____
Manufacturer: _____ Winery: _____
                                  Appellation: _____
☐ Soft   ☐ Creamy   Vintage: _____
☐ Semi-soft   ☐ Crumbly   Cost: _____
☐ Firm   ☐ Young
☐ Hard   ☐ Aged   ☐ White
☐ Salt brined   ☐ Blue   ☐ Red   ☐ Dessert
☐ Triple cream ☐ Fresh   ☐ Rosé   ☐ Sparkling

Milk: ☐ Cow ☐ Goat ☐ Sheep   Nose (Aroma & Bouquet): _____

Comments: _____   Flavor: _____
_____   Balance: _____
_____   Finish: _____
Date: By: Comments:

Cheese: _____ Wine: _____
Manufacturer: _____ Winery: _____
                                  Appellation: _____
☐ Soft   ☐ Creamy   Vintage: _____
☐ Semi-soft   ☐ Crumbly   Cost: _____
☐ Firm   ☐ Young
☐ Hard   ☐ Aged   ☐ White
☐ Salt brined   ☐ Blue   ☐ Red   ☐ Dessert
☐ Triple cream ☐ Fresh   ☐ Rosé   ☐ Sparkling

Milk: ☐ Cow ☐ Goat ☐ Sheep   Nose (Aroma & Bouquet): _____

Comments: _____   Flavor: _____
_____   Balance: _____
_____   Finish: _____
Date: By: Comments:

Cheese: _____ Wine: _____
Manufacturer: _____ Winery: _____
                                  Appellation: _____
☐ Soft   ☐ Creamy   Vintage: _____
☐ Semi-soft   ☐ Crumbly   Cost: _____
☐ Firm   ☐ Young
☐ Hard   ☐ Aged   ☐ White
☐ Salt brined   ☐ Blue   ☐ Red   ☐ Dessert
☐ Triple cream ☐ Fresh   ☐ Rosé   ☐ Sparkling

Milk: ☐ Cow ☐ Goat ☐ Sheep   Nose (Aroma & Bouquet): _____

Comments: _____   Flavor: _____
_____   Balance: _____
_____   Finish: _____
Date: By: Comments:

Cheese: _____
Manufacturer: _____

☐ Soft   ☐ Creamy
☐ Semi-soft   ☐ Crumbly
☐ Firm   ☐ Young
☐ Hard   ☐ Aged
☐ Salt brined   ☐ Blue
☐ Triple cream   ☐ Fresh

Milk: ☐ Cow   ☐ Goat   ☐ Sheep

Comments: _____
_____
_____

Date: By:

Wine: _____
Winery: _____
Appellation: _____
Vintage: _____
Cost: _____

☐ White
☐ Red   ☐ Dessert
☐ Rosé   ☐ Sparkling

Nose (Aroma & Bouquet): _____
_____

Flavor: _____
Balance: _____
Finish: _____
Comments:

Cheese: _____
Manufacturer: _____

☐ Soft   ☐ Creamy
☐ Semi-soft   ☐ Crumbly
☐ Firm   ☐ Young
☐ Hard   ☐ Aged
☐ Salt brined   ☐ Blue
☐ Triple cream   ☐ Fresh

Milk: ☐ Cow   ☐ Goat   ☐ Sheep

Comments: _____
_____
_____

Date: By:

Wine: _____
Winery: _____
Appellation: _____
Vintage: _____
Cost: _____

☐ White
☐ Red   ☐ Dessert
☐ Rosé   ☐ Sparkling

Nose (Aroma & Bouquet): _____
_____

Flavor: _____
Balance: _____
Finish: _____
Comments:

Cheese: _____
Manufacturer: _____

☐ Soft   ☐ Creamy
☐ Semi-soft   ☐ Crumbly
☐ Firm   ☐ Young
☐ Hard   ☐ Aged
☐ Salt brined   ☐ Blue
☐ Triple cream   ☐ Fresh

Milk: ☐ Cow   ☐ Goat   ☐ Sheep

Comments: _____
_____
_____

Date: By:

Wine: _____
Winery: _____
Appellation: _____
Vintage: _____
Cost: _____

☐ White
☐ Red   ☐ Dessert
☐ Rosé   ☐ Sparkling

Nose (Aroma & Bouquet): _____
_____

Flavor: _____
Balance: _____
Finish: _____
Comments:

Cheese: _____ Wine: _____
Manufacturer: _____ Winery: _____
                                  Appellation: _____
☐ Soft   ☐ Creamy   Vintage: _____
☐ Semi-soft   ☐ Crumbly   Cost: _____
☐ Firm   ☐ Young   ☐ White
☐ Hard   ☐ Aged   ☐ Red   ☐ Dessert
☐ Salt brined ☐ Blue   ☐ Rosé   ☐ Sparkling
☐ Triple cream ☐ Fresh
                                  Nose (Aroma & Bouquet): _____
Milk: ☐ Cow ☐ Goat ☐ Sheep

Comments: _____   Flavor: _____
_____   Balance: _____
_____   Finish: _____
Date: By: Comments:

Cheese: _____ Wine: _____
Manufacturer: _____ Winery: _____
                                  Appellation: _____
☐ Soft   ☐ Creamy   Vintage: _____
☐ Seml-soft   ☐ Crumbly   Cost: _____
☐ Firm   ☐ Young   ☐ White
☐ Hard   ☐ Aged   ☐ Red   ☐ Dessert
☐ Salt brined ☐ Blue   ☐ Rosé   ☐ Sparkling
☐ Triple cream ☐ Fresh
                                  Nose (Aroma & Bouquet): _____
Milk: ☐ Cow ☐ Goat ☐ Sheep

Comments: _____   Flavor: _____
_____   Balance: _____
_____   Finish: _____
Date: By: Comments:

Cheese: _____ Wine: _____
Manufacturer: _____ Winery: _____
                                  Appellation: _____
☐ Soft   ☐ Creamy   Vintage: _____
☐ Semi-soft   ☐ Crumbly   Cost: _____
☐ Firm   ☐ Young   ☐ White
☐ Hard   ☐ Aged   ☐ Red   ☐ Dessert
☐ Salt brined ☐ Blue   ☐ Rosé   ☐ Sparkling
☐ Triple cream ☐ Fresh
                                  Nose (Aroma & Bouquet): _____
Milk: ☐ Cow ☐ Goat ☐ Sheep

Comments: _____   Flavor: _____
_____   Balance: _____
_____   Finish: _____
Date: By: Comments:

Cheese: _____ Wine: _____

Manufacturer: _____ Winery: _____

Appellation: _____

- [ ] Soft [ ] Creamy
- [ ] Semi-soft [ ] Crumbly
- [ ] Firm [ ] Young
- [ ] Hard [ ] Aged
- [ ] Salt brined [ ] Blue
- [ ] Triple cream [ ] Fresh

Vintage: _____

Cost: _____

- [ ] White
- [ ] Red [ ] Dessert
- [ ] Rosé [ ] Sparkling

Milk: [ ] Cow [ ] Goat [ ] Sheep

Nose (Aroma & Bouquet): _____

Comments: _____

Flavor: _____

Balance: _____

Finish: _____

Date: By:

Comments:

Cheese: _____ Wine: _____

Manufacturer: _____ Winery: _____

Appellation: _____

- [ ] Soft [ ] Creamy
- [ ] Semi-soft [ ] Crumbly
- [ ] Firm [ ] Young
- [ ] Hard [ ] Aged
- [ ] Salt brined [ ] Blue
- [ ] Triple cream [ ] Fresh

Vintage: _____

Cost: _____

- [ ] White
- [ ] Red [ ] Dessert
- [ ] Rosé [ ] Sparkling

Milk: [ ] Cow [ ] Goat [ ] Sheep

Nose (Aroma & Bouquet): _____

Comments: _____

Flavor: _____

Balance: _____

Finish: _____

Date: By:

Comments:

Cheese: _____ Wine: _____

Manufacturer: _____ Winery: _____

Appellation: _____

- [ ] Soft [ ] Creamy
- [ ] Semi-soft [ ] Crumbly
- [ ] Firm [ ] Young
- [ ] Hard [ ] Aged
- [ ] Salt brined [ ] Blue
- [ ] Triple cream [ ] Fresh

Vintage: _____

Cost: _____

- [ ] White
- [ ] Red [ ] Dessert
- [ ] Rosé [ ] Sparkling

Milk: [ ] Cow [ ] Goat [ ] Sheep

Nose (Aroma & Bouquet): _____

Comments: _____

Flavor: _____

Balance: _____

Finish: _____

Date: By:

Comments:

Cheese: _____ Wine: _____
Manufacturer: _____ Winery: _____
                                 Appellation: _____
☐ Soft   ☐ Creamy   Vintage: _____
☐ Semi-soft   ☐ Crumbly   Cost: _____
☐ Firm   ☐ Young
☐ Hard   ☐ Aged   ☐ White
☐ Salt brined   ☐ Blue   ☐ Red   ☐ Dessert
☐ Triple cream ☐ Fresh   ☐ Rosé   ☐ Sparkling

Milk: ☐ Cow ☐ Goat ☐ Sheep   Nose (Aroma & Bouquet): _____

Comments: _____ Flavor: _____
_____ Balance: _____
                                 Finish: _____
Date: By: Comments:

Cheese: _____ Wine: _____
Manufacturer: _____ Winery: _____
                                 Appellation: _____
☐ Soft   ☐ Creamy   Vintage: _____
☐ Semi-soft   ☐ Crumbly   Cost: _____
☐ Firm   ☐ Young
☐ Hard   ☐ Aged   ☐ White
☐ Salt brined   ☐ Blue   ☐ Red   ☐ Dessert
☐ Triple cream ☐ Fresh   ☐ Rosé   ☐ Sparkling

Milk: ☐ Cow ☐ Goat ☐ Sheep   Nose (Aroma & Bouquet): _____

Comments: _____ Flavor: _____
_____ Balance: _____
                                 Finish: _____
Date: By: Comments:

Cheese: _____ Wine: _____
Manufacturer: _____ Winery: _____
                                 Appellation: _____
☐ Soft   ☐ Creamy   Vintage: _____
☐ Semi-soft   ☐ Crumbly   Cost: _____
☐ Firm   ☐ Young
☐ Hard   ☐ Aged   ☐ White
☐ Salt brined   ☐ Blue   ☐ Red   ☐ Dessert
☐ Triple cream ☐ Fresh   ☐ Rosé   ☐ Sparkling

Milk: ☐ Cow ☐ Goat ☐ Sheep   Nose (Aroma & Bouquet): _____

Comments: _____ Flavor: _____
_____ Balance: _____
                                 Finish: _____
Date: By: Comments:

Cheese: _____ Wine: _____
Manufacturer: _____ Winery: _____
                                 Appellation: _____
☐ Soft   ☐ Creamy   Vintage: _____
☐ Semi-soft   ☐ Crumbly   Cost: _____
☐ Firm   ☐ Young
☐ Hard   ☐ Aged   ☐ White
☐ Salt brined ☐ Blue   ☐ Red   ☐ Dessert
☐ Triple cream ☐ Fresh   ☐ Rosé   ☐ Sparkling

Milk: ☐ Cow ☐ Goat ☐ Sheep   Nose (Aroma & Bouquet): _____

Comments: _____   Flavor: _____
_____   Balance: _____
_____   Finish: _____
Date: By: Comments:

Cheese: _____ Wine: _____
Manufacturer: _____ Winery: _____
                                 Appellation: _____
☐ Soft   ☐ Creamy   Vintage: _____
☐ Semi-soft   ☐ Crumbly   Cost: _____
☐ Firm   ☐ Young
☐ Hard   ☐ Aged   ☐ White
☐ Salt brined ☐ Blue   ☐ Red   ☐ Dessert
☐ Triple cream ☐ Fresh   ☐ Rosé   ☐ Sparkling

Milk: ☐ Cow ☐ Goat ☐ Sheep   Nose (Aroma & Bouquet): _____

Comments: _____   Flavor: _____
_____   Balance: _____
_____   Finish: _____
Date: By: Comments:

Cheese: _____ Wine: _____
Manufacturer: _____ Winery: _____
                                 Appellation: _____
☐ Soft   ☐ Creamy   Vintage: _____
☐ Semi-soft   ☐ Crumbly   Cost: _____
☐ Firm   ☐ Young
☐ Hard   ☐ Aged   ☐ White
☐ Salt brined ☐ Blue   ☐ Red   ☐ Dessert
☐ Triple cream ☐ Fresh   ☐ Rosé   ☐ Sparkling

Milk: ☐ Cow ☐ Goat ☐ Sheep   Nose (Aroma & Bouquet): _____

Comments: _____   Flavor: _____
_____   Balance: _____
_____   Finish: _____
Date: By: Comments:

Cheese: _____
Manufacturer: _____

☐ Soft ☐ Creamy
☐ Semi-soft ☐ Crumbly
☐ Firm ☐ Young
☐ Hard ☐ Aged
☐ Salt brined ☐ Blue
☐ Triple cream ☐ Fresh

Milk: ☐ Cow ☐ Goat ☐ Sheep

Comments: _____
_____
_____
Date: By:

Wine: _____
Winery: _____
Appellation: _____
Vintage: _____
Cost: _____
☐ White
☐ Red ☐ Dessert
☐ Rosé ☐ Sparkling
Nose (Aroma & Bouquet): _____
_____
Flavor: _____
Balance: _____
Finish: _____
Comments:

Cheese: _____
Manufacturer: _____

☐ Soft ☐ Creamy
☐ Semi-soft ☐ Crumbly
☐ Firm ☐ Young
☐ Hard ☐ Aged
☐ Salt brined ☐ Blue
☐ Triple cream ☐ Fresh

Milk: ☐ Cow ☐ Goat ☐ Sheep

Comments: _____
_____
_____
Date: By:

Wine: _____
Winery: _____
Appellation: _____
Vintage: _____
Cost: _____
☐ White
☐ Red ☐ Dessert
☐ Rosé ☐ Sparkling
Nose (Aroma & Bouquet): _____
_____
Flavor: _____
Balance: _____
Finish: _____
Comments:

Cheese: _____
Manufacturer: _____

☐ Soft ☐ Creamy
☐ Semi-soft ☐ Crumbly
☐ Firm ☐ Young
☐ Hard ☐ Aged
☐ Salt brined ☐ Blue
☐ Triple cream ☐ Fresh

Milk: ☐ Cow ☐ Goat ☐ Sheep

Comments: _____
_____
_____
Date: By:

Wine: _____
Winery: _____
Appellation: _____
Vintage: _____
Cost: _____
☐ White
☐ Red ☐ Dessert
☐ Rosé ☐ Sparkling
Nose (Aroma & Bouquet): _____
_____
Flavor: _____
Balance: _____
Finish: _____
Comments:

Cheese: _____ Wine: _____
Manufacturer: _____ Winery: _____
                         Appellation: _____
☐ Soft   ☐ Creamy   Vintage: _____
☐ Semi-soft ☐ Crumbly   Cost: _____
☐ Firm   ☐ Young   ☐ White
☐ Hard   ☐ Aged   ☐ Red   ☐ Dessert
☐ Salt brined ☐ Blue   ☐ Rosé   ☐ Sparkling
☐ Triple cream ☐ Fresh
                         Nose (Aroma & Bouquet): _____
Milk: ☐ Cow ☐ Goat ☐ Sheep
                         Flavor: _____
Comments: _____ Balance: _____
_____ Finish: _____
Date: By: Comments:

Cheese: _____ Wine: _____
Manufacturer: _____ Winery: _____
                         Appellation: _____
☐ Soft   ☐ Creamy   Vintage: _____
☐ Semi-soft ☐ Crumbly   Cost: _____
☐ Firm   ☐ Young   ☐ White
☐ Hard   ☐ Aged   ☐ Red   ☐ Dessert
☐ Salt brined ☐ Blue   ☐ Rosé   ☐ Sparkling
☐ Triple cream ☐ Fresh
                         Nose (Aroma & Bouquet): _____
Milk: ☐ Cow ☐ Goat ☐ Sheep
                         Flavor: _____
Comments: _____ Balance: _____
_____ Finish: _____
Date: By: Comments:

Cheese: _____ Wine: _____
Manufacturer: _____ Winery: _____
                         Appellation: _____
☐ Soft   ☐ Creamy   Vintage: _____
☐ Semi-soft ☐ Crumbly   Cost: _____
☐ Firm   ☐ Young   ☐ White
☐ Hard   ☐ Aged   ☐ Red   ☐ Dessert
☐ Salt brined ☐ Blue   ☐ Rosé   ☐ Sparkling
☐ Triple cream ☐ Fresh
                         Nose (Aroma & Bouquet): _____
Milk: ☐ Cow ☐ Goat ☐ Sheep
                         Flavor: _____
Comments: _____ Balance: _____
_____ Finish: _____
Date: By: Comments:

Cheese: _____   Wine: _____
Manufacturer: _____   Winery: _____
                                    Appellation: _____
☐ Soft   ☐ Creamy   Vintage: _____
☐ Semi-soft   ☐ Crumbly   Cost: _____
☐ Firm   ☐ Young
☐ Hard   ☐ Aged   ☐ White
☐ Salt brined   ☐ Blue   ☐ Red   ☐ Dessert
☐ Triple cream ☐ Fresh   ☐ Rosé   ☐ Sparkling

Milk: ☐ Cow ☐ Goat ☐ Sheep   Nose (Aroma & Bouquet): _____

Comments: _____   Flavor: _____
_____   Balance: _____
_____   Finish: _____
Date: By: Comments:

Cheese: _____   Wine: _____
Manufacturer: _____   Winery: _____
                                    Appellation: _____
☐ Soft   ☐ Creamy   Vintage: _____
☐ Semi-soft   ☐ Crumbly   Cost: _____
☐ Firm   ☐ Young
☐ Hard   ☐ Aged   ☐ White
☐ Salt brined   ☐ Blue   ☐ Red   ☐ Dessert
☐ Triple cream ☐ Fresh   ☐ Rosé   ☐ Sparkling

Milk: ☐ Cow ☐ Goat ☐ Sheep   Nose (Aroma & Bouquet): _____

Comments: _____   Flavor: _____
_____   Balance: _____
_____   Finish: _____
Date: By: Comments:

Cheese: _____   Wine: _____
Manufacturer: _____   Winery: _____
                                    Appellation: _____
☐ Soft   ☐ Creamy   Vintage: _____
☐ Semi-soft   ☐ Crumbly   Cost: _____
☐ Firm   ☐ Young
☐ Hard   ☐ Aged   ☐ White
☐ Salt brined   ☐ Blue   ☐ Red   ☐ Dessert
☐ Triple cream ☐ Fresh   ☐ Rosé   ☐ Sparkling

Milk: ☐ Cow ☐ Goat ☐ Sheep   Nose (Aroma & Bouquet): _____

Comments: _____   Flavor: _____
_____   Balance: _____
_____   Finish: _____
Date: By: Comments:

Cheese: _____ Wine: _____
Manufacturer: _____ Winery: _____
                            Appellation: _____
☐ Soft   ☐ Creamy   Vintage: _____
☐ Semi-soft   ☐ Crumbly   Cost: _____
☐ Firm   ☐ Young   ☐ White
☐ Hard   ☐ Aged   ☐ Red   ☐ Dessert
☐ Salt brined ☐ Blue   ☐ Rosé   ☐ Sparkling
☐ Triple cream ☐ Fresh
                            Nose (Aroma & Bouquet): ____
Milk: ☐ Cow ☐ Goat ☐ Sheep
                            _____
Comments: _____ Flavor: _____
_____ Balance: _____
_____ Finish: _____
Date: By: Comments:

Cheese: _____ Wine: _____
Manufacturer: _____ Winery: _____
                            Appellation: _____
☐ Soft   ☐ Creamy   Vintage: _____
☐ Semi-soft   ☐ Crumbly   Cost: _____
☐ Firm   ☐ Young   ☐ White
☐ Hard   ☐ Aged   ☐ Red   ☐ Dessert
☐ Salt brined ☐ Blue   ☐ Rosé   ☐ Sparkling
☐ Triple cream ☐ Fresh
                            Nose (Aroma & Bouquet): ____
Milk: ☐ Cow ☐ Goat ☐ Sheep
                            _____
Comments: _____ Flavor: _____
_____ Balance: _____
_____ Finish: _____
Date: By: Comments:

Cheese: _____ Wine: _____
Manufacturer: _____ Winery: _____
                            Appellation: _____
☐ Soft   ☐ Creamy   Vintage: _____
☐ Semi-soft   ☐ Crumbly   Cost: _____
☐ Firm   ☐ Young   ☐ White
☐ Hard   ☐ Aged   ☐ Red   ☐ Dessert
☐ Salt brined ☐ Blue   ☐ Rosé   ☐ Sparkling
☐ Triple cream ☐ Fresh
                            Nose (Aroma & Bouquet): ____
Milk: ☐ Cow ☐ Goat ☐ Sheep
                            _____
Comments: _____ Flavor: _____
_____ Balance: _____
_____ Finish: _____
Date: By: Comments:

Cheese: _____   Wine: _____

Manufacturer: _____   Winery: _____

Appellation: _____

☐ Soft   ☐ Creamy   Vintage: _____

☐ Semi-soft   ☐ Crumbly   Cost: _____

☐ Firm   ☐ Young

☐ Hard   ☐ Aged   ☐ White

☐ Salt brined   ☐ Blue   ☐ Red   ☐ Dessert

☐ Triple cream   ☐ Fresh   ☐ Rosé   ☐ Sparkling

Milk: ☐ Cow   ☐ Goat   ☐ Sheep   Nose (Aroma & Bouquet): _____

Comments: _____   Flavor: _____

_____   Balance: _____

_____   Finish: _____

Date: _____ By: _____   Comments:

Cheese: _____   Wine: _____

Manufacturer: _____   Winery: _____

Appellation: _____

☐ Soft   ☐ Creamy   Vintage: _____

☐ Semi-soft   ☐ Crumbly   Cost: _____

☐ Firm   ☐ Young

☐ Hard   ☐ Aged   ☐ White

☐ Salt brined   ☐ Blue   ☐ Red   ☐ Dessert

☐ Triple cream   ☐ Fresh   ☐ Rosé   ☐ Sparkling

Milk: ☐ Cow   ☐ Goat   ☐ Sheep   Nose (Aroma & Bouquet): _____

Comments: _____   Flavor: _____

_____   Balance: _____

_____   Finish: _____

Date: _____ By: _____   Comments:

Cheese: _____   Wine: _____

Manufacturer: _____   Winery: _____

Appellation: _____

☐ Soft   ☐ Creamy   Vintage: _____

☐ Semi-soft   ☐ Crumbly   Cost: _____

☐ Firm   ☐ Young

☐ Hard   ☐ Aged   ☐ White

☐ Salt brined   ☐ Blue   ☐ Red   ☐ Dessert

☐ Triple cream   ☐ Fresh   ☐ Rosé   ☐ Sparkling

Milk: ☐ Cow   ☐ Goat   ☐ Sheep   Nose (Aroma & Bouquet): _____

Comments: _____   Flavor: _____

_____   Balance: _____

_____   Finish: _____

Date: _____ By: _____   Comments:

Cheese: _____
Manufacturer: _____

- ☐ Soft
- ☐ Semi-soft
- ☐ Firm
- ☐ Hard
- ☐ Salt brined
- ☐ Triple cream
- ☐ Creamy
- ☐ Crumbly
- ☐ Young
- ☐ Aged
- ☐ Blue
- ☐ Fresh

Milk: ☐ Cow ☐ Goat ☐ Sheep

Comments: _____
_____
_____

Date: _____ By: _____

Wine: _____
Winery: _____
Appellation: _____
Vintage: _____
Cost: _____

- ☐ White
- ☐ Red
- ☐ Rosé
- ☐ Dessert
- ☐ Sparkling

Nose (Aroma & Bouquet): _____
_____
Flavor: _____
Balance: _____
Finish: _____
Comments:

Cheese: _____
Manufacturer: _____

- ☐ Soft
- ☐ Semi-soft
- ☐ Firm
- ☐ Hard
- ☐ Salt brined
- ☐ Triple cream
- ☐ Creamy
- ☐ Crumbly
- ☐ Young
- ☐ Aged
- ☐ Blue
- ☐ Fresh

Milk: ☐ Cow ☐ Goat ☐ Sheep

Comments: _____
_____
_____

Date: _____ By: _____

Wine: _____
Winery: _____
Appellation: _____
Vintage: _____
Cost: _____

- ☐ White
- ☐ Red
- ☐ Rosé
- ☐ Dessert
- ☐ Sparkling

Nose (Aroma & Bouquet): _____
_____
Flavor: _____
Balance: _____
Finish: _____
Comments:

Cheese: _____
Manufacturer: _____

- ☐ Soft
- ☐ Semi-soft
- ☐ Firm
- ☐ Hard
- ☐ Salt brined
- ☐ Triple cream
- ☐ Creamy
- ☐ Crumbly
- ☐ Young
- ☐ Aged
- ☐ Blue
- ☐ Fresh

Milk: ☐ Cow ☐ Goat ☐ Sheep

Comments: _____
_____
_____

Date: _____ By: _____

Wine: _____
Winery: _____
Appellation: _____
Vintage: _____
Cost: _____

- ☐ White
- ☐ Red
- ☐ Rosé
- ☐ Dessert
- ☐ Sparkling

Nose (Aroma & Bouquet): _____
_____
Flavor: _____
Balance: _____
Finish: _____
Comments:

Cheese: _____ Wine: _____
Manufacturer: _____ Winery: _____
Appellation: _____
☐ Soft ☐ Creamy Vintage: _____
☐ Semi-soft ☐ Crumbly Cost: _____
☐ Firm ☐ Young
☐ Hard ☐ Aged ☐ White
☐ Salt brined ☐ Blue ☐ Red ☐ Dessert
☐ Triple cream ☐ Fresh ☐ Rosé ☐ Sparkling

Milk: ☐ Cow ☐ Goat ☐ Sheep Nose (Aroma & Bouquet): _____

Comments: _____ Flavor: _____
_____ Balance: _____
_____ Finish: _____
Date: By: Comments:

Cheese: _____ Wine: _____
Manufacturer: _____ Winery: _____
Appellation: _____
☐ Soft ☐ Creamy Vintage: _____
☐ Semi-soft ☐ Crumbly Cost: _____
☐ Firm ☐ Young
☐ Hard ☐ Aged ☐ White
☐ Salt brined ☐ Blue ☐ Red ☐ Dessert
☐ Triple cream ☐ Fresh ☐ Rosé ☐ Sparkling

Milk: ☐ Cow ☐ Goat ☐ Sheep Nose (Aroma & Bouquet): _____

Comments: _____ Flavor: _____
_____ Balance: _____
_____ Finish: _____
Date: By: Comments:

Cheese: _____ Wine: _____
Manufacturer: _____ Winery: _____
Appellation: _____
☐ Soft ☐ Creamy Vintage: _____
☐ Semi-soft ☐ Crumbly Cost: _____
☐ Firm ☐ Young
☐ Hard ☐ Aged ☐ White
☐ Salt brined ☐ Blue ☐ Red ☐ Dessert
☐ Triple cream ☐ Fresh ☐ Rosé ☐ Sparkling

Milk: ☐ Cow ☐ Goat ☐ Sheep Nose (Aroma & Bouquet): _____

Comments: _____ Flavor: _____
_____ Balance: _____
_____ Finish: _____
Date: By: Comments:

Cheese: _____   Wine: _____
Manufacturer: _____   Winery: _____
                                   Appellation: _____
☐ Soft   ☐ Creamy   Vintage: _____
☐ Semi-soft   ☐ Crumbly   Cost: _____
☐ Firm   ☐ Young
☐ Hard   ☐ Aged   ☐ White
☐ Salt brined   ☐ Blue   ☐ Red   ☐ Dessert
☐ Triple cream ☐ Fresh   ☐ Rosé   ☐ Sparkling

Milk: ☐ Cow ☐ Goat ☐ Sheep   Nose (Aroma & Bouquet): _____
                                   _____
Comments: _____   Flavor: _____
_____   Balance: _____
_____   Finish: _____
Date: _____ By: _____   Comments:

Cheese: _____   Wine: _____
Manufacturer: _____   Winery: _____
                                   Appellation: _____
☐ Soft   ☐ Creamy   Vintage: _____
☐ Semi-soft   ☐ Crumbly   Cost: _____
☐ Firm   ☐ Young
☐ Hard   ☐ Aged   ☐ White
☐ Salt brined   ☐ Blue   ☐ Red   ☐ Dessert
☐ Triple cream ☐ Fresh   ☐ Rosé   ☐ Sparkling

Milk: ☐ Cow ☐ Goat ☐ Sheep   Nose (Aroma & Bouquet): _____
                                   _____
Comments: _____   Flavor: _____
_____   Balance: _____
_____   Finish: _____
Date: _____ By: _____   Comments:

Cheese: _____   Wine: _____
Manufacturer: _____   Winery: _____
                                   Appellation: _____
☐ Soft   ☐ Creamy   Vintage: _____
☐ Semi-soft   ☐ Crumbly   Cost: _____
☐ Firm   ☐ Young
☐ Hard   ☐ Aged   ☐ White
☐ Salt brined   ☐ Blue   ☐ Red   ☐ Dessert
☐ Triple cream ☐ Fresh   ☐ Rosé   ☐ Sparkling

Milk: ☐ Cow ☐ Goat ☐ Sheep   Nose (Aroma & Bouquet): _____
                                   _____
Comments: _____   Flavor: _____
_____   Balance: _____
_____   Finish: _____
Date: _____ By: _____   Comments:

Cheese: _____ Wine: _____

Manufacturer: _____ Winery: _____

Appellation: _____

☐ Soft   ☐ Creamy   Vintage: _____

☐ Semi-soft   ☐ Crumbly   Cost: _____

☐ Firm   ☐ Young

☐ Hard   ☐ Aged   ☐ White

☐ Salt brined ☐ Blue   ☐ Red   ☐ Dessert

☐ Triple cream ☐ Fresh   ☐ Rosé   ☐ Sparkling

Milk: ☐ Cow ☐ Goat ☐ Sheep Aroma: _____

Comments: _____ Bouquet: _____

Balance: _____

_____ Finish: _____

Comments: _____

Date: _____ By: _____

Cheese: _____ Wine: _____

Manufacturer: _____ Winery: _____

Appellation: _____

☐ Soft   ☐ Creamy   Vintage: _____

☐ Semi-soft   ☐ Crumbly   Cost: _____

☐ Firm   ☐ Young

☐ Hard   ☐ Aged   ☐ White

☐ Salt brined ☐ Blue   ☐ Red   ☐ Dessert

☐ Triple cream ☐ Fresh   ☐ Rosé   ☐ Sparkling

Milk: ☐ Cow ☐ Goat ☐ Sheep Aroma: _____

Comments: _____ Bouquet: _____

Balance: _____

_____ Finish: _____

Comments: _____

Date: _____ By: _____

Cheese: _____ Wine: _____

Manufacturer: _____ Winery: _____

Appellation: _____

☐ Soft   ☐ Creamy   Vintage: _____

☐ Semi-soft   ☐ Crumbly   Cost: _____

☐ Firm   ☐ Young

☐ Hard   ☐ Aged   ☐ White

☐ Salt brined ☐ Blue   ☐ Red   ☐ Dessert

☐ Triple cream ☐ Fresh   ☐ Rosé   ☐ Sparkling

Milk: ☐ Cow ☐ Goat ☐ Sheep Aroma: _____

Comments: _____ Bouquet: _____

Balance: _____

_____ Finish: _____

Comments: _____

Date: _____ By: _____

"Oops! I Won't Pair These Again" Journal

Cheese: _____   Wine: _____

Manufacturer: _____   Winery: _____

Appellation: _____

☐ Soft   ☐ Creamy   Vintage: _____

☐ Semi-soft   ☐ Crumbly   Cost: _____

☐ Firm   ☐ Young

☐ Hard   ☐ Aged   ☐ White

☐ Salt brined   ☐ Blue   ☐ Red   ☐ Dessert

☐ Triple cream   ☐ Fresh   ☐ Rosé   ☐ Sparkling

Milk: ☐ Cow ☐ Goat ☐ Sheep   Nose (Aroma & Bouquet): _____

Comments: _____   Flavor: _____

_____   Balance: _____

_____   Finish: _____

Date: By: Comments:

Cheese: _____   Wine: _____

Manufacturer: _____   Winery: _____

Appellation: _____

☐ Soft   ☐ Creamy   Vintage: _____

☐ Semi-soft   ☐ Crumbly   Cost: _____

☐ Firm   ☐ Young

☐ Hard   ☐ Aged   ☐ White

☐ Salt brined   ☐ Blue   ☐ Red   ☐ Dessert

☐ Triple cream   ☐ Fresh   ☐ Rosé   ☐ Sparkling

Milk: ☐ Cow ☐ Goat ☐ Sheep   Nose (Aroma & Bouquet): _____

Comments: _____   Flavor: _____

_____   Balance: _____

_____   Finish: _____

Date: By: Comments:

Cheese: _____   Wine: _____

Manufacturer: _____   Winery: _____

Appellation: _____

☐ Soft   ☐ Creamy   Vintage: _____

☐ Semi-soft   ☐ Crumbly   Cost: _____

☐ Firm   ☐ Young

☐ Hard   ☐ Aged   ☐ White

☐ Salt brined   ☐ Blue   ☐ Red   ☐ Dessert

☐ Triple cream   ☐ Fresh   ☐ Rosé   ☐ Sparkling

Milk: ☐ Cow ☐ Goat ☐ Sheep   Nose (Aroma & Bouquet): _____

Comments: _____   Flavor: _____

_____   Balance: _____

_____   Finish: _____

Date: By: Comments:

Cheese: _____ Wine: _____
Manufacturer: _____ Winery: _____
                             Appellation: _____
- [ ] Soft   - [ ] Creamy   Vintage: _____
- [ ] Semi-soft   - [ ] Crumbly   Cost: _____
- [ ] Firm   - [ ] Young
- [ ] Hard   - [ ] Aged   - [ ] White
- [ ] Salt brined - [ ] Blue   - [ ] Red   - [ ] Dessert
- [ ] Triple cream - [ ] Fresh   - [ ] Rosé   - [ ] Sparkling

Milk: - [ ] Cow   - [ ] Goat   - [ ] Sheep   Nose (Aroma & Bouquet): _____

Comments: _____ Flavor: _____
_____   Balance: _____
_____   Finish: _____
Date: _____ By: _____ Comments:

Cheese: _____ Wine: _____
Manufacturer: _____ Winery: _____
                             Appellation: _____
- [ ] Soft   - [ ] Creamy   Vintage: _____
- [ ] Semi-soft   - [ ] Crumbly   Cost: _____
- [ ] Firm   - [ ] Young
- [ ] Hard   - [ ] Aged   - [ ] White
- [ ] Salt brined - [ ] Blue   - [ ] Red   - [ ] Dessert
- [ ] Triple cream - [ ] Fresh   - [ ] Rosé   - [ ] Sparkling

Milk: - [ ] Cow   - [ ] Goat   - [ ] Sheep   Nose (Aroma & Bouquet): _____

Comments: _____ Flavor: _____
_____   Balance: _____
_____   Finish: _____
Date: _____ By: _____ Comments:

Cheese: _____ Wine: _____
Manufacturer: _____ Winery: _____
                             Appellation: _____
- [ ] Soft   - [ ] Creamy   Vintage: _____
- [ ] Semi-soft   - [ ] Crumbly   Cost: _____
- [ ] Firm   - [ ] Young
- [ ] Hard   - [ ] Aged   - [ ] White
- [ ] Salt brined - [ ] Blue   - [ ] Red   - [ ] Dessert
- [ ] Triple cream - [ ] Fresh   - [ ] Rosé   - [ ] Sparkling

Milk: - [ ] Cow   - [ ] Goat   - [ ] Sheep   Nose (Aroma & Bouquet): _____

Comments: _____ Flavor: _____
_____   Balance: _____
_____   Finish: _____
Date: _____ By: _____ Comments:

Cheese: _____ Wine: _____
Manufacturer: _____ Winery: _____
                                 Appellation: _____
☐ Soft   ☐ Creamy   Vintage: _____
☐ Semi-soft   ☐ Crumbly   Cost: _____
☐ Firm   ☐ Young
☐ Hard   ☐ Aged   ☐ White
☐ Salt brined   ☐ Blue   ☐ Red   ☐ Dessert
☐ Triple cream ☐ Fresh   ☐ Rosé   ☐ Sparkling

Milk: ☐ Cow ☐ Goat ☐ Sheep   Nose (Aroma & Bouquet): _____

Comments: _____ Flavor: _____
_____ Balance: _____
_____ Finish: _____
Date: By: Comments:

Cheese: _____ Wine: _____
Manufacturer: _____ Winery: _____
                                 Appellation: _____
☐ Soft   ☐ Creamy   Vintage: _____
☐ Semi-soft   ☐ Crumbly   Cost: _____
☐ Firm   ☐ Young
☐ Hard   ☐ Aged   ☐ White
☐ Salt brined   ☐ Blue   ☐ Red   ☐ Dessert
☐ Triple cream ☐ Fresh   ☐ Rosé   ☐ Sparkling

Milk: ☐ Cow ☐ Goat ☐ Sheep   Nose (Aroma & Bouquet): _____

Comments: _____ Flavor: _____
_____ Balance: _____
_____ Finish: _____
Date: By: Comments:

Cheese: _____ Wine: _____
Manufacturer: _____ Winery: _____
                                 Appellation: _____
☐ Soft   ☐ Creamy   Vintage: _____
☐ Semi-soft   ☐ Crumbly   Cost: _____
☐ Firm   ☐ Young
☐ Hard   ☐ Aged   ☐ White
☐ Salt brined   ☐ Blue   ☐ Red   ☐ Dessert
☐ Triple cream ☐ Fresh   ☐ Rosé   ☐ Sparkling

Milk: ☐ Cow ☐ Goat ☐ Sheep   Nose (Aroma & Bouquet): _____

Comments: _____ Flavor: _____
_____ Balance: _____
_____ Finish: _____
Date: By: Comments:

Cheese: _____ Wine: _____
Manufacturer: _____ Winery: _____
                          Appellation: _____
☐ Soft   ☐ Creamy   Vintage: _____
☐ Semi-soft ☐ Crumbly   Cost: _____
☐ Firm   ☐ Young
☐ Hard   ☐ Aged   ☐ White
☐ Salt brined ☐ Blue   ☐ Red   ☐ Dessert
☐ Triple cream ☐ Fresh   ☐ Rosé   ☐ Sparkling

Milk: ☐ Cow ☐ Goat ☐ Sheep   Nose (Aroma & Bouquet): _____

Comments: _____   Flavor: _____
_____   Balance: _____
                          Finish: _____
Date: By: Comments:

Cheese: _____ Wine: _____
Manufacturer: _____ Winery: _____
                          Appellation: _____
☐ Soft   ☐ Creamy   Vintage: _____
☐ Semi-soft ☐ Crumbly   Cost: _____
☐ Firm   ☐ Young
☐ Hard   ☐ Aged   ☐ White
☐ Salt brined ☐ Blue   ☐ Red   ☐ Dessert
☐ Triple cream ☐ Fresh   ☐ Rosé   ☐ Sparkling

Milk: ☐ Cow ☐ Goat ☐ Sheep   Nose (Aroma & Bouquet): _____

Comments: _____   Flavor: _____
_____   Balance: _____
                          Finish: _____
Date: By: Comments:

Cheese: _____ Wine: _____
Manufacturer: _____ Winery: _____
                          Appellation: _____
☐ Soft   ☐ Creamy   Vintage: _____
☐ Semi-soft ☐ Crumbly   Cost: _____
☐ Firm   ☐ Young
☐ Hard   ☐ Aged   ☐ White
☐ Salt brined ☐ Blue   ☐ Red   ☐ Dessert
☐ Triple cream ☐ Fresh   ☐ Rosé   ☐ Sparkling

Milk: ☐ Cow ☐ Goat ☐ Sheep   Nose (Aroma & Bouquet): _____

Comments: _____   Flavor: _____
_____   Balance: _____
                          Finish: _____
Date: By: Comments:

Cheese: _____   Wine: _____

Manufacturer: _____   Winery: _____

     Appellation: _____

☐ Soft   ☐ Creamy   Vintage: _____

☐ Semi-soft   ☐ Crumbly   Cost: _____

☐ Firm   ☐ Young

☐ Hard   ☐ Aged   ☐ White

☐ Salt brined   ☐ Blue   ☐ Red   ☐ Dessert

☐ Triple cream   ☐ Fresh   ☐ Rosé   ☐ Sparkling

Milk: ☐ Cow ☐ Goat ☐ Sheep   Nose (Aroma & Bouquet): _____

Comments: _____   Flavor: _____

_____   Balance: _____

_____   Finish: _____

Date: By: Comments:

Cheese: _____   Wine: _____

Manufacturer: _____   Winery: _____

     Appellation: _____

☐ Soft   ☐ Creamy   Vintage: _____

☐ Semi-soft   ☐ Crumbly   Cost: _____

☐ Firm   ☐ Young

☐ Hard   ☐ Aged   ☐ White

☐ Salt brined   ☐ Blue   ☐ Red   ☐ Dessert

☐ Triple cream   ☐ Fresh   ☐ Rosé   ☐ Sparkling

Milk: ☐ Cow ☐ Goat ☐ Sheep   Nose (Aroma & Bouquet): _____

Comments: _____   Flavor: _____

_____   Balance: _____

_____   Finish: _____

Date: By: Comments:

Cheese: _____   Wine: _____

Manufacturer: _____   Winery: _____

     Appellation: _____

☐ Soft   ☐ Creamy   Vintage: _____

☐ Semi-soft   ☐ Crumbly   Cost: _____

☐ Firm   ☐ Young

☐ Hard   ☐ Aged   ☐ White

☐ Salt brined   ☐ Blue   ☐ Red   ☐ Dessert

☐ Triple cream   ☐ Fresh   ☐ Rosé   ☐ Sparkling

Milk: ☐ Cow ☐ Goat ☐ Sheep   Nose (Aroma & Bouquet): _____

Comments: _____   Flavor: _____

_____   Balance: _____

_____   Finish: _____

Date: By: Comments:

Cheese: _____ Wine: _____
Manufacturer: _____ Winery: _____
Appellation: _____
☐ Soft   ☐ Creamy   Vintage: _____
☐ Semi-soft   ☐ Crumbly   Cost: _____
☐ Firm   ☐ Young   ☐ White
☐ Hard   ☐ Aged   ☐ Red   ☐ Dessert
☐ Salt brined ☐ Blue   ☐ Rosé   ☐ Sparkling
☐ Triple cream ☐ Fresh   Nose (Aroma & Bouquet): _____
Milk: ☐ Cow ☐ Goat ☐ Sheep _____
Comments: _____ Flavor: _____
_____ Balance: _____
_____ Finish: _____
Date: By: Comments:

Cheese: _____ Wine: _____
Manufacturer: _____ Winery: _____
Appellation: _____
☐ Soft   ☐ Creamy   Vintage: _____
☐ Semi-soft   ☐ Crumbly   Cost: _____
☐ Firm   ☐ Young   ☐ White
☐ Hard   ☐ Aged   ☐ Red   ☐ Dessert
☐ Salt brined ☐ Blue   ☐ Rosé   ☐ Sparkling
☐ Triple cream ☐ Fresh   Nose (Aroma & Bouquet): _____
Milk: ☐ Cow ☐ Goat ☐ Sheep _____
Comments: _____ Flavor: _____
_____ Balance: _____
_____ Finish: _____
Date: By: Comments:

Cheese: _____ Wine: _____
Manufacturer: _____ Winery: _____
Appellation: _____
☐ Soft   ☐ Creamy   Vintage: _____
☐ Semi-soft   ☐ Crumbly   Cost: _____
☐ Firm   ☐ Young   ☐ White
☐ Hard   ☐ Aged   ☐ Red   ☐ Dessert
☐ Salt brined ☐ Blue   ☐ Rosé   ☐ Sparkling
☐ Triple cream ☐ Fresh   Nose (Aroma & Bouquet): _____
Milk: ☐ Cow ☐ Goat ☐ Sheep _____
Comments: _____ Flavor: _____
_____ Balance: _____
_____ Finish: _____
Date: By: Comments:

Cheese: _____

Manufacturer: _____

☐ Soft   ☐ Creamy
☐ Semi-soft   ☐ Crumbly
☐ Firm   ☐ Young
☐ Hard   ☐ Aged
☐ Salt brined ☐ Blue
☐ Triple cream ☐ Fresh

Milk: ☐ Cow   ☐ Goat   ☐ Sheep

Comments: _____

_____

_____

Date: By:

Wine: _____

Winery: _____

Appellation: _____

Vintage: _____

Cost: _____

☐ White
☐ Red   ☐ Dessert
☐ Rosé   ☐ Sparkling

Nose (Aroma & Bouquet): _____

_____

Flavor: _____

Balance: _____

Finish: _____

Comments:

Cheese: _____

Manufacturer: _____

☐ Soft   ☐ Creamy
☐ Semi-soft   ☐ Crumbly
☐ Firm   ☐ Young
☐ Hard   ☐ Aged
☐ Salt brined ☐ Blue
☐ Triple cream ☐ Fresh

Milk: ☐ Cow   ☐ Goat   ☐ Sheep

Comments: _____

_____

_____

Date: By:

Wine: _____

Winery: _____

Appellation: _____

Vintage: _____

Cost: _____

☐ White
☐ Red   ☐ Dessert
☐ Rosé   ☐ Sparkling

Nose (Aroma & Bouquet): _____

_____

Flavor: _____

Balance: _____

Finish: _____

Comments:

Cheese: _____

Manufacturer: _____

☐ Soft   ☐ Creamy
☐ Semi-soft   ☐ Crumbly
☐ Firm   ☐ Young
☐ Hard   ☐ Aged
☐ Salt brined ☐ Blue
☐ Triple cream ☐ Fresh

Milk: ☐ Cow   ☐ Goat   ☐ Sheep

Comments: _____

_____

_____

Date: By:

Wine: _____

Winery: _____

Appellation: _____

Vintage: _____

Cost: _____

☐ White
☐ Red   ☐ Dessert
☐ Rosé   ☐ Sparkling

Nose (Aroma & Bouquet): _____

_____

Flavor: _____

Balance: _____

Finish: _____

Comments:

Cheese: _____
Manufacturer: _____

☐ Soft   ☐ Creamy
☐ Semi-soft   ☐ Crumbly
☐ Firm   ☐ Young
☐ Hard   ☐ Aged
☐ Salt brined   ☐ Blue
☐ Triple cream ☐ Fresh

Milk: ☐ Cow   ☐ Goat   ☐ Sheep

Comments: _____
_____
_____
Date: _____ By: _____

Wine: _____
Winery: _____
Appellation: _____
Vintage: _____
Cost: _____
☐ White
☐ Red   ☐ Dessert
☐ Rosé   ☐ Sparkling
Nose (Aroma & Bouquet): _____
_____
Flavor: _____
Balance: _____
Finish: _____
Comments:

Cheese: _____
Manufacturer: _____

☐ Soft   ☐ Creamy
☐ Semi-soft   ☐ Crumbly
☐ Firm   ☐ Young
☐ Hard   ☐ Aged
☐ Salt brined   ☐ Blue
☐ Triple cream ☐ Fresh

Milk: ☐ Cow   ☐ Goat   ☐ Sheep

Comments: _____
_____
_____
Date: _____ By: _____

Wine: _____
Winery: _____
Appellation: _____
Vintage: _____
Cost: _____
☐ White
☐ Red   ☐ Dessert
☐ Rosé   ☐ Sparkling
Nose (Aroma & Bouquet): _____
_____
Flavor: _____
Balance: _____
Finish: _____
Comments:

Cheese: _____
Manufacturer: _____

☐ Soft   ☐ Creamy
☐ Semi-soft   ☐ Crumbly
☐ Firm   ☐ Young
☐ Hard   ☐ Aged
☐ Salt brined   ☐ Blue
☐ Triple cream ☐ Fresh

Milk: ☐ Cow   ☐ Goat   ☐ Sheep

Comments: _____
_____
_____
Date: _____ By: _____

Wine: _____
Winery: _____
Appellation: _____
Vintage: _____
Cost: _____
☐ White
☐ Red   ☐ Dessert
☐ Rosé   ☐ Sparkling
Nose (Aroma & Bouquet): _____
_____
Flavor: _____
Balance: _____
Finish: _____
Comments:

Cheese: _____ Wine: _____
Manufacturer: _____ Winery: _____
                                 Appellation: _____
☐ Soft   ☐ Creamy   Vintage: _____
☐ Semi-soft   ☐ Crumbly   Cost: _____
☐ Firm   ☐ Young
☐ Hard   ☐ Aged   ☐ White
☐ Salt brined   ☐ Blue   ☐ Red   ☐ Dessert
☐ Triple cream ☐ Fresh   ☐ Rosé   ☐ Sparkling

Milk: ☐ Cow ☐ Goat ☐ Sheep   Nose (Aroma & Bouquet): _____

Comments: _____   Flavor: _____
_____   Balance: _____
_____   Finish: _____
Date: By: Comments:

Cheese: _____ Wine: _____
Manufacturer: _____ Winery: _____
                                 Appellation: _____
☐ Soft   ☐ Creamy   Vintage: _____
☐ Semi-soft   ☐ Crumbly   Cost: _____
☐ Firm   ☐ Young
☐ Hard   ☐ Aged   ☐ White
☐ Salt brined   ☐ Blue   ☐ Red   ☐ Dessert
☐ Triple cream ☐ Fresh   ☐ Rosé   ☐ Sparkling

Milk: ☐ Cow ☐ Goat ☐ Sheep   Nose (Aroma & Bouquet): _____

Comments: _____   Flavor: _____
_____   Balance: _____
_____   Finish: _____
Date: By: Comments:

Cheese: _____ Wine: _____
Manufacturer: _____ Winery: _____
                                 Appellation: _____
☐ Soft   ☐ Creamy   Vintage: _____
☐ Semi-soft   ☐ Crumbly   Cost: _____
☐ Firm   ☐ Young
☐ Hard   ☐ Aged   ☐ White
☐ Salt brined   ☐ Blue   ☐ Red   ☐ Dessert
☐ Triple cream ☐ Fresh   ☐ Rosé   ☐ Sparkling

Milk: ☐ Cow ☐ Goat ☐ Sheep   Nose (Aroma & Bouquet): _____

Comments: _____   Flavor: _____
_____   Balance: _____
_____   Finish: _____
Date: By: Comments:

Cheese: _____   Wine: _____
Manufacturer: _____   Winery: _____
                                       Appellation: _____

- [ ] Soft   [ ] Creamy   Vintage: _____
- [ ] Semi-soft   [ ] Crumbly   Cost: _____
- [ ] Firm   [ ] Young
- [ ] Hard   [ ] Aged   [ ] White
- [ ] Salt brined   [ ] Blue   [ ] Red   [ ] Dessert
- [ ] Triple cream   [ ] Fresh   [ ] Rosé   [ ] Sparkling

Milk: [ ] Cow   [ ] Goat   [ ] Sheep   Nose (Aroma & Bouquet): _____

Comments: _____   Flavor: _____
_____   Balance: _____
_____   Finish: _____
Date: By: Comments:

Cheese: _____   Wine: _____
Manufacturer: _____   Winery: _____
                                         Appellation: _____

- [ ] Soft   [ ] Creamy   Vintage: _____
- [ ] Semi-soft   [ ] Crumbly   Cost: _____
- [ ] Firm   [ ] Young
- [ ] Hard   [ ] Aged   [ ] White
- [ ] Salt brined   [ ] Blue   [ ] Red   [ ] Dessert
- [ ] Triple cream   [ ] Fresh   [ ] Rosé   [ ] Sparkling

Milk: [ ] Cow   [ ] Goat   [ ] Sheep   Nose (Aroma & Bouquet): _____

Comments: _____   Flavor: _____
_____   Balance: _____
_____   Finish: _____
Date: By: Comments:

Cheese: _____   Wine: _____
Manufacturer: _____   Winery: _____
                                         Appellation: _____

- [ ] Soft   [ ] Creamy   Vintage: _____
- [ ] Semi-soft   [ ] Crumbly   Cost: _____
- [ ] Firm   [ ] Young
- [ ] Hard   [ ] Aged   [ ] White
- [ ] Salt brined   [ ] Blue   [ ] Red   [ ] Dessert
- [ ] Triple cream   [ ] Fresh   [ ] Rosé   [ ] Sparkling

Milk: [ ] Cow   [ ] Goat   [ ] Sheep   Nose (Aroma & Bouquet): _____

Comments: _____   Flavor: _____
_____   Balance: _____
_____   Finish: _____
Date: By: Comments:

About the Authors

Norm and Barbara Ray, authors of several wine-and-food cookbooks, have a passion for excellent wine and fine food. They have an intimate knowledge of wine and food, having grown up in Sonoma County, California, both working on local ranches from early childhood. Norm's grandparents, Logan and Daisy Moody, owned a small ranch in Geyserville, where as a youth, Norm became skilled in the numerous tasks required for successful ranching, especially pruning and harvesting. It was during those years that Norm (and Barbara during their teen-age courtship) learned to appreciate the variety and exciting flavors of grapes, particularly those that "Grandpa Moody" grew — Cabernet Sauvignon, Petite Sirah, Carignane, Muscat, Tokay, Concord — as well as many others grown in Sonoma County. Barbara's background includes a heritage of women who were excellent, creative cooks. Her family lived in Dry Creek Valley, where Barbara (and Norm during their teen-age courtship) savored meals prepared from home-grown produce, livestock, poultry, wild game, and fresh fish. Norm and Barbara married while students at U.C. Berkeley, their alma mater, lived many years in the San Francisco bay area, and returned to Sonoma County during the early 1980s.

☆ *Cooking With Wine*
by Virginia and Robert Hoffman

Eighty-six American winery chefs share 172 of their best recipes for cooking with wine and pairing food with wine in this excellent cookbook. Whether you are a novice or an expert in the kitchen, you'll enjoy these great recipes. But that's not all. You'll also learn how cooking with wine can be good for your health! Included is a glossary of American wines and suggested pairings of wine and food. This bestselling cookbook is considered a classic.

ISBN 0-9629927-3-9, softcover, 7 x 10, 206 pages   **$15.95**

☆ *The Great Little Food With Wine Cookbook, 2nd Edition*
by Virginia and Robert Hoffman

There's a lot of information in this cookbook! You'll enjoy excellent recipes by some of America's finest winery chefs, tips on how and where to buy wine, guidelines for selecting wine in restaurants, helpful hints on deciphering wine labels so you know what you're buying, and how to select wines to go with your meals ... and the wines are all American.

ISBN 1-877810-70-3, softcover, 6 x 9, 128 pages   **$9.95**

☆ *The California Wine Country Cookbook II*

by Virginia and Robert Hoffman

Here are 172 exciting recipes from the most creative chefs of the California wine country. Recipes for appetizers, soups, salads, pastas, meats, seafood, poultry, vegetables and desserts — each an exciting addition to your culinary repertoire. Some recipes are quite simple, easy and fast to prepare. Others require more time and effort. All are innovative and will bring the cuisine of the California Wine Country into your home.

ISBN 0-9629927-6-3, softcover, 7 x 10, 208 pages   **$12.95**

☆ *The California Wine Country Herbs & Spices Cookbook, New Revised Edition*

by Virginia and Robert Hoffman

Herbs and spices are the theme of this collection of recipes by 96 of the foremost chefs in the California wine country. You'll enjoy 212 of the best recipes that made them world famous for their cuisine. You'll discover exciting new ways to use 37 herbs and spices, how to make your own spice mixes, and how to make herbed and spiced oils and vinegars.

ISBN 0-9629927-7-1, softcover, 7 x 10, 240 pages   **$14.95**

☆ *Great Salsas!*

by Virginia and Robert Hoffman

This collection of 96 salsa recipes takes you from mild and mellow to very hot. You will discover delicious recipes from Latin America, the Caribbean, Africa, the Far East, and the American Southwest. Each recipe is simple and easy to make ... and guaranteed to tantalize your taste buds. Come with us on a culinary adventure using exotic but easy-to-find ingredients, and enjoy new and exciting flavors, aromas to make your mouth water, and excitement in every taste!

ISBN 1-893718-05-0, softcover, 5½ x 8½, 96 pages   **$7.95**

☆ *The Wine-Lover's Holidays Cookbook*

by Virginia and Robert Hoffman

You'll enjoy happier holidays with this timesaving collection of menus, recipes and wine recommendations. The book includes 13 seasonal holiday menus, with recipes and suggested American wines to accompany them, for Thanksgiving, Christmas, Chanukah, Passover, Easter and the 4th of July. Each is easy to prepare and appropriate for the selected holiday. This charming book is a perfect gift or remembrance for any special occasion.

ISBN 1-893718-03-4, softcover, 6 x 9, 144 pages   **$9.95**

☆ Pairing Wine With Food

by Virginia and Robert Hoffman

In this handy bestselling book, more than 500 foods are paired with American wines. You'll learn where and how to buy wine, how to select wine in a restaurant, and even the right wines to pair with fast- and takeout foods such as nachos, Kentucky Fried Chicken, and pizza. In addition, there's a helpful guide to American wines, and even a Winespeak Dictionary. With this unique book, you'll discover everything you've always wanted to know about pairing wine with food ... and more.

ISBN 1-893718-01-8, softcover, 5½ x 8½, 96 pages   **$8.95**

☆ Nancy's Candy Cookbook: How to Make Candy at Home the Easy Way, 2nd Edition

by Nancy Shipman

Have fun and save money by making top-quality candy at home. In this step-by-step guidebook, candy specialist Nancy Shipman takes you through the candy-making process and shares favorite recipes —fudge, divinity, brittles, barks, caramels, nougats, nut clusters, creams, fruit and nut centers, mints, and many more. More than 100 excellent recipes plus information on types of chocolate, candy-making equipment, dipping, coating, and much more. You'll become an expert candy maker in no time. How sweet it is!

ISBN 1-877810-64-9, softcover. 8½ x 11, 192 pages   **$15.95**

☆ *Wine & Cheese Pairing Guide: Your Exciting Search for Wow! Combinations*

by Norm and Barbara Ray

☑ Pairing recommendations for over 150 wines & 340 cheeses of the world, presented in two convenient formats:
  • Cheese & Wine Pairings
  • Wine & Cheese Pairings
☑ Valuable tips for finding perfect pairings
☑ Efficient, easy-to-use journals that help you remember your tasting experiences.
  •"My Favorite Pairings" Journal
  •"Oops! I won't Pair These Again" Journal

It's great fun to discover a taste sensation that makes you say "Wow! This is fantastic!" and this extremely informative guidebook gives you a running start in finding your exciting and perfect pairings. Let your quest begin.

ISBN 1-877810-00-2, softcover, 6 x 9, 224 pages **$15.95**

☆ *The Great Turkey Cookbook CD*

by Virginia and Robert Hoffman

Discover turkey — delicious, versatile, low in calories and cholesterol, and less espensive than most meats. This Compact Disc (CD) contains 120 turkey recipes for traditiional holiday meals, not-so-traditional dinner roasts, and turkey makeovers of favorite dishes customarily made with pork, lamb, or beef. It also includes a section on how to buy, cook, carve, and store turkey. The original Great Turkey Cookbook, which was a Book-of-the-Month Club selection for two years, sold more than 100,000 copies. The book is no longer in print but the CD is still available. Don't miss out on this classic!

ISBN 0-917413-05-9 **Compact Disk (CD)** (Windows 3.1 up) **$14.95**

☆ Cooking with Chardonnay: 75 Sensational Chardonnay Recipes

by Barbara and Norm Ray

Chardonnay is one of the most popular white table wines worldwide. Its unique flavors are ideal for drinking and cooking, many excellent vintages are readily available at reasonable prices, and it pairs well with today's lighter cuisine. In this cookbook you'll enjoy 75 sensational, easy-to-prepare recipes, each of which is flavored with Chardonnay — soups, pastas and grains, meats, poultry, seafood, and desserts. In addition, you'll appreciate the introduction to Chardonnay, helpful guides on how to cook with wine, decipher wine labels, and serve wine, a glossary and pronunciation guide for wine cooking terms ... and more.

ISBN 1-877810-54-1, softcover, 6 x 9, 128 pages   **$9.95**

☆ Cooking with Merlot: 75 Marvelous Merlot Recipes

by Barbara and Norm Ray

If you, your family, and friends enjoy moderately heavy cuisine with rich wine overtones, think Merlot! This exciting cookbook contains 75 marvelous, easy-to-prepare recipes, each of which is flavored with Merlot — soups, pastas and grains, meats, poultry, seafood, and desserts. In addition, there's an informative introduction to Merlot, helpful guides on how to cook with Merlot, decipher wine labels, and serve wine, a glossary and pronunciation guide for wine cooking terms ... and more.

ISBN 1-877810-53-3, softcover, 6 x 9, 128 pages   **$9.95**

☆ *Cooking with Riesling:*
75 Remarkable Riesling Recipes

by Barbara and Norm Ray

Riesling wines, which range from very dry to very sweet, are praised for their delicate yet complex characteristics and their delightful versatility. Rieslings are delicious alone, in cooking, or as an accompaniment to a wide variety of foods, from mild appetizers to spicy exotic cuisine. In this cookbook, you'll discover for yourself Riesling's remarkable versatility as you choose from among 75 delicious recipes that feature Riesling wine. And, as in the other books in this series, Cooking with Riesling contains an introduction to Riesling, helpful guides on how to cook with wine, decipher wine labels, and serve wine, a glossary and pronunciation guide for wine cooking terms ... and more.

ISBN 1-877810-56-8, softcover, 6 x 9, 128 pages   **$9.95**

☆ *Cooking with Varietals: Three*
Book Set

This special, shrinkwrapped set includes the three excellent cookbooks in our varietals cookbook series. It is ideal for your personal use or for gift-giving, and you'll save money, too.

☑ **Cooking with Chardonnay**
   75 Sensational Chardonnay Recipes
☑ **Cooking with Merlot**
   75 Marvelous MerlotRecipes
☑ **Cooking with Riesling**
   75 Remarkable Riesling Recipes

SAVE 5% from single-book prices

ISBN 1-877810-63-0   **$28.50**

ORDER

To order Rayve Productions cookbooks through the mail, please complete this order form and forward with check, money order or credit card information to Rayve Productions, POB 726, Windsor CA 95492. If paying with a credit card, you can call us toll-free at 800.852.4890 or fax this completed form to Rayve Productions at 707.838.2220.

We invite you to visit the Rayve Productions website and view our cookbooks at www.foodandwinebooks.com.

☐ Please send me the following books:

Title _____ Price _____ Qty ___ Amount $ _____

Title _____ Price _____ Qty ___ Amount _____

Title _____ Price _____ Qty ___ Amount _____

Quantity Discount: 4 items @ 10%; 7 items @ 15%; 10 items @ 20% **NOTE:** Discounts do not apply to multiple-item packages	Subtotal _____ Discount _____ Shipping _____

Sales Tax: Californians please add 7.75% sales tax **Shipping & Handling** Media rate — $4 for first book + $1 each additional Priority — $5.50 for first book + $1 each additional	Subtotal _____ Sales Tax _____ (*Calif. only*)

Total $ _____

Name _____ Phone _____

Address _____

City State Zip _____

☐ Check enclosed $ _____   Date _____

☐ Charge my Visa/MC/Discover/AMEX $ _____

Credit card # _____   Exp. _____

Signature _____   *Thank you!*

WCPG06